Lecture Notes in Computer Science 2978

Edited by G. Goos, J. Hartmanis, and J. van Leeuwen

Springer

Berlin
Heidelberg
New York
Hong Kong
London
Milan
Paris
Tokyo

Roland Groz   Robert M. Hierons (Eds.)

Testing
of Communicating
Systems

16th IFIP International Conference, TestCom 2004
Oxford, UK, March 17-19, 2004
Proceedings

 Springer

Series Editors

Gerhard Goos, Karlsruhe University, Germany
Juris Hartmanis, Cornell University, NY, USA
Jan van Leeuwen, Utrecht University, The Netherlands

Volume Editors

Roland Groz
LSR-IMAG
681, rue de la Passerelle, 38402 St Martin d'Hères Cedex, France
E-mail: Roland.Groz@imag.fr

Robert M. Hierons
Brunel University, Department of Information Systems and Computing
Uxbridge, Middlesex, UB8 3PH, United Kingdom
E-mail: rob.hierons@brunel.ac.uk

Cataloging-in-Publication Data applied for

A catalog record for this book is available from the Library of Congress.

Bibliographic information published by Die Deutsche Bibliothek
Die Deutsche Bibliothek lists this publication in the Deutsche Nationalbibliografie;
detailed bibliographic data is available in the Internet at <http://dnb.ddb.de>.

CR Subject Classification (1998): D.2.5, D.2, C.2

ISSN 0302-9743
ISBN 3-540-21219-1 Springer-Verlag Berlin Heidelberg New York

Springer-Verlag is a part of Springer Science+Business Media

springeronline.com

© 2004 IFIP International Federation for Information Processing, Hofstrasse 3, 2361 Laxenburg, Austria
Printed in Germany

Typesetting: Camera-ready by author, data conversion by PTP-Berlin, Protago-TeX-Production GmbH
Printed on acid-free paper   SPIN: 10988343   06/3142   5 4 3 2 1 0

Preface

This volume contains the proceedings of the 16th IFIP TC6/WG6.1 International Conference on Testing of Communicating Systems (TestCom 2004). This conference was held at St Anne's College, Oxford, UK, from March 17 to March 19, 2004.

TestCom 2004 was the sixteenth in a series of IFIP-sponsored events that started in 1988. The previous events were held in Vancouver, Canada (1988); Berlin, Germany (1989); McLean, USA (1990); Leidschendam, Netherlands (1991); Montreal, Canada (1992); Pau, France (1993); Tokyo, Japan (1994); Evry, France (1995); Darmstadt, Germany (1996); Cheju Island, Korea (1997); Tomsk, Russia (1998); Budapest, Hungary (1999); Ottawa, Canada (2000); Berlin, Germany (2002); and Sophia Antipolis, France (2003). TestCom was not held in 2001 since at this point the conference moved from autumn to spring.

TestCom 2004 was organized by Brunel University, UK and LSR-IMAG, France and was sponsored by IFIP. Support was also provided by the Engineering and Physical Sciences Research Council (EPSRC). We are grateful to the keynote speaker, Prof. Sir Tony Hoare, FRS, and our invited speakers for agreeing to address TestCom 2004.

TestCom focuses on the testing of communicating systems within all application domains. Examples of such application domains include, but are not limited to, the automobile industry, avionics, banking, e-commerce, health, military, and telecommunications systems. The 14 papers contained in this volume are largely motivated by problems within the telecommunications domain, which is not surprising given the origins of TestCom. However, a number of papers cover topics outside of telecommunications, such as the testing of reactive systems and testing from UML. This is encouraging and we hope that it indicates the beginning of a closer dialogue between the telecommunications testing community and the general software testing community.

We are grateful to the many people who contributed to the activities required in order for TestCom 2004 to be held. These people include the members of the steering committee, who provided invaluable advice, and the members of the organizing committee, who were responsible for the smooth running of TestCom 2004. As ever, the referees were given the vital task of reviewing many papers in a short period of time. The individuals who contributed to this are listed in the following pages. We would also like to thank Ursula Barth of Springer-Verlag for her assistance in the production of this volume.

January 2004

Roland Groz
Robert M. Hierons

Conference Committees

Conference Chairs

R.M. Hierons (Brunel University, UK)
R. Groz (LSR-IMAG, France)

Steering Committee

S.T. Chanson (Hong Kong University, China)
R. Groz (LSR-IMAG, France)
G. Leduc, Chairman (University of Liège, Belgium)
A. Petrenko (CRIM, Canada)

Technical Programme Committee

G. von Bochmann, University of Ottawa, Canada
A.R. Cavalli, INT, France
J. Clark, York University, UK
R. Dssouli, Concordia University, Canada
S. Dibuz, Ericsson, Hungary
P. Frankl, Polytechnic University, USA
J. Grabowski, University of Göttingen, Germany
M. Harman, Brunel University, UK
K. Harrison, Praxis Critical Systems, UK
T. Higashino, Osaka University, Japan
D. Hogrefe, University of Göttingen, Germany
T. Jéron, IRISA, France
M. Kim, ICU University, Korea
D. Lee, Bell Labs Research, USA
G. Maggiore, TIM, Italy
J. Offutt, George Mason University, USA
I. Schieferdecker, Fraunhofer FOKUS, Germany
K. Suzuki, Kennisbron Co., Ltd., Japan
J. Tretmans, University of Nijmegen, The Netherlands
A. Ulrich, Siemens, Germany
H. Ural, University of Ottawa, Canada
M.U. Uyar, City University of New York, USA
J. Wegener, DaimlerChrysler AG, Germany
A. Wiles, ETSI, France
J. Wu, Tsinghua University, China
N. Yevtushenko, Tomsk State University, Russia

Additional Reviewers

S. Balon, University of Liège, Belgium
A. Baresel, DaimlerChrysler AG, Berlin, Germany
E. Bayse, INT, France
M. van der Bijl, University of Twente, The Netherlands
S. Boroday, CRIM, Canada
D. Chen, Tsinghua University, Beijing, China
B. Daou, University of Ottawa, Canada
A. Duale, IBM, USA
M. Ebner, University of Göttingen, Germany
K. El-Fakih, American University of Sharjah, United Arab Emirates
M. Fecko, Telcordia Technologies, USA
J.-M. François, University of Liège, Belgium
L. Frantzen, University of Nijmegen, The Netherlands
R. Gecse, Ericsson, Hungary
A. Gotlieb, IRISA/INRIA, Rennes, France
H. Hallal, CRIM, Canada
T. Hasegawa, KDDI R&D Laboratories, Japan
L. Hélouët, IRISA/INRIA, Rennes, France
J.L. Huo, McGill University, Canada
A. Idoue, KDDI R&D Laboratories, Japan
Z. Janos Szabo, Ericsson, Hungary
C. Jard, IRISA/ENS, Cachan/Rennes, France
S. Kang, Information and Communications University, Korea
P. Kremer, Ericsson Hungary
K. Li, Bell Labs Research, China
Z. Li, Tsinghua University, China
F. Liu, Bell Labs Research, China
H. Neukirchen, University of Göttingen, Germany
J.-M. Orset, INT, France
S. Prokopenko, Tomsk State University, Russia
A. Riedel, University of Göttingen, Germany
S. Seol, Information and Communications University, Korea
F. Skivée, University of Liège, Belgium
N. Sptisyna, Tomsk State University, Russia
V. Trenkaev, Tomsk State University, Russia
V. Tschaen, IRISA, France
E.R. Vieira, INT, France
R.G. de Vries, University of Nijmegen, The Netherlands
D. Wang, Bell Labs Research, China
X. Yin, Tsinghua University, China
C. Werner, University of Göttingen, Germany
M. Zibull, University of Göttingen, Germany

Organization Committee

Sponsoring Institutions

Table of Contents

Implementation of an Open Source Toolset for CCM Components and Systems Testing [*]

Harold Batteram[1], Wim Hellenthal[1], Willem Romijn[1],
Andreas Hoffmann[2], Axel Rennoch[2], Alain Vouffo[2]

[1]Bell Labs Advanced Technologies Nederland,
Larenseweg 50, NL-1200 BD Hilversum, The Netherlands
{batteram, whellenthal, romijn}@lucent.com
www.lucent.nl/bell-labs
[2]Fraunhofer FOKUS, Competence Center TIP,
Kaiserin-Augusta-Allee 31, D-10589 Berlin, Germany
{a.hoffmann, rennoch, vouffo}@fokus.fhg.de
www.fokus.fhg.de/tip/

Abstract. Following the success of CORBA based systems the OMG has standardized the CORBA Component Model (CCM) to improve the implementation process of large distributed systems. The European project COACH [16] has been set up to build an Open Source development platform to construct CCM applications. As part of COACH a toolset for CCM components and system testing has been defined and implemented. This paper introduces the various components and features which have been foreseen and implemented for test activities such as interactive component testing, test trace visualization, or the application of abstract test specifications. The resulting test infrastructure addresses the CCM specifics but also benefits from CCM, e.g. by incorporating component communication facilities.

1 Introduction

This contribution presents a framework for testing software components and systems that are based on the CORBA Component Model (CCM)[17] standard. An important aspect of CCM based systems is that the system must be verifiable and testable at the abstraction level of its design and independent of the chosen component implementation language. Component based systems allow the development and testing of components to be partitioned across development groups, working in parallel. However, dependencies between separately developed components may cause delay in testing. Component oriented software engineering has enjoyed an increasing interest in research and industry over the last decade. Component oriented software engineering focuses on system composition from components as elementary building blocks. This approach has many advantages and is generally regarded as an efficient way to handle complexity in large systems and (when properly applied) to

---

* This work is partly sponsored by the European IST Project Coach (IST-2001-34445, Component Based Open Source Architecture for Distributed Telecom Applications).

R. Groz and R.M. Hierons (Eds.): TestCom 2004, LNCS 2978, pp. 1-16, 2004.

improve overall system quality. Component frameworks such as Enterprise Java Beans (EJB) from Sun Microsystems, COM (and more recently .NET) from Microsoft have gained widespread acceptance in software development communities in a short time. The CCM is the component model proposed by the Object Management Group (OMG). As opposed to EJB and .NET the CCM is not proprietary but is an open industry standard. While EJB and .NET are usually applied in web based, client-server application domains, the CCM can be applied in many industrial domains including the telecommunication industry.

Using the CCM requires a different approach to the development cycle. Software systems are now composed from multiple components and separate the task of component development from system composition. This also requires a different approach for the testing of CCM based systems.

There are multiple parts during the whole development cycle of a CCM based system where testing is needed. For example, a component developer needs to test individual components, or small clusters of components working together. System developers compose systems from readily available components but must test the various interaction scenarios for the specific composition in which the components are used. Finally, with large and complex systems integration and conformance testing is often done by specialized system testers and not by developers.

In the context of testing CCM components there is less related work to be mentioned. The majority of the CCM implementers did not address testing by specific techniques or tools. Furthermore we did not assume the availability of an UML specification of the System under Test (SUT) as it has been done in other approaches [4][6].

We have only found the following work carried out by L. Johnson and E. Teiniker on a project called CORBA Component Model Tools [12]. Their aim is to provide tools used for generating CORBA components, test components, and test programs based on source IDL files. Testing has been identified as an important issue. They intend to test their applications on different levels during development: Every class of the business logic that will be part of a component has to be tested (Class Level Testing). For every component a counter component that looks like a mirror to the original component will be created. This counter component has a receptacle for every facet of the original component and vice versa (Component Level Testing). Testing should include a set of connected components (Assembly Level Testing).

Johnson and Teiniker follow the methodology of Beck [3] who introduces the Test Driven Development and starts implementing the test before implementing the application. A test client coordinates creating and connecting the components, as well as the test calls to the facets of a given component C. The mirror component C' and the test client are always generated at the same time as the component itself, without additional development effort. The process begins automatically after compiling. The development of the local component is separated from the development of the test client. A deployed component can be used in different applications at the same time. Currently there are no test tools documented in the project that have been started recently in 2003.

From this latest survey of existing testing tools no test implementations do fit the requirements stated within the COACH project [1][9] and there is still the need to build an appropriate CCM testing environment.

The test architecture described in this paper addresses two distinct test audiences, developers and system testers. Although both groups have a common goal of testing the overall quality of a CCM system, each group has a different focus and a different approach to reach that goal. Component programmers are concerned with testing at a lower level and have to take infrastructure specifics into account such as concurrency, performance, stress testing etc. During the development cycle, component programmers also often use test tools as a debugging facility to locate implementation errors in components, or for regression testing to verify modifications done on a component implementation has not affected other component functions.

Considering system testing there is a special need to compare application tests and the test results gathered from test campaigns executed with different vendor implementations and heterogeneous user environments. In this context the conformance to (standardized) system requirements has to be shown and an international standardized test notation has to be applied. Test languages such as TTCN-3 [13] are specifically designed by ETSI and ITU-T for such kind of testing.

Our CCM test architecture describes a full set of tools that cover both component developer oriented testing and system integration and conformance testing for system testers.

This paper is organised as follows: Section 2 specifies the component test framework describing the different parts of our framework. Section 3 addresses test notations which can be applied to the components under test in order to automate the tests. Section 4 investigates in the test trace viewing facilities. Section 5 describes an application of the test tools. And finally the conclusions will summarise the major results of this paper.

2   Component Test Framework Description

Our test framework, i.e. the COACH test framework, is only concerned with testing CCM components and interactions between CCM components. This means that the framework can be used to identify components that do not behave according to their specifications. Once a component containing a fault has been identified, further localization of the fault within the component can be done using the test and debug facilities that are usually part of the implementation language specific development environment. This implementation language specific testing and debugging is outside the scope of the test framework specified in this contribution.

Tests on CCM components and the observation of interactions between components are expressed using IDL data types and are independent of the data types of the implementation language of the component. Our CCM test framework provides the testers with the following essential capabilities:

- The ability to invoke CORBA operations on selected component facets and observe the response, using a so-called Actor component.

- The ability to intercept CORBA operations on two different levels:

  - Inside a component using the portable interceptors

  - Outside the component using so-called Proxy Components

- The ability to extend the range of test scenarios for components that have dependencies with other components whose implementation is unavailable; using so-called Reactor components as substitutes.

- The ability to visualize causality relations between invocations at runtime.

- The ability to run standardized abstract TTCN-3 test cases against CCM applications under test.

The following figure gives an overview of the test framework. The elements that are above and on the right side of the SUT are used during the development phase of the system under test. The elements left from the SUT are used after the SUT is finished and ready for deployment.

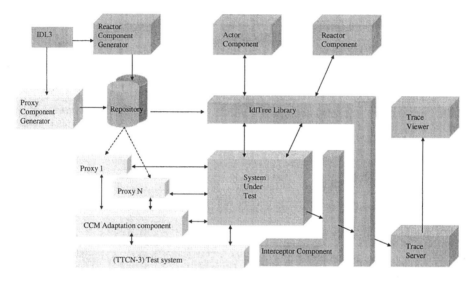

Fig. 1. Component Test Framework

The CCM test framework addresses each capability as will be explained further in the next sections.

2.1 Developers Testing Tools

The CCM is well suited to develop large-scale distributed applications. Teams of developers typically develop these types of applications where each team is responsible for a subsystem. One developer may be responsible for the development of a group of components that will eventually need to be integrated into the system. A developer will need to test the set of components (s)he is responsible for as much as possible before integrating them into the whole system.

The ability to test components may be severely restricted when the components under test depend on interactions between other components that are not yet implemented. To reduce this restriction, the dependent components can be substituted by, so-called, Reactor components for the purpose of testing only. Reactor components must provide the same set of facets, operations and events as their real counterparts. If the IDL specification is known, Reactor component implementations can be generated automatically.

The Reactor-implementation-generation process is similar to the generation of Stub, Skeleton and other implementation classes by the IDL compiler. The IDL specification is read as input and Reactor implementation classes are produced as output that then needs to be compiled by the implementation language compiler. Although IDL can be translated into different kind of implementation languages, the Reactor components do not necessarily need to be implemented in the same language as the components they are substituting. After all, one of the strengths of CORBA systems is heterogeneity. It does not matter in what language a component is implemented as long as it supports the same IDL interfaces. For practical purposes we have chosen to generate Reactor components in Java.

The implementation of the Reactor component must be configurable to allow different kind of responses. The response may be interactive allowing the tester to examine the parameter values and construct a reply using an interactive IDL type editor, or the response is automated. The Reactor can be hard-coded to give an automated response, or by executing a general purpose scripting language that can be loaded and interpreted by the Reactor at runtime. The latter is obviously more flexible but may not be necessary for simple test cases or may have an unacceptable performance penalty. In any case, the tester must be able to make the choice. When an invocation arrives on a Reactor component facet it can reply (within limits) as if the real component is in place. The range of possible test scenarios is now extended for the components under test and can reduce the probability of errors when the final components replace the Reactor components when they are available.

Of course, the behavior of Reactor components is determined by the interactive or programmed response and will most likely differ from their real implementation. Nevertheless, the presence of Reactor components can demonstrate correct behavior of the components under test for various interaction scenarios. In particular error conditions occurring in the Reactor components can usually be simulated more easily using Reactors then real implementations. Even when real implementations become available, Reactor components are still useful for regression testing.

Another part of the test framework is the Actor component that acts as a general purpose CCM client component that can invoke operations on other components. The Actor can also load and execute test scripts or can be run in interactive mode. In interactive mode the tester can interactively fill in parameter values for a selected operation, invoke the operation and examine the result. In order to invoke an operation on a facet of a target component, the Interoperable Object Reference (IOR) of the component must be obtainable. In CCM systems, key components usually publish their IORs using a naming server. References to other components may be passed as return values of operations. References to component facets can be obtained by using the navigation operations provided by the component interface.

In addition to providing the tester with a means of testing components using an actor and reactor, the CCM test framework allows the tester to trace and visualize the propagation of invocations between CCM components, see section 4 for the details.

With the combination of Actor, Reactor, and Invocation tracing viewer the implementers of CCM components have a powerful set of tools available to test their CCM components at an early stage.

To illustrate the developers' test approach with an example, suppose a developer has implemented components C1 and C2 as depicted in Figure 2. Component C1 interacts with C2 using facet f3. The implementation of C1 also needs to interact with facet f5 of component R1 and facet f6 of component R2 as shown in Figure 2. This figure also shows that component C2 interacts with facet f7 of component R2. The implementation of R1 and R2 is outside the scope of our developer and the implementation may not become available for some time. This situation limits the test scenario possibilities for components C1 and C2 since the test scenarios in which invocations of R1 and R2 occur must be omitted. However, with the IDL specification known for R1 and R2, Reactor components are generated and instantiated as part of the test system. The test scenarios for C1 and C2 are now extended to include invocations to R1 and R2.

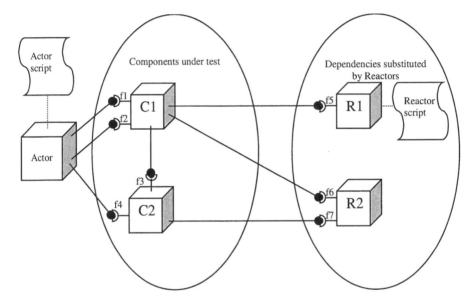

Fig. 2. Actor-reactor test environment

To test C1 and C2 the Actor is used. Figure 2 shows how the Actor user interface is used to invoke operations on the facets of the components under test C1 and C2 interactively. The Actor includes a naming server browser that allows the tester to examine the content of the naming server and to select one of the registered references. If the selected reference is a component reference, the Actor will introspect the component to obtain information about the facets it supports and will display a new window that allows the tester to select a target facet reference. Once a target facet is selected, another window is shown in which parameter values can be interactively filled in. The signatures of the operations and the structure of the parameters is obtained from an interface repository. In this example Figure 3 shows the selected operation of facet f2 of C1 on the left panel. After 'method3' has been invoked the result of the operation is shown on the right panel.

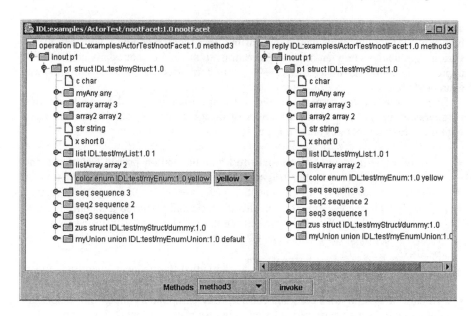

Fig. 3. Actor invocation dialog

After the test scenarios for C1 and C2 are completed by repeating the method described above for each step in the scenario the tester can visualize the propagation of invocations between C1 and C2, this invocation trace is presented in standard web browser. Figure 7 shows a similar trace from another example. The tester can now compare this message sequence chart with the same chart in the specification and verify if the components behave accordingly.

2.2   Systems Testing Tools

System testers are more engaged in the acceptance of the complete (customers) target application. The requirements and test purposes from the application users are different from the developer's viewpoint. System testers focus on the whole system or at least a meaningful subsystem that fulfills a particular work. The in-depth testing phase of the component developer using such test tools as described in the previous section is a prerequisite for the examination of a large composed system. Single components A and B have to operate according to their interface definitions and semantics specification. A system including multiple components A and B interworking possibly with each other and further components of different type fulfills an overall functionality which has to be evaluated and/or demonstrated according to an unambiguous test plan and has to deliver a meaningful test report.

It is often sufficient to run applications tests at the API provided for end-customers only. In this situation the test engineers have a choice between lots of test tools provided at the software market. An easy approach to integrate observation points into component-based system implementation is proposed for system testing: We have implemented CCM components that can be introduced at communication points between components under test (SUT components). The primary task of such so-called *proxy* components is the collection of proper information about the interaction between SUT components and the distribution of corresponding notifications to various applications (e.g. an arbiter). In contrast to the interceptor approach the proxy approach is more flexible (e.g. if C++ is used it does not need any component sources).

Due to the expressiveness of the IDL specification of the involved SUT components we had to address a number of design questions which we considered with the following features and decisions for the proxy components:

- One proxy component will cover a full communication profile (interfaces and event sinks) provided by one original SUT component; i.e. the proxy reflects the "incoming" side of a SUT component.
- It is subject to the test engineer (i.e. his interests and preferred test configuration) to couple (deploy) all or only parts of the proxy interfaces (e.g. in the following Figure 4 a proxy for component C2 is introduced, but only one facet will be used).
- Each proxy component requires an individual component identifier to be identified within the SUT after deployment.
- In case of synchronous communication proxy components should not block any interaction during waiting for a reaction in response to an operation invocation.

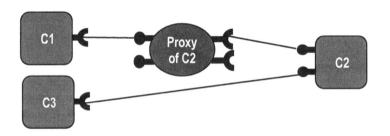

Fig. 4. Sample proxy configuration

Other major questions address the test system applications that should take care on the observations of the proxy component and how to distribute the proxy notifications. The approach depends on the facilities and intention of the test engineers. Conceptionally a specific test system component is foreseen to adapt the preferred test system application responsible for filtering, analysis or presentation of the observations (see the following sections for sample applications).

A comprehensive IDL3 event type has been defined to serve as a common interface for the different adaptation approaches. Such proxy notifications are delivered using CCM event channels. In our implementation we've distinguished *proxy_request, proxy_reply* and *proxy_exception* notifications for synchronous SUT interaction (see Figure 5) and a single *proxy_event* notification for asynchronous SUT interaction. Transported data comprise details on operation name, parameters (in/out, results), location (proxy identifier) and timestamps of the observations.

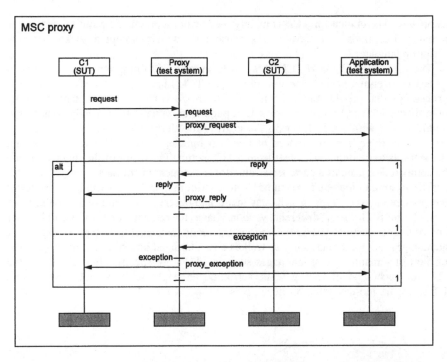

Fig. 5. Proxy component interactions

With the broadcast (publishing) feature of the CCM event communication it is possible to use different concurrent adaptation components, i.e. evaluation systems. Such adaptation components fulfill a bridge function to a non CCM-based test equipment. Unfortunately it is required to implement the specific needs for each application. On the other hand there is no implementation necessary to get the proxy components: We've selected the Open source CCM development environment Qedo [21] to generate proxy source code which can be compiled, linked and deployed with conventional tools. Due to the CCM standardized interfaces the SUT components can be based on any implementation language and do not need to be developed with Qedo.

Our implementation extends the Qedo compiler in such a way that it is sufficient to list the components (using the new "- - *proxy*" option) for which proxies should be build when Qedo is called for an IDL3 specification of the SUT. Proxy components will be generated once and can be instantiated and deployed multiple times.

3   Test Definition Languages

The COACH test framework contains a library, which allows scripts written in the popular TCL language to interact with the CCM environment. The TCL library works closely with the IdlTree library and uses the freely available Jacl [8] implementation of TCL written in Java. Although TCL is currently used for the COACH test tools, libraries for other scripting languages such as Python [2] can easily be used in the same way. The choice for TCL is mainly made from a pragmatic point of view since it easily integrates with Java and because it is widely accepted as an effective scripting language.

The goal of the COACH TCL library is to support CCM programmers, which need to test their components in an easy way. The TCL library consists of a set of TCL procedures that provide an API with the CORBA and CCM environment. With the help of the IdlTree library, complex IDL parameter values can be easily constructed and modified within a TCL script. These API procedures allow CCM components to be located, their facet references obtained, parameter values to be constructed and invocations to be done on a facet from a TCL script. The result of the invocation can be compared or used as a parameter value for subsequent operations.

The Actor can load and execute TCL test script in a TCL shell window. The tester can also interactively type in TCL statements and observe the result in the shell.

If large SUT from different vendors have to be validated in multiple user environments abstract test specifications are recommended for system testing. Their advantages are good readability as well as a standardized and common understanding of the test semantics. Test languages such as TTCN are specifically designed by the ITU for such kind of testing while scripting languages such as TCL, Python and IDLscript are more suitable for developers.

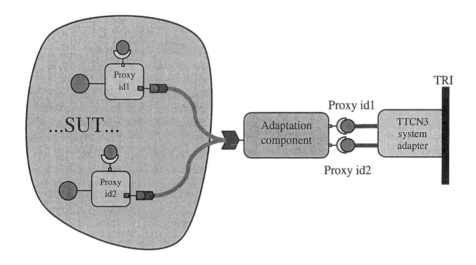

Fig. 6. TTCN-3 test system adaptation sample

Standardized test notations like TTCN-3 [13] or the testing profile for UML [18] are mature candidates and go beyond XML-based test notations as proposed in [5]. Message-based protocol conformance testing and operation-based CORBA application tests have already been done with TTCN-3 [10][11]. The UML testing profile was another alternative test notation but it was due to the incomplete standardization process of UML2.0 within the OMG not available at the beginning of our work.

In principle a TTCN-3 based test system can access operations under test at every known (or registered) CCM component. Initial trails for the application of TTCN-3 to test CCM applications have been already presented in [7], but have been limited to operation-based component interfaces and did not consider the proxy components introduced above. Furthermore, in the meanwhile the IDL2.* to TTCN-3 mapping standard from ETSI [14] could be used and requires only small additions for covering IDL3 event communication: Events can be exchanged at message-based TTCN-3 ports. Event types can be expressed by TTCN-3 record structures. The TTCN-3 *group* definition may collect all data types and templates that are related to an event type.

Our CCM adaptation component for TTCN-3 assumes a CORBA interface (for each proxy) provided by the TTCN-3 system adapter that collects (incoming) operation calls to related port instances defined in the TTCN-3 abstract test suite. Figure 6 illustrates the situation and the interfaces exemplarily involving two proxy components with a TTCN-3 system adapter that provides the related CORBA interfaces and applies to the TTCN-3 runtime interface (TRI) [15].

4   Test Trace Viewing Facilities

In addition to providing the tester with a means of testing components using an actor and reactor, the CCM test framework allows the tester to trace and visualize the propagation of invocations between CCM components. Invocation tracing is useful for such things as comparing the runtime behavior of a planned system with its design specifications. The Tracer framework presented in this section consists of two parts:

- TraceServer

- TraceViewer

The TraceServer is a CCM component that contains a collection of events that occurred within the system under test. An event basically is an interaction between CCM components. The TraceServer responds to queries by returning the requested event data formatted in XML, including complex parameter data types.

The TraceViewer (see Figure 7) is a combination of a web server and a web client. The web server acts as an intermediary between the TraceServer and the web client. It translates HTTP requests from the web client into TraceServer queries using CORBA invocations. The result is send back to the web client as plain text XML. The web client is the vehicle to visualize the data received from the web server in a user-friendly manner. The client depends heavily on JavaScript code, not only for dynamic SVG [24] creation but also for user control about how the information is presented.

Events are part of an invocation trail with a start point and an end point. As an invocation propagates through a CCM system it carries context information. This context information is extracted and updated at each interaction point.

The trace framework is generally concerned with tracing and visualizing invocations between CCM components. However, in a CCM system several communicating entities can be distinguished such as facets, receptacles event sources, event sinks, components, containers and plain CORBA objects. In order to present a meaningful picture of the various interactions we must know what the relation between an event and the communication entity is.

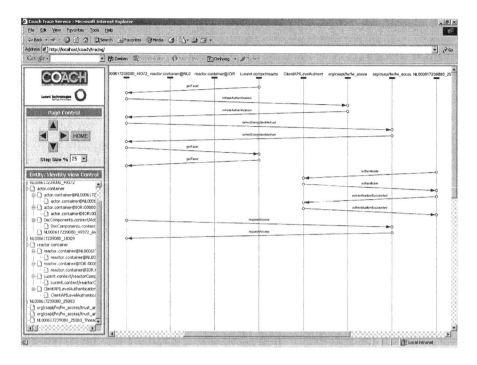

Fig. 7. Invocation tracing viewer

The underlying communication mechanism in CCM is still based on standard CORBA. The CORBA IDL compiler generates stubs and skeletons. An invocation on a CORBA object passes through a stub instance on exit and passes through a skeleton on entry. At the CORBA level, an invocation enters an entity at the POA_IN. It leaves an entity at the STUB. This results in the definition of the interaction points as shown in Listing 1. Each trace event contains information from which interaction point it was sent.

```
module tracing {
    enum InteractionPoint {
        STUB_OUT,
        POA_IN,
        POA_OUT,
        POA_OUT_EXCEPTION,
        STUB_IN,
        STUB_IN_EXCEPTION,
        ONEWAY_STUB_OUT,
        ONEWAY_POA_IN
    };
};
```

Listing 1. IDL Interaction points specification

At each interaction point a trace event must be send to the TraceServer component with timing and identity information about the interaction. This requires that the invocation flow at the interactions points is intercepted to allow for the additional actions to collect and sent the trace information. The CORBA Portable Interceptor (PI) specification [19] defines a portable mechanism to intercept the invocation flow of an operation on a CORBA object. Since CCM Component facets are implemented as normal CORBA objects, this mechanism is also suitable for the implementation of invocation tracing for CCM component interactions. The PI mechanism also allows additional service data to be propagated transparently between CORBA invocations. This is used for example with a transaction service to propagate a transaction context. For the purpose of invocation tracing, a TraceService can be created which propagates tracing context information between CORBA invocations. The IDL specification of the propagation context is shown in Listing 2.

```
struct PropagationContext {
    // user defined indentification string to mark a segment of an invocation trail
    string trail_label;

    // Id of the originating thread at the start of the invocation chain.
    string trail_id;
    long interaction_counter;
};
```

Listing 2. IDL Propagation Context specification.

The originator_id field is initialised at the start of an invocation trail and uniquely labels the trail as it propagates through distributed components. The interaction_counter field is incremented at each interaction point and is used to determine the proper order between interactions. The trailLabel field is an optional, additional label to mark an invocation trail. It can be used in combination with the Actor and the scripting environment to highlight specific sections of an invocation trail with a user defined label. TraceViewer applications can use this label to visualize such segment in the graphical output.

5   Application of the Test Tools

Due to the scope of the different test tools introduced above there are various possibilities for test engineers to benefit, i.e. the tools can be combined according to the specific needs (e.g. see Figure 8 which illustrates a combination of the proxy components with the tracing tools). The preliminary version of the test tools are an input to the COACH project workpackages developing large CCM based applications for the telecom domain (a Network Management Framework and a Parlay Platform) which are due to the COACH project termination in spring 2004. At the time of writing the experiences with the usage of our toolset are restricted to our own test applications.

The developers testing tools have been already successfully used during the implementation of some own components like e.g. the TraceServer. Predecessors of the Actor and Reactor test components were already successfully used in the

WINMAN project [23] starting at the specification phase until the final integration phase. During the integration phase they used Reactor components to isolate part of the system without disturbing the operation of the rest of the system. The actor was used to execute acceptance test scripts.

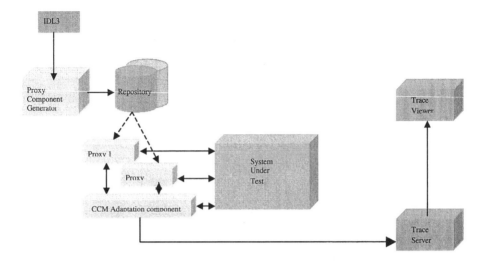

Fig. 8. Sample test configuration for online monitoring

The systems testing tools have been applied to the standard CCM examples supplied by the OMG (e.g. "dining philosophers"). It has been already demonstrated within the project how proxy components are suitable for feeding there observations to the COACH TraceServer (see section 4) and also in combination with a TTCN-3 based online monitoring system that compares observed interactions from the SUT based on abstract TTCN-3 test definitions. In the latter case the proxy components which had been generated once have been applied in multiple test cases and address various test purposes according to the selected test configurations.

6   Summary and Conclusions

The area of component based testing is a rather new area in the sense that there are almost no specialized tools in testing the development or acceptance of CCM components. The work presented in this paper is a first step to realize a test and acceptance framework for these components. A comprehensive set of testing tools have been described and implemented which can be used at an early stage of the production of CCM based applications as well as during the system acceptance testing because its scope covers the needs of component software implementers and the requirements of system test engineers.

Test concepts like the Actor and Reactor have already proven their usefulness. Visualization techniques as implemented in the trace viewer provide useful feedback for verifying the correctness of the implementation. Although two distinct user groups have been identified the test framework is flexible enough to allow other usage as well. It is at the discretion of the user whether to use the proxy based approach that can be used without modifying the component under test or the interceptor approach that allows for a rich choice in interaction points in the component under test at any stage of the development or acceptance.

The use of test scripts allows for test automation and a reproducible way of testing the components. Different needs such as monitoring, trace visualization and adaptation of well accepted (standardized) test notations have been considered and satisfied. The availability and active usage of such test tools in the CCM based software production shall support the quality, confidence and acceptance of CORBA components applications.

The Open Source implementations developed in the COACH project have been adopted and extended to create a meaningful test environment. The test facilities will be available with the CCM platforms OpenCCM [20] and Qedo [21].

References

1. H.J. Batteram and W.A. Romijn (editors), "Telecom domain requirements upon component architectures". COACH deliverable D1.1.
2. D. Beazley, "Python Essential Reference", ISBN: 0735710910, New Riders, 416 pages (June 2001)
3. K. Beck. Test-Driven Development by Example. Addison Wesley, 2003.
4. A. Bertolino, A. Polini: A Framework for Component Deployment Testing. Proceedings of the 25th International Conference on Software engineering, Portland, Oregon, Oct. 2003.
5. G. Bundell et al.: A Software component Verification Tool. SMT'00. Wollongong (AUS) Nov. 2000.
6. J. Hartmann et al.: UML-Based Integration Testing. ISSTA'00. Portland, Oregon, Aug. 2000.
7. A. Hoffmann et al.: CCM testing environment. ICSSEA'2002, Paris, Dec.2002.
8. R. Johnson, "Tcl and Java Integration", Sun Microsystems Laboratories, February 3, 1998 http://www.tcl.tk/software/java/tcljava.pdf
9. J. Reznik (editor), "Requirements for the component tool chain and the component architecture", COACH deliverable D1.3.
10. M. Schünemann et al.: Improving test software using TTCN-3, GMD Report No. 153, Dec. 2001. http://www.gmd.de/publications/report/0153/
11. A. Yin et al.: Operation-based interface testing on different abstraction levels. ICSSEA'2001, Paris, Dec.2001.
12. CCMtools project: http://sourceforge.net/projects/ccmtools
13. ETSI: Testing and Test Control Notation (TTCN-3). http://www.etsi.org/ptcc/ptccttcn3.htm
14. ETSI TS 102 219: Methods for Testing and Specification (MTS): The IDL to TTCN-3 Mapping, V1.1.1, 2003-06.
15. ETSI: TTCN-3 Runtime Interface (TRI). ES 201 873-5, Feb. 2003.
16. IST Project COACH web site, http://www.ist-COACH.org/
17. OMG, formal/02-06-65: CORBA Components, v3.0 full specification
18. OMG ADTF: UML testing profile. http://www.fokus.fhg.de/tip/u2tp/
19. OMG: Portable interceptors. TC Document orbos/99-12-02, December 1999.

20. Open CORBA Component Model Platform (OpenCCM)
    http://corbaweb.lifl.fr/OpenCCM
21. The QEDO project http://www.qedo.org/
22. W3C Note on VML http://www.w3.org/TR/NOTE-VML
23. WDM and IP Network Management (WINMAN) project: http://www.winman.org/
24. Mozilla SVG project, http://www.mozilla.org/projects/svg/

A Multi-service and Multi-protocol Validation Platform – Experimentation Results

Ana Cavalli[1], Amel Mederreg[1], Fatiha Zaïdi[1], Pierre Combes[2], Wei Monin[3],
Richard Castanet[4], Marcien MacKaya[4], and Patrice Laurençot[5]

[1]Institut National des Télécommunications- CNRS Samovar
9 rue Charles Fourier 91011 Evry Cedex
{ana.cavalli, amel.mederreg, fatiha.zaidi}@int-evry.fr
[2]France Telecom R&D/DTL
38,40, rue du Général Leclerc, 92794, Issy les moulineaux, France
pierre.combes@rd.francetelecom.fr
[3]France Télécom R&D, Technopole Anticipa
2, avenue Pierre Marzin, 22307, Lannion Cedex, France
wei.monin@rd.francetelecom.fr
[4]Université de Bordeaux 1 -Labri
351, cours de la libération 33405 Talence Cedex
{richard.castanet, marcien.mackaya}@labri.u-bordeaux.fr
[5]Université de Clermont-Ferrand- Limos
34, Avenue Carnot, 63000, Clermont-Ferrand, France
laurenco@isima.fr

Abstract. This article presents the implementation of a validation platform
based on formal methods and the experimental results obtained. This platform
allows performing conformance and interoperability tests, analysing the
specification and constructing a performance model for the services. It covers
all stages of the validation which are: formal specification, test architecture
definition, test generation and execution for the defined architecture, and performance evaluation. The test methods and architectures used here make it easier to detect and localise errors. The platform has been constructed within the
framework of the RNRT (National Telecommunications Research Network)
platform project, PLATONIS. This platform is composed of a network integrating the different sites of the project partners. The principal application domains
for the platform are telecommunication systems and mobile telephony. In particular, two different cases study are presented that illustrate the platform's applicability to the test of mobile 3rd generation protocols and services using
WAP[1], GPRS[2] and UMTS[3]. Nevertheless, the platform is generic and can be
used for other types of communication protocols and services.

---

[1] Wireless Application Protocol
[2] General Packet Radio Service
[3] Universal Mobile Telecommunication System

R. Groz and R.M. Hierons (Eds.): TestCom 2004, LNCS 2978, pp. 17–32, 2004.
© IFIP 2004

1 Introduction

In the last few years major progress has been achieved in the area of networks and computers, particularly concerning Internet and mobile networks. This evolution has strengthened the idea of mobile telephony over Internet. This last has entailed the design of new protocols and services. However, the architectures implemented by using these protocols and services interconnect heterogeneous elements that needs to be tested in order to validate their interoperability. Tests and trials on real platforms is crucial for all the actors involved, such as, operators, service providers and equipment manufacturers.

This article presents the implementation and the experimentation results of the PLATONIS multi-protocol and multi-service validation and experimentation platform [9], [14]. The work has been approved and financed by the RNRT program and is the result of the collaboration between several research labs and industrial groups. The objective of PLATONIS platform is to help industry (operators, service providers and equipment manufacturers) and research to test the conformance, the interoperability and evaluate the performance of new communication protocols and services. It assures the reliability by detecting functional errors (output and transmission errors) and performance problems. The platform has been deployed over several sites: Evry (at INT), Bordeaux (at LABRI), Clemont Ferrand (at LIMOS) and Issy-les-Molineaux (at France Telecom R&D).

The implementation of the platform integrates the network configuration part and the open source WAP protocol stack called Kannel [12]. This implementation respects the standard established by the WAP Forum. The results obtained by applying the platform encompass all test phases: specification, test generation, test execution and, also, specification analysis. These results also include the definition of new test methods and architectures. Indeed, in the cases studied, it has been noted that an implementation under test is often embedded in a complex system that does not provide a directly accessible interface to the implementation under test. This is the case with the different WAP protocol layers. The fact that there is no direct access makes it impossible to rely only on classical test methods. This makes it necessary to define test architectures that incorporate Points of Control and Observation (PCO) and Points of Observation (PO) in the implementation and use appropriate test methods.

Concerning the formal specification of the protocols, the WAP protocols were described using formal methods in order to make it easier to apply automated methods for test generation. These specifications were done for the different layers involved and in particular for WSP[4], WTP[5] and a simplified version of WAE[6].

This article also presents the formal specification of new services for cellular phones that require Internet access for their provision. In the project, the services chosen were based on the location of the subscriber and ran with WAP over GSM, GPRS and UMTS infrastructure. The services were formally described, implemented

---

[4] Wireless Session Protocol
[5] Wireless Transport Protocol
[6] Wireless Application Environment

and validated. The validation was done using test scenarios that were generated from the specifications (an approach based on an XML parser have been followed).

The generation of test scenarios was also done for the protocols. The execution of these scenarios was done on the protocol stack and using simulated and real terminal devices (cellular phone and PDA's -Personal Digital Assistants).

The article also presents the elements forming the approach that allows integrating the functional validation and the performance evaluation in the same environment. This approach was used on the same protocols and location services. Let us note that the performance evaluation of a system needs to be considered as soon as from the conception phase and stay coherent with the functional validation.

In the following sections the article first introduces the configuration of the platform and presents the new test architectures (section 2). In section 3, the formal specification of the WAP protocols and the location based services are presented. In section 4, the derived performance model is explained. In section 5, the experimental results obtained using the implemented services and protocol stack, are presented. Finally, in section 6 the conclusions and perspectives for the work are given.

2   Test Methodology and Architecture

2.1   Platform Configuration

The platform includes several sites corresponding to the partners involved in the project. Only the academic sites are open. The platform can be accessed through a mobile phone, a PDA or a simulated mobile terminal. In the case of the mobile phones or the PDA's, the access is authenticated using a RAS (Remote Access Service). This service allows the access to the Open Source Kannel WAP protocol stack. This stack connects the mobile terminals to the different HTTP servers available on the platform (Apache server, IIS 4.0) and also to the WAP service provider servers (see Fig. 1). A detailed description of the installation for each site is given in section 2.3.2.

2.2   Test Methodology

The objective is to define a methodology and the architectures for the validation and trial of the protocols and services. It is also a goal to cover and automate all phases of the test process: from the specification of the system under test to its execution on the real platform. This last allows performing conformance and interoperability tests. The interoperability tests serve to validate that different implementations interact correctly, that is, the implementations provide the global service as expected and conform to the standard. This type of tests allow verifying the interoperability between, for instance, an application running on the terminal and another on the server. On the other hand, conformance tests verify that the implementation under test follows the standard, as for instance, verifying that one of the WAP protocol layers functions correctly.

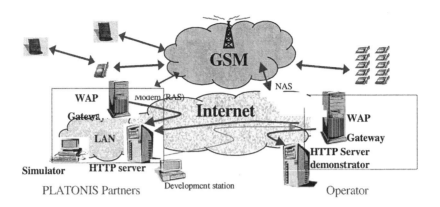

Fig. 1. The PLATONIS platform.

The test methodology used here is based on two main elements: generation methods and architectures. Below are described the different steps that constitute this methodology:

1. First, a precise representation of the system is provided. The description language used is SDL [4]. The specification needs to take into account the test architecture and the interactions with the environment.
2. Next, the tests that need to be made are selected by defining test objectives. It means choosing a strategy for the selection of tests using predefined criteria. To generate the tests, test generation algorithms are used that have been conceived for embedded testing and can be easily adapted to objectives based testing. [1] provides a detailed description of these algorithms.
3. The generated tests are then executed over the test architectures that are proposed in this article and that are described in detail in the following section.

2.3   Test Architectures

At first, the PLATONIS platform has been applied to validate and trial services for mobile networks based on WAP, GPRS and UMTS. Due to the heterogeneity and the complexity of the network elements involved, the classical architectures are not applicable [7]. This is because several entities in the network must cooperate to provide the desired service. For this reason, the authors propose a test architecture based on PCO's and PO's. This architecture is represented in figure 1.

One needs to observe the transit at different strategic points in order to be able to analyse the data exchanged. This leads to the introduction of Points of Observation (PO). A PO needs to be set between the mobile terminal and the gateway. In this way it will be able to collect the data carried by the radio link and the interoperability between the equipment can be verified. The second PO needs to be located between the gateway and the server in order to verify that the data transmitted from the gateway to the server is correct. The Point of Control and Observation (PCO) found up-stream to the mobile device allows initiating transactions and injecting valid, unexpected or invalid events, as well as recuperating the results obtained.

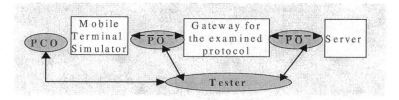

Fig. 2. Generic architecture for testing a mobile application.

With this architecture, error detection is powerful and allows capturing all the data exchanged for a given service. If an error occurs between the gateway and the server, the PO will immediately detect it. It is not necessary to place all the PO's but leaving one out reduces the observation capability. There is the possibility of optimising the tests scenarios by removing all the PO's and if a test fails, to reinstall them in order to make a diagnosis and more easily locate the error or errors. This introduces an incremental test methodology based on the degree of test detection capability.

2.3.1   Obtained Verdict

Each PO is coupled with an interface that allows verifying the progress of the test which leads to installing one per zone. In figure 2 we need two interfaces: one between the terminal and the gateway and the other between the gateway and the server. From each PO we will have a file of saved traces. The properties coming from the test objectives will be checked over these traces and in this way errors will be detected and localised. Local verdicts will be pronounced. On the other hand, each PCO will be able to give a local verdict for its zone by using the test scenario of the property being verified. The set of all local verdicts is gathered by a central tester that is in charge of pronouncing the final verdict which will be FAIL, INCONCLUSIVE or PASS.

2.3.2   Test Architectures for the WAP Protocols and Services

In the beginning, the PLATONIS project partners were interested in the mobile WAP protocol in order to verify that the implemented platform functioned correctly. This protocol was selected because the standard is stable and can be modelled (see next section) and the material that uses it exists and is commercialised.

The test architecture presented in figure 3 is the direct implementation of the model described before.

Above we find the different PO's and PCO's that are responsible for performing the local verdicts. The WAP protocol uses a gateway that transforms the data coming from a WAP navigator (in WML format) to data compatible with the Web servers (in

HTTP format). This gateway thus implements the different protocol layers that are required (WDP/UDP[7], WTP, WSP) in the WAP protocol.

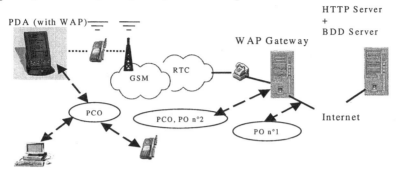

Fig. 3. Test architecture for the WAP.

Knowing that the objective is to test a mobile application, it is necessary to obtain the final result on a mobile terminal. For this several options exist:

- Create a secondary network that connects the different testers. In this way one can recuperate the different verdicts without interfering with the application. This solution requires additional equipment: a mobile terminal that can manage simultaneous communications with different mediums. This is not always possible and depends on what protocols are being tested.
- Give the mobile terminal the role of test coordinator and send to it the local results obtained from the different communication mediums that are part of the system under test. This solution does not perturb the test since the results are sent after it is completed, with the bandwidth available to send this data being a client-server type architecture.

Here we use this second solution for testing the WAP services.

It is also possible to give the gateway the role of remote tester when testing the WAP protocol stack from the client side. In this case one should follow the test architecture of figure 3 and add a PCO at the WAP gateway level. In this way all mobiles can be tested.

3   Functional Verification Model

3.1   Formal Modeling of the Protocol Layers

The modelling of the WAP protocol stack was essentially done for the WTP and WSP layers as well as a simplified version of WAE. This last layer was necessary to be able to dynamically control the system under test. The WAP system was studied for the transmission of messages in connection mode. Following are some important comments on the modelling process:

---

[7] Wireless Datagram Protocol, often replaced by UDP (Unit Datagram Protocol)

- The WAP standard describes protocols whose behaviour is very complex. This is particularly the case of WTP. This complexity has resulted in 35 000 lines of SDL code for the WTP and WSP layers.
- The abstract ASN.1 notation [2] was used to describe the parameter structures associated to the messages exchanged between protocol layers.
- Effort was made so that the modelling resulted in a modular and flexible one. This was important so that it could be easily adapted to the different test architectures defining where the PCO's and PO's are located. The use of the object oriented SDL 2000 made this modularisation possible.

The specifications were found incomplete and often ambiguous. This was particularly true with respect to error behaviour and the parameters corresponding to the error codes. The specification does not specify and leaves up to the implementation most non-nominal behaviours. For instance, the behaviour of the WAP protocol receiving a signal in a state that did not expect it. This type of behaviour can occur very often due partly to the asynchronous nature of exchanges.

Another case is, for example, when the timer overflows while waiting for a server-side user action. Here, the processes INITIATOR and RESPONDER, that manage the transaction, are killed (return to the NULL state according to the specification). Nothing prevents receiving a signal resulting from an user action, though late, particularly in an asynchronous system. The standard does not give any precisions on this making it possible for different implementations to resolve the problem differently. This could create interoperability problems. Formal modelling of the protocols using languages such as SDL helps eliminating these ambiguities.

3.2   Modeling of the Location Based Services

This section presents the location based services (LBS). These services depend on the geographical positioning of the user terminal and bring a value added to the service offer by the mobile phones. An LBS service can be described in the following way: a mobile phone sends a request to the WAP server via a gateway that transforms the WAP request into HTTP. The WAP server (LCS -LoCation Services - client) sends a request to the LCS server in order to locate the phone. The LCS server lies in the public mobile network PLMN (Public Land Mobile Network). The location of the terminal is calculated using one of the following technologies: GPS, A-GPS, E-OTD, CGI-TA or TOA [13]. Once this location established, the WAP server replies the phone's position.

The knowledge of the user's location allows to develop a new set of applications. The authors have selected and specified, by using SDL, the following services: Nearness Service (for detecting proximity), Itinerary Service (for providing best itinerary to a given place), Emergency Help Service (with location information), Road Traffic Service and Search Service (for searching in a data base associated with the preceding services by using key words).

These services can be integrated on any of the network infrastructures considered (GSM, GPRS and UMTS). However, the methods applied to calculate the user position depends on the type of network. For each network type, different components are used to perform the calculations. In this section, we first present the SDL description of these services independent of the underlying network. Then, the SDL description of the calculation of the position at the operator level for an UMTS network. The UMTS case is presented here to illustrate this level of description because it has well defined LCS interfaces for both types of network switching modes: circuit and packet modes. For UMTS, the location information is significant and testing its underlying mechanisms is necessary for guaranteeing the reliability of the network.

3.2.1   SDL Description of Services

The services were specified using the SDL 96 description language in order to make it easier to modify the specification by adding or eliminating some functionalities. Data types were defined using ASN.1 allowing the use of variable types such as lists and tables.

The specification of the services was done in two parts. The first part includes the behaviour of the users, the mobile terminals, the application server, the WAP gateway and the LCS server. The second part includes the behaviour of the PLMN for calculating the locations.

Part 1: SDL Description of the LBS Services
The specification consists of four main blocks . Each block describes respectively: the behaviour of the terminal or of several terminals (using dynamic instantiation); the network including the location server and the operator (who gives the temporary terminal id and the SIM id corresponding to the LCS); the WAP gateway; and, the application server (hosting the services introduced before). The SDL specification was developed from an informal description of the services provided by the mobile telephone operators. The modularity followed allows to easily add new services and, in accordance to the services one is subscribed to, modify the subscriber profiles. The specification resulted in a little bit more than 11 000 lines of SDL.

In order to verify that the specification is free from *livelocks* or *deadlocks* [15], the system was simulated using the exhaustive mode.

Part 2: SDL Description of the PLMN Location
In the framework of the UMTS access network and from a LCS [5] perspective, a public mobile network is composed of a core network (CN) and an access network (AN). These interact through the *Le* interface. The GMLC (*Gateway Mobile Location Centre*) is the first node in the CN. The LCS client accesses the network through the *Le* interface. The routing information is provided by the HLR (*Home Location Register*) via the *Lh* interface. The GMLC controls the user rights and then transfers the request to the MSC (*Mobile Switching Center*) or the SGSN (Serving GPRS Support Node) via the *Lg* interface. The SRNC (*Serving Radio Network Controller*) in the AN receives the authenticated request from the CN through the *Iu* interface. The RNC (Radio Network Controller) manages the AN's resources (i.e. the LMU's - *Location Mesurement Unit*), the mobile and the calculations. The LMU recuperates the meas-

urements from the signals used for determining the location. These entities communicate by messages sent through the *Iur*, *Iub* and *Uu* interfaces.

The SDL specification of LCS was done taking into consideration the location service architecture as found in UMTS and is briefly described bellow. The system is comprised of two functional blocks [5]. They are:

- The CN block, CoreNetwork, is composed of the processes that describe the behaviour of the GMLC, the HLR and the MSC. In this block, the GMLC process communicates with the HLR and MSC processes through the *Lj* and *Lg* interfaces.
- The AN block, AssessNetwork, is composed of the processes that describe the behaviour of the SRNC and the NodeB.

4   Performance Evaluation

Performance evaluation allows, first, to avoid system malfunctions caused by over-congestion of resources. Second, it allows to identify satisfactory system configurations with respect to some well-defined QoS requirements. System performance engineering has been neglected by software engineers primarily due to the difficulty encountered in using the methods required for performance modelling. It must be noted that 80% of the client/server systems need to be rebuilt due to the lower performance obtained over that required. This should be compared to the cost of performance evaluation that only represents 3% of the total cost of the development. It would be of unique interest to develop tools that better integrate performance engineering in the development process. Particularly in the following aspects: trying to consolidate the link between performance models and functional models; making performance evaluation more accessible to non-specialists, improving efficiency in the development process; and, integrating event simulation techniques. In this last point, it should be noted that design of the simulation model is not expressed using mathematical formulas but by programming. This allows constructing a model as close to reality as possible without making its complete development necessary. It also adapts very well when the objective is to compare different technologies or products or when dimensioning the system being conceived. Other elements, such as the end to end distribution of response time or the loss rate, are very difficult to quantify, making simulation necessary. The performance models for commercial simulators are based essentially on queuing theory. Such a system can be represented by a set of material resources (CPU, buffers, network, ...) accessed by applications (programs or tasks). Eventually, tasks will concur when accessing forcibly limited resources. This type of problem is resolved by scheduling mechanisms that can be associated to the access queues. In the context of the work presented in this article, SES_Workbench [8] was used.

Studying the way to derive a performance model from the functional model was carried out in order to integrate the functional verification with the performance evaluation [6]. MSC (Message Sequence Charts) and SDL (Specification Description Language) are the formalisms that we propose for the specification of the functional aspects. The use of MSC [3] is particularly useful in the case of a service platform where the use of the system can most often be resumed to a limited set of use cases.

Several notations are added to the functional model. These are:

- The *EXEC (uni x, y)* clause on a component means that the computing resources associated with the component are busy for length of time uniformly varying between x and y.
- In a similar way, the *DELAY* clause indicates a delay but concerning external activity to the studied system (i.e. protocol interfaces).
- Other syntax structures allow expressing, for instance, the synchronisation between execution paths, the triggering conditions.

An important point of which we must be aware of here is that a functional model expresses "what a system does" or the functionality it offers, while the performance model describes "the use that is made of resources". Therefore, in the case of the performance model, the functional aspects of the system only appear if they influence the consumption of the resources. The procedure followed here becomes clearer if one considers the following elements:

- When modelling, first one must select the software entities associated to the resources (i.e. the CPU that hosts it) and determine the scenarios that describe the system's common use cases. The software entities are selected according to the desired level of granularity of the results obtained by simulation and of the initial data (unitary measures) that can be procured.
- An exhaustive simulation of a model, such as the location service model, lead to an enormous number of different scenarios. Nevertheless, these scenarios are often redundant from the performance point of view. The choice of one emergency service over another does not modify the performance characteristics unless, of course, one needs to consider different reply times for different service data treatments. Thus, one needs to simplify the model by applying restrictions. This is done by identifying, in the functional model, the external conditions that influence the behaviour of the system being validated, the execution delays and making sure that the data ranges are of pertinence.

The simpler model obtained gives more manageable results when (exhaustively) simulated. Identification of the behaviour needed for performance evaluation can be made as well as the decision branch construction for each behaviour. These decisions are weighted according to the probability and constitute the different performance simulation request types.

In the case of a service platform, the goal of performance evaluation is to improve the configuration sizing with respect to the resources allocated for the different services running on the same platform. For instance, emergency calls should not be affected due to an overload of lower priority services. Figure 4 gives a simplified annotated view of a scenario of an emergency service obtained from the SDL specification described in section 3. Delays are depicted on the instances corresponding to the environment of the platform being validated (here only consisting of a location server). The condition represents a decision branch of the logical behaviour of the service for the scenario.

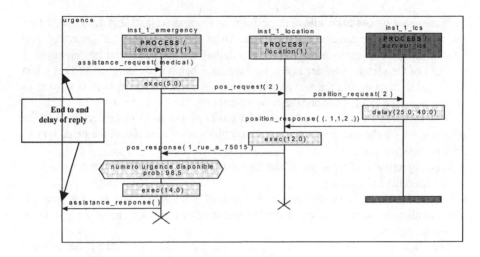

Fig. 4. Emergency Help Service notations.

5   Experimental Results

5.1   Test Generation Experiments

Two approaches to test generation of location based applications are presented in this section. The first approach relies on the automatic test generation from the SDL specification of the services and by using a test algorithm. The second approach uses a WML parser to generate the tests from the WML application. The results obtained from the generation of tests for the protocols is also presented in this section.

5.1.1   Test Generation for the *Nearness* Service

In this section we present the test of the *Nearness* service. The scenario generated allows verifying the behaviour of the service in a context with the other services. The test of the other services was performed in a similar manner.

The embedded testing techniques developed at the INT [1] was used for generating the tests of the service without direct access. Starting from the formal specification of the LBS application, a set of test scenarios was automatically generated for the *Nearness* service. To do this, the test objectives were defined. These test objectives are represented in the service specification by a set of transitions to be tested. The method used allows generating test scenarios with the test objectives as a guide for their generation.

This method constructs the test scenario from partial simulations of the specification, to avoid the state's explosion problem.

The scenarios obtained allow to perform conformance tests and to detect errors due to erroneous or unexpected messages. Once the test have been generated and following the architecture defined in section 2, they are applied to the implementation in WLM of the service in order to test its functional behaviour. Only the PCO is taken into consideration during the test of the services, the remaining network is viewed as a black box. The PO's in the architecture are not used for this type of test.

The first step of this method is the definition of the test objectives. For lack of space, here we only give a selection of these objectives that illustrate the behaviour of the Nearness service:

- **Test objective 1:** Test to see if the application server makes a request for a position from the LCS server.
- **Test objective 2:** Once the location is obtained from the LCS server, test to see if the application server requests from the user a selection from one of the proximity interest points.
- **Test objective 3:** Once the user has made his selection, test to see if the application server requests from the user to end the connection or to switch to the *Itinerary* service to obtain the itinerary to the interest point selected.
- **Test objective 4:** Test to see if the application server switches from the *Nearness* service to the *Itinerary* service.

Once all the transitions corresponding to the test objectives have been covered, we obtain a test scenario. We have obtained a test scenario that covers all these objectives. It corresponds to the path that has been followed from the environment to the last test objective and has a length of 46 transitions.

5.1.2   Test Generation Method Using an WML Parser

Here we are only interested in the WML application. In this case, the terminal, the gateway and the HTTP server are viewed as a black box. For this, we make the assumption that the information regarding the location is already available and that the network is reliable in the sense that the communication between the HTTP server and the terminal works correctly. The test architecture followed is the one presented in section 2, using only the PCO on the mobile terminal side. The procedure to test the WML application is as follows:

- Generation of the automata for the WML application: The first step is to generate the automata representing the behaviour of the application. For this, a tool called *GenTree* [5] was developed. This tool takes as input the WML application, performs a lexical and syntactical analysis, generates a behaviour tree, visualises it and saves it in the form of an automata.
- Conversion of the automata to SDL: The second step is to take the behaviour automata and convert it to SDL. Work on how to transform an EFSM (Extended Finite State Machine) to SDL is described in [11]. Using tools available on the platform, the resulting SDL description is used to automatically generate the tests.

5.1.3   Test Generation for the WSP and WTP Protocols

As explained before, the WTP and WSP layers are not directly accessible. Therefore, to test them we must also use the embedded testing techniques. The tests also allow testing the interoperability between the protocol layers.

For the generation of the tests, test objectives were defined based on the WTP and WSP specifications from the WAP Forum [10]. The following table gives some insight on the results obtained for the test generation of the standards.

Table 1. Test objectives for the WSP and WTP layers.

	Test Objectives	Test scenario length (in n° of transitions)
WSP	Session connection and disconnection phase	53
	Refused session connection phase	121
	Moved session connection phase	29
	Complete transaction phase	98
	Transaction abortion phase	144
	Session suspension and reactivation phase	93
	Session suspension and refused reactivation phase	93
	Session suspension and termination phase	67
	Complete PUSH transaction without confirmation phase	60
	Complete PUSH transaction with confirmation phase	63
	PUSH confirmation interruption phase	68
WTP	Basic transaction class 0	52
	Basic transaction class 1	100
	Basic transaction class 2 without validation from initiator	135
	Basic transaction class 2 with validation from initiator	38
	Basic transaction class 2 with interruption from initiator	67
	Basic transaction class 2 with interruption from replier	69

5.2   Test Architecture Experiments

In this section we present the deployment of the different PO's and PCO's that make up the test architecture (figure 3, section 2). Each PO is made up of two parts: PO_trace for traffic inspection and PO_analysis for giving the local verdict.

In general, the WAP gateways are connected to Internet via a local network. In this type of network, all the machines can capture the exchanged data. Thus, the PO_trace can be based on a "sniffer" that will not perturb the network. For portability reasons, the "sniffer" was implemented in Java using *Jpcap*. *Jpcap* is based on *Winpcap* for Windows and *Lipcap* for Unix. On the other hand, PO_analysis has a set of defined properties that it needs to verify. It will verify them on the trace provided by PO_trace. Once the verification is done, PO_analysis will produce the local verdict and send it to the tester that centralises all the verdicts.

The PO n°2 (see Figure 3) observes the traffic received and emitted by the WAP gateway. The open source Kannel gateway was used allowing the code modifications needed for installing the trace tools. The Kannel software is structured as different layers, each implemented as a thread that communicates with the others by exchanging messages. Following this architecture, PCO's have been located between the different layers. The installed PO is made up of a PO_trace_in that recuperates incoming traffic, a PO_trace_out that recuperates outgoing traffic and a PO_analysis that inspects all the traces and gives out the local verdict. These PO's can be used to test the behaviour of the gateway when there is no possibility of incorporating the PCO inside the gateway. The information recuperated by the PO's is very descriptive and includes the name of primitives, the data transferred, the states reached, etc. Figure 5 depicts a sample of the trace obtained from the WSP layer PO. The WSP layer is the one that allows setting up and releasing a session between the client and the server using one of the two connection modes. In figure 5 one can see the connection between the client (the PCO program running on the PDA: *PDA_Tool-Kit*) and the server (with the IP address *157.159.100.113*) using the connection oriented mode (*9201*). The message *TR-Invoke.ind* is used to open the *welcome.wml* page.

```
2003-04-22 11:23:43 [1] INFO: From WTP: Primitive Name: TR-Invoke.ind
2003-04-22 11:23:43 [1] INFO: From WTP: Ack Type: 0x01
2003-04-22 11:23:43 [1] INFO: From WTP: WTP Class: 2
2003-04-22 11:23:43 [1] INFO: From WTP: WAPAddrTuple 0x823e5d0 =
<157.159.100.113:2761> - <0.0.0.0:9201>
2003-04-22 11:23:43 [1] INFO: From WTP: Handle: 9
2003-04-22 11:23:43 [1] INFO: WSP Get PDU at 0x821d908:
2003-04-22 11:23:43 [1] INFO: GET, OPTIONS, HEAD, DELETE, or TRACE: 0
2003-04-22 11:23:43 [1] INFO: Length of URI: 28
2003-04-22 11:23:43 [1] INFO: URI:
2003-04-22 11:23:43 [1] INFO: Octet string at 0x8217f70:
2003-04-22 11:23:43 [1] INFO:         len:   28
2003-04-22 11:23:43 [1] INFO:         size:  29
2003-04-22 11:23:43 [1] INFO:         immutable: 0
2003-04-22 11:23:43 [1] INFO:         data: 68 74 74 70 3a 2f 2f 6c    http://l
2003-04-22 11:23:43 [1] INFO:         data: 6f 74 69 3a 38 30 30 30    oti:8000
2003-04-22 11:23:43 [1] INFO:         data: 2f 77 65 6c 63 6f 6d 65    /welcome
2003-04-22 11:23:43 [1] INFO:         data: 2e 77 6d 6c                .wml
2003-04-22 11:23:43 [1] INFO: Octet string dump ends.
2003-04-22 11:23:43 [1] INFO: Request headers:
2003-04-22 11:23:43 [1] INFO: Octet string at 0x82448a0:
2003-04-22 11:23:43 [1] INFO:         len:   230
2003-04-22 11:23:43 [1] INFO:         size:  231
2003-04-22 11:23:43 [1] INFO:         immutable: 0
2003-04-22 11:23:43 [1] INFO:         data: 81 83 81 84 81 85 81 86    ........
.....
2003-04-22 11:23:43 [1] INFO:         data: 74 2d 72 65 73 70 6f 6e    Projet_P
2003-04-22 11:23:43 [1] INFO:         data: 73 65 00 80 9e a9 4e 6f    latonis/
2003-04-22 11:23:43 [1] INFO:         data: 6b 69 61 2d 4d 49 54 2d    PDA-Tool
2003-04-22 11:23:43 [1] INFO:         data: 42 72 6f 77 73 65 72 2f    -Kit/V1.
2003-04-22 11:23:43 [1] INFO:         data: 33 2e 30 00 83 99          0.......
2003-04-22 11:23:43 [1] INFO: Octet string dump ends.
2003-04-22 11:23:43 [1] INFO: WSP PDU dump ends.

2003-04-22 11:23:43 [1] INFO: From WTP: Primitive Name: TR-Result.cnf
```

Fig. 5. WSP PO in the Kannel WAP gateway.

The PCO must be capable of sending and receiving different frames as well as the different local verdicts. A PDA running Windows CE was used making it easier to program and establishing either a direct connection to GSM or through a mobile phone equipped with a *Irda* port. A WAP navigator was developed that implements the WTP and WSP layers (standard WAP version 1.1) and provides a graphical user interface that allows loading the test files.

While the test is being performed, the PDA waits for data that is either information feedback or a local verdict. At the end of the test, it waits until it receives all the verdicts and only then produces the final one based on the rule stated previously. Figure 6 bellow shows the beginning of a test, including the request for the connection of figure 5 but seen from another perspective.

Also, to test the protocols found on the client side (mobile), a PCO has been installed at the WAP Kannel gateway level. The test scenarios produced as presented in section 4 are executed on the platform using the PCO at the gateway level, but also using the PDA as previously described.

To give an example, a test scenario produced as presented in section 5.3 will be described. This scenario is injected at the PCO level and allows testing the "class 2 transaction with interruption from replier". As seen in figure 7, one can observe the PO level exchanges. In this way we are able to check that the mobile behaves correctly when an unexpected message is received during the exchanges. Resulting from this injected error, the existing WML page (that the terminal wanted to access) cannot be opened due to the message sent via the PCO.

Fig. 6. WSP PCO at the PDA

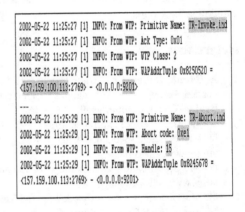

Fig. 7. WSP PO with injected message

6   Conclusion

The platform presented in this article allows performing conformance and interoperability tests, analyse the specification and produce a performance model for the services. It covers all of the validation phases: formal specification, test architecture definition, test generation and execution for the given architecture and performance evaluation. Its originality lies in its ability to cover several different aspects that start with the formal specification and end with the incremental implementation of the tests following an innovative test architecture. It has allowed to experiment with embedded test techniques and is designed to allow end-users to test real applications in their environment. It also shows the scalability of the proposed methods.

Complementary research on several aspects is being carried out. The test of an WML application is currently based on a behaviour tree extracted from the specification. To be able to use automatic generation tools, this tree is translated to SDL. Calculating test coverage also becomes necessary. Introduction of control and observation events in the specification is being studied in order to increase the testing capability of an application.

The complexity of the architecture must be considered in the performance modelling. The architecture is composed of many components and is always evolving (i.e. adding/removing services, evolution of standards). Thus, another important aspect that is being studied is the component modelling and composition rules and how they take into account performance and resources.

Finally, the techniques presented here will be applied to other types of mobile networks, as for instance, ad-hoc networks. This type of networks do not require (or preferably don't depend on) a centralised management or a fixed network infrastructure, such as, base stations and fixed access points. Furthermore, dynamic reconfiguration of the network becomes necessary in order to adapt to eventual context changes. These new characteristics make it necessary to adapt existing test methods and devise new ones.

References

1. A. Cavalli, D. Lee, Ch. Rinderknecht, and F. Zaïdi. Hit-or-Jump: An Algorithm for Embedded Testing with Applications to IN Services. In Proceedings of FORTE/PSTV'99, Beijing, China, Octobre 1999.
2. O.Dubuisson. ASN.1. Springer, 1999.
3. ITU-T, Message Sequence Chart (MSC), Recommendation Z.120, November, 1999, http://www.sdl-forum.org
4. ITU-T, Specification and Description Language, Recommandation Z.100, Nov. 1999, http://www.sdl-forum.org
5. M. Mackaya, R. Castanet. Modelling and Testing Location Based Application in UMTS Networks. IEEE Contel, Zagreb, Croatia, June 2003.
6. W. Monin, F. Dubois, D. Vincent , P. Combes, Looking for a better integration of design and performance engineering, SDL Forum 2003.
7. O. Rafiq, R. Castanet and C. Chraibi. Towards an environment for testing OSI protocols. Proc of the International Workshop on Protocol Specification, testing and Verification, Toulouse, France, 1985.
8. SES Inc. SES WorkBench Modelling Reference manual, 1998.
9. The PLATONIS Consortium. The platonis project. In First International Workshop on Services Applications in the Wireless Public Infrastructure, Mai 2001. http: //www-lor.int-evry.fr/platonis.
10. WAP spécification, http://www.wapforum.org.
11. YoungJoon Byun, Beverly A. Sanders, Chang-Sup Keum, Design Patterns of Communicating Extended Finite State Machines in SDL, PloP 2001 conference
12. http://www.kannel.org.
13. http://www.wirelessdevnet.com/channels/lbs/features/mobilepositioning.html.
14. http://www-lor.int-evry.fr/platonis
15. http://www.telelogic.com

From Design to Test with UML
Applied to a Roaming Algorithm
for Bluetooth Devices

Zhen Ru Dai[1], Jens Grabowski[2], Helmut Neukirchen[2], and Holger Pals[3]

[1] Fraunhofer FOKUS, Competence Center TIP, Kaiserin-Augusta-Allee 31,
D-10589 Berlin, Germany, dai@fokus.fraunhofer.de
[2] Institute of Computer Engineering, University of Lübeck, Ratzeburger Allee 160
D-23538 Lübeck, Germany, pals@iti.uni-luebeck.de
[3] Institute for Informatics, Software Engineering for Distributed Systems Group,
University of Göttingen, Lotzestrasse 16-18, D-37083 Göttingen, Germany
{grabowski,neukirchen}@cs.uni-goettingen.de

Abstract. The UML Testing Profile provides support for UML based model-driven testing. This paper introduces a methodology of how to use the testing profile in order to modify and extend an existing UML design model for test issues. As a case study, a new roaming algorithm for bluetooth devices has been developed at the *University of Lübeck*, is modelled using UML. The usability of the UML Testing Profile will be explained by applying it to this model.

1   Introduction

The Unified Modeling Language (UML) is a visual language to support the design and development of complex object-oriented systems [1]. While UML models focus primarily on the definition of system structure and behaviour, they provide only limited means for describing test objectives and test procedures. Furthermore, the growing system complexity increases the need for solid testing. Thus, in 2001, a consortium is built by the Object Management Group (OMG) in order to develop a UML 2.0[1] profile for the testing domain [3,4]. Currently, the UML Testing Profile project [5] is at its finalization stage.

A UML profile provides a generic extension mechanism for building UML models in particular domains. The UML Testing Profile is such an extension developed for the testing domain. It bridges the gap between designers and testers by providing a means for using UML for both system modeling and test specification. This allows a reuse of UML design documents for testing and enables test development in an early system development phase [6].

---

[1] UML 2.0 has been adopted by the OMG in June 2003. Currently, it is at its standardization finalization stage. In this paper, we follow the approach of *U2 Partners* consortium [2], who is the main submitter of UML 2.0. When talking about UML, we only refer to version 2.0.

R. Groz and R.M. Hierons (Eds.): TestCom 2004, LNCS 2978, pp. 33–49, 2004.

In this paper, we provide a methodology of how to apply UML Testing Profile concepts to an existing UML design model effectively. As a case study, the methodology will be evaluated by applying it to a UML model for roaming with Bluetooth devices.

This paper is structured as follows: After a short introduction of UML Testing Profile in the next section, a methodology will be provided (Section 3) where mandatory and optional test aspects of UML Testing Profile are discussed. In Section 4, we will introduce potential roaming techniques for data transfer scenarios using Bluetooth hardware devices as a case study. A corresponding UML model is given in Section 5. Section 6 evaluates our testing methodology by applying it to the UML model. Some conclusions are drawn in Section 7.

2   The UML Testing Profile (UTP)

The UML Testing Profile provides concepts to develop test specifications and test models for black-box testing [7]. The profile introduces four logical concept groups covering the aspects: *test architecture, test behavior, test data* and *time* (Figure 1) [8]. Together, these concepts define a modeling language for visualizing, specifying, analyzing, constructing and documenting a test system.

Test Architecture Concepts	Test Behavior Concepts	Test Data Concepts	Time Concepts
SUT	Test objective	Wildcards	Timer
Test components	Test case	Logical partition	Time zone
Test suite	Defaults	Coding rules	
Test configuration	Verdicts		
Test control	Validation action		
Arbiter	Test trace		
Utility part	Log action		

Fig. 1. UML Testing Profile Concepts

The test architecture group covers the concepts for specifying test components, the interfaces of and connections among test components and between test components and System Under Test (SUT). The test behavior group embodies concepts of specifying actions necessary to evaluate the objective of a test. Test behaviors can be defined by any behavioral diagram of UML 2.0, e.g. as interaction diagrams or state machines. The test data group includes concepts for specifying test data. The time group defines concepts to constrain and control test behavior with regard to time.

3   A Methodology for UML Testing Profile

In this section, we introduce a methodology for using the UML Testing Profile effectively after having received a detailed design model which should be tested. In the following, we determine *design model* to be the system design model in UML and the *test model* to be the UML model enriched with UML Testing Profile concepts.

Having a design model, a tester may have to specify tests for the system. This can be done by extending the design model with UML Testing Profile concepts. The following aspects must be considered when transforming a design model into a test model:

First of all, define a new UML package as the test package of the system. Import the classes and interfaces from the system design package in order to get access to message and data types in the test specification. Next, start with the specification of the *test architecture* and continue with *test behavior* specifications. Test data and time are mostly already comprised in either the test architecture (e.g. timezone or data pool) or test behavior (e.g. timer or data partitioning) specifications.

Below, issues regarding test architecture and test behavior specifications are listed. They are subdivided into two categories: mandatory issues and optional issues. *Mandatory* issues can normally be retrieved directly from the design model, while *optional* issues are specific to test requirements and, therefore, can seldom be retrieved from existing UML diagrams. However, they are not always needed for the test model. The most important issues are the specification of SUT components, test components, test cases and verdict settings:

I. Test architecture:
   i. Mandatory:
      - Assign the system component(s) you would like to test to *SUT*.
      - Depending on their functionalities, test components have to be defined. Try to group the system components (except the SUT) to *test components*.
      - Specify a *test suite* class listing the test attributes and test cases, also possible test control and test configuration.
   ii. Optional:
      - In order to define the ordering of test case execution, specify the *test control*. The simplest way is to string the test cases together. In more complex test controls, loops and conditional test execution may be specified.
      - *Test configuration* can be easily retrieved by means of existing interaction diagrams: Whenever two components exchange messages with each other, assign a communication channel between the components. If there is no interaction diagram defined in the design model, connect the test components and SUT to an appropriate *test configuration* so that the configuration is relevant for all test cases included in the test suite.

- Determine *utility parts* within the test configuration.
- Determine an *arbiter* for test verdict arbitration.
- Assign *timezones* to the components. Timezones are normally needed if a distributed test system is built and time values of different components need to be compared.
- Provide *coding rule* specifications.

II. Test behavior:

  i. Mandatory:

- For designing the *test cases*, take the given interaction diagrams of the design model and change (i.e. rename or group) the instances and assign them with stereotypes of the UML Testing Profile (i.e. test component or SUT) according to their functionalities.
- Assign *verdicts* at the end of each test case specification. Usually, the verdict in a test case is set to pass.

  ii. Optional:

- Specify *default* behaviors using *wildcards* for setting a fail or inconclusive verdict.
- Define time events by means of *timers* or *time constraints*.

4   A Case Study: Roaming with Bluetooth Devices

Bluetooth is an established standard for short-range wireless communication. The Bluetooth specification enables small devices to interact within a short range. The standards related to Bluetooth include both the hardware (radio, baseband and hardware interface) and basic protocol layers that allow Bluetooth software to run on different Bluetooth enabled devices.

The current Bluetooth standard does not support roaming of Bluetooth devices [9]. If a device is losing the link to its master, no provision is made to transfer the connection to another master. Nevertheless, roaming within Bluetooth piconets might be useful in some cases, e.g. for Bluetooth-enabled network access using LAN access points. Assuming having more than one Bluetooth LAN access point, roaming might be useful for having a seamless connection even while moving.

4.1   The Application

The need for a basic roaming support for Bluetooth devices descends from a project at the *University of Lübeck* and several other academic and industrial partners [10]. The project is situated in medical environment. Its goal is to replace the traditional cable-based monitoring of patients during surgical treatments with a wireless transmission of the patient's monitoring data using Bluetooth hardware devices. By transmitting the sensor data via radio, the mobility of the patient will be increased significantly, the number of artifacts (often caused by the cables themselves) are reduced as well as the overall cost for the replacement of broken cables.

Sensor data like electrocardiogram (ECG), temperature or blood pressure are gathered at a *mobile device*, digitized and transmitted via radio to fixed units (*receivers*). The mobile device is fixed at the patient's bed (or the patient itself) which may be moved during the entire monitoring period. One of the advantages of this wireless monitoring is a continuous data transmission throughout all the different stages the patient passes through (e.g. preparation, anesthesiology, surgery, wake up, intensive care). Thus, the connection between the mobile devices and the receivers mounted at the hospital's walls or ceilings must be handed over from one receiver to the next while the patient is moving. The receivers have to be mounted in such a way that the entire area the mobile device can reach is covered. To allow a seamless connection, the areas covered by the antennas of two adjacent receivers are overlapping.

In this scenario, different units (e.g. sensor units, digitizing unit and radio transmission unit) share the same rechargeable battery pack. The electric power consumption plays an important role in the design of the system. As a consequence, a mobile device only consists of a small embedded device including the Bluetooth chipset and a low-current microcontroller without a complete Bluetooth protocol stack running on it. From now on the term *Bluetooth device* denominates a device using a Bluetooth hardware unit to send and receive data without necessarily using the complete Bluetooth protocol stack.

4.2   Roaming for Bluetooth

Our roaming approach assumes that all masters are connected to a fixed network. The mobile devices are usually moving along the masters. If a slave runs the risk of losing connection to its actual master, the connection must be handed over to the next master. The slave prevents the loss by periodically checking the quality of the link to the master. This can be done using the *HCI_Get_Link_Quality* command defined in the Bluetooth standard [9]. If the quality drops below a certain threshold value the next master will be chosen. The slave tries to connect directly to the next master using the Bluetooth paging mechanism, knowing to which master it has to contact to next. Herefore, movements of the slave are tracked by a *Location Server*, which updates and provides slave's spacial information in form of a *roaming list* whenever the slave changes its master. The current master receives the roaming list from Location Server and forwards it to the slave [11].

The Activity Diagram in Figure 2 shows the activities of a slave necessary for roaming. The slave tries to connect to a master. If the connection is successful, the updated roaming list is transferred to the slave and data can be sent. In parallel, the link quality between slave and master is observed. If the quality gets bad, the slave will look in the roaming list for a new master and try to connect to that master directly. If, for any reason, no connection can be established, a warning message is sent to the user (e.g. by a warning light or a special sound indicating that a problem has occurred). Another warning message is sent to the last master. If the connection to the last master is still alive, the reception

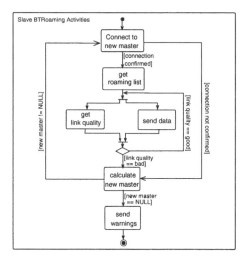

Fig. 2. Roaming Algorithm as Activity Diagram

of a warning message can be used to initiate appropriate exception handling mechanisms.

Figure 3 shows the design of the protocol stack resulting from the proposed roaming approach: Special roaming layers (*Slave Roaming Layer* and *Master Roaming Layer*) are added. They take care of the correct transfer of the connections. Our roaming approach makes no use of the higher protocol stacks of Bluetooth. Therefore, the roaming layers are implemented directly on the hardware interface called *Host Controller Interface* (HCI). The application layers are set upon the roaming layers. The interface from roaming layer to application layer is called *Slave Roaming Interface* (SRI) and *Master Roaming Interface* (MRI), respectively.

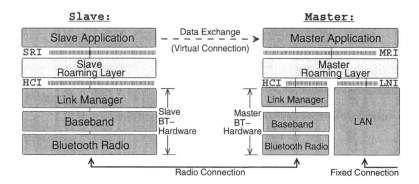

Fig. 3. Protocol Stack with Roaming Layer

Additionally, a master is specified as a fixed network node. Thus, it also embodies the LAN protocol stacks to be able to communicate with the local network. The interface between the *Master Roaming Layer* and the Ethernet is called *Local Network Interface* (LNI).

5   From Design ...

In addition to the Bluetooth roaming algorithm presented in the previous section, we also investigated the applicability of UML 2.0 [4,12,1] for modeling our roaming approach. The usage of a standardized and widely accepted modeling language like UML has several advantages: It supports the communication among soft- and hardware designers, avoids ambiguities in the description and allows the usage of commercial tools for documentation, analysis, implementation and testing during system development. In this section, we describe an architectural view on our Bluetooth roaming scenario by means of a UML package diagram, show the communication among the UML Bluetooth classes in form of sequence diagrams and present the local behavior of a slave by using a UML state machine.

Figure 4 shows a UML package diagram with different classes involved in our Bluetooth roaming approach. Similarity can be recognized between the classes in Figure 4 and the Bluetooth protocol stacks in Figure 3. The slave classes are called Slave Application, Slave BTRoaming and Slave BT-HW (Bluetooth Hardware). The interfaces SRI and HCI connect the class components with each other. A Slave BT-HW is connected to one Master BT-HW. Similar to the slave classes and interfaces, there are the classes Master Application, Master BTRoaming and Master BT-HW and the interfaces MRI and HCI on the master's side.

Master BTRoaming class is connected to the Location Server, which represents a node in the local network, by means of the interface LNI. Location Server owns a Net_Struct_Table and several Slave_Roaming_Lists. There is exactly one roaming list for each slave. The Net_Struct_Table is a static table which provides information

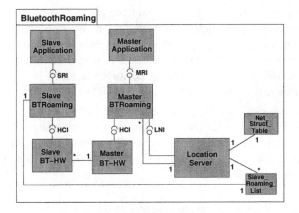

Fig. 4. Bluetooth Roaming Package

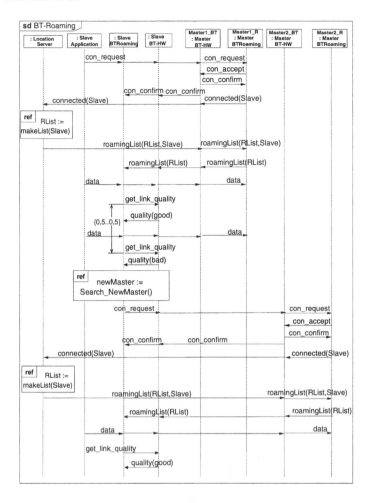

Fig. 5. Roaming Scenario Design

about the structure of the local network and the physical position of the masters as necessary for calculating each Slave_Roaming_List. In contrast, the instances of Slave_Roaming_List are changing dynamically. The Slave_Roaming_List is updated by the Location Server whenever a slave roams to a new master. Since a copy of each updated Slave_Roaming_List is transferred to its slave there is also a one-to-one association between Slave_Roaming_List and Slave BTRoaming.

In Figure 5, the sequence diagram depicts a detailed roaming scenario. There are eight different instances in the diagram: One location server instance called Location Server, three slave instances named Slave Application, Slave BTRoaming, Slave BT-HW, and four masters instances with BT-HW and BTRoaming instances for each of Master1 and Master2.[2]

---

[2] The application instances of Master1 and Master2 are not shown because roaming is independent from the application layers.

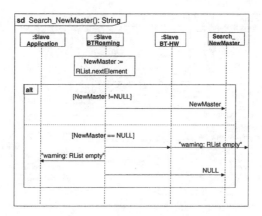

Fig. 6. *Search_NewMaster()* Function

The scenario starts with a connection request from the application instance of the Slave to Master1.[3] The hardware instance Master1_BT confirms the connection establishment and the roaming instance Master1_R informs the Location Server that Slave is now under its responsibility.[4]

Hence, the Location Server calculates and updates the roaming list RList of the Slave and sends it to Master1_R. Master1_R forwards the RList immediately to the Slave Roaming instance. Now, data can be exchanged between Slave and Master1 until the link quality becomes bad.

The verification of the link quality is performed periodically every 0.5s between the Slave BTRoaming instance and the Slave BT-HW Instance. If the link quality is proved to be bad, a new master is needed. For that, the function Search_NewMaster() is called by Slave BTRoaming. This function looks up in the RList and picks out the name of the next neighbouring master and returns the name of the new Master to Slave BTRoaming (Figure 6). In case that RList is empty, a warning signal will be sent to both the Slave Application and the old Master (if it is still possible).

In our scenario (in Figure 5), the new Master is Master2. Thus, a connection request will be sent from Slave Roaming instance to Master2_R instance. If Master2 BT-HW confirms a successful connection establishment, the Location Server will again be informed about the new status of Slave. It updates the roaming list and sends it to the roaming instance of the new master. Master2_R forwards the list to Slave BTRoaming and data exchange can be started.

A set of scenarios, like the ones presented in Figures 5 and 6, can be analyzed and used to generate local views of class behaviors. One possibility of UML to describe such local behaviors are state machines.

---

[3] In order to provide an intuitive understanding of the signals, we abstracted from the signal names in the Bluetooth specification [9].

[4] Since there is a lot forwarding traffic between the instances, we only describe the source and the destination instances of a message.

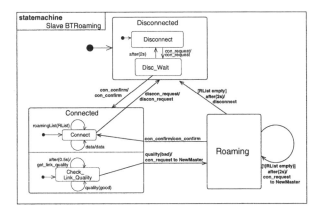

Fig. 7. Statemachine of class Slave BTRoaming

As an example, Figure 7 shows a state machine of the slave roaming instance Slave BTRoaming. This instance receives messages from the Slave Application instance and the slave hardware (Slave BT-HW) instance. The diagram contains the states Disconnected, Connected and Roaming. Disconnected is a composite state with multiple sub-states, Connected has orthogonal sub-states running in parallel.

In the beginning, the Slave BTRoaming instance is in the sub-state Disconnect of state Disconnected. If it receives a connection request from the application instance, it forwards the request to the hardware instance and goes into the sub-state Disc_Wait, waiting for a connection confirmation from the hardware. If the confirmation message does not arrive within 2 seconds, Slave BTRoaming instance goes back to the Disconnect state. If the confirmation is received by the roaming instance within time limit, the slave is Connected and goes into the sub-state Connect. In this state, data can be received from the application instance and is forwarded to the hardware instance. In parallel, link quality is verified every 0.5s (state Check_Link_Quality). The Roaming state will be reached, if the link quality becomes bad. Herein, a new master is picked out and a connection between the slave and the new master will be established. From state Roaming, the roaming instance can either get connected to a new Master or be disconnected again, if the roaming list has been exhaustively searched and no master was be found.

Even though the newest version of UML is still under development, we got the impression that UML is very well suited to model roaming for Bluetooth devices. The different kinds of diagrams force us to describe the roaming from different perspectives and on different levels of abstraction. We believe that UML improved the modeling process and helped to avoid ambiguities in the description.

6 ... to Test with UML 2.0

In this section, we will show how to design tests and modify an existing design model to obtain a test model. As a case study, we take the UML model for roaming with Bluetooth devices which is introduced in Section 5. For the model modification, we will apply step by step the methodology introduced in Section 3. One focus of this case study is to show that classes and interfaces specified in the design model can be re-used in the test model.

6.1   Test Preparation

Before augmenting the design model, the focus of the test must be defined, i.e. which classes should be tested and which interfaces does the tester need in order to get access to these classes. For our case study, the functionalities of the Slave BTRoaming layer[5] is subject of test.

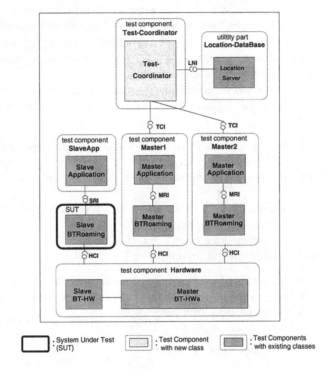

Fig. 8. Role Assignment for System Components

Figure 8[6] presents the test configuration with one slave and two masters.The classes originate from the BluetoothRoaming package of the design model in Section 5: The focus of our tests is the Slave BTRoaming layer. Thus, the Slave Application layer is one test component. Other test components are the underlying Bluetooth Hardware layer and the master components Master1 and Master2.

---

[5] *Layer* is a term used in the context of communication protocols. In this paper, we will use it as a synonym to *component* within an object-oriented system.

[6] This diagram is not a UML diagram.

On the top of the slave and the masters, we specified a new test component of class Test-Coordinator. This test component is the main test component which administrates and instructs the other test components during the test execution. The coordinator is also responsible for the setting of the test verdicts during test case execution. The coordinator has access to the utility part Location-DataBase. This data base embodies the Location Server, which owns the slave roaming lists and the network structure table. Communication between the Test-Coordinator and the masters is performed via the Test Coordination Interface (TCI).

This test configuration is very flexible: The Bluetooth Hardware layer used in a test configuration might either be real Bluetooth (i.e. consisting of the slave's Bluetooth hardware SlaveBT-HW and the master's Bluetooth hardware MasterBT-HW) or emulated by software. Moreover, different multi party test configurations can easily be obtained by adding further masters. Even the master test component can be regarded as sub-divided into a Master Roaming and Master Application layer. This allows to re-use all the classes specified in the design model. Additionally, in a different test stage, it would be possible to replace more and more of the emulated test components with real implementations. Consequently, it is easy to perform integration tests with such a test configuration, as well.

In our case study, the following functionalities of the Slave Roaming layer should be tested:

– Is the Slave Roaming layer able to choose a new master by looking up its roaming list when the connection with its current master gets weak?
– Does the Slave Roaming layer request a connection establishment to the chosen master?
– Does the Slave Roaming layer wait for a connection confirmation of the master when the connection has been established?
– Does the Slave Roaming layer send a warning to the environment, when no master can be found and the roaming list is empty?

These test objectives assume that basic functionalities of the Slave Roaming layer like data forwarding from the application layer to the hardware layer have already been tested in a preceding capability test.

6.2   Test Architecture Specification

First of all, a test package for the test model must be defined. Our package is named BluetoothTest (Figure 9a). The test package imports the classes and interfaces from the BluetoothRoaming package in Section 5 in order to get access to the classes to be tested.

In Section 6.1, we have assigned the Slave BTRoaming layer to *SUT* and other system components to *test components*. The test package consists of five test component classes, one utility part and one test suite class. The test suite class is called BluetoothSuite. It shows various test attributes, some test functions and two test cases (Figure 9b).

Test configuration and test control are also specified in the test suite class. The *test configuration* (Figure 10a) corresponds with the test configuration in

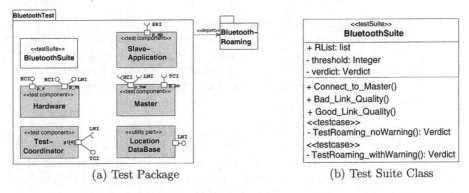

Fig. 9. Test Package & Test Suite Class

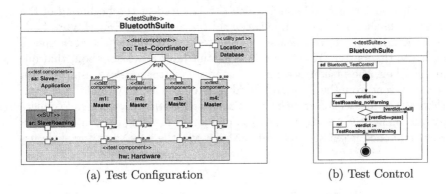

(a) Test Configuration   (b) Test Control

Fig. 10. Test Configuration & Test Control

Figure 8, except that it consists of one slave and four masters m1–m4. Ports with interfaces connect the test components and the SUT to each other.

Figure 10b illustrates the *test control*, indicating the execution order of the test cases: First, test case TestRoaming_noWarning is executed. If the test result is pass, the second test case TestRoaming_withWarning will also be executed. Otherwise, the test is finished.

6.3 Test Behavior Specification

Our test cases are all derived from the sequence diagrams, state machines and activity diagrams of the design model presented in Section 5. Only little effort was necessary for deriving the test case specifications. Some of the test cases may also be generated automatically.

In Section 6.1, we have listed the test objectives of the case study. As an example, we will present a test case for the following scenario:

After the exchange of two data packages, the link quality between Slave and its current master m1 becomes bad. The first alternative master in the roaming list m2 cannot be reached since the link quality is also weak. Thus, after at most two seconds, a further master m3 is chosen from the roaming list and the connection is established successfully.

Figure 11 depicts the test case for the scenario above. Test case TestRoaming_NoWarning starts with the activation of the timer T1 of six seconds. T1 is a guarding timer which is started at the beginning and stopped at the end of a test case. It assures that the test finishes properly even if e.g. the SUT crashes and does not respond anymore. In this case, the timeout event is caught by a default behavior.

The function Connect_To_Master, which is referenced at the beginning of the test case establishes a connection between the Slave and Master m1 (Figure 12a): The connection request (con_request) is initiated by the Slave-Application and is forwarded to the master. The master informs the Test-Coordinator about that observation. Then, the master accepts the connection (con_accept), resulting in a confirmation sent from the Bluetooth hardware to both the slave and the master. Thereupon, the master informs the Test-Coordinator about the successful connection, which allows the Test-Coordinator to build a new roaming list containing the masters (reference makeList) and to transfer it via the master to the slave us-

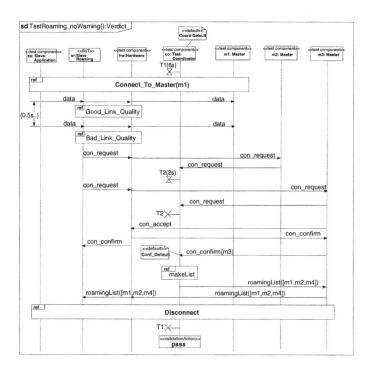

Fig. 11. Test Scenario

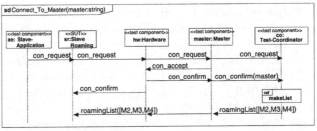

(a) Connect to Master Function

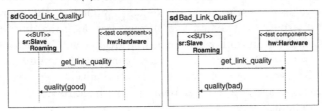

(b) Link Quality Evaluation Functions

Fig. 12. Test Functions

ing the message roamingList([M2,M3,M4]). The entries of the roaming list indicate that if the connection between slave and its current master gets weak, master m2 should be tried next. If this connection cannot be established, master m3 should contacted. As a last alternative, m4 should be chosen. If none of the alternative masters can be connected to, warnings would be sent out.

When the referenced behavior of Connect_to_Master has finished in Figure 11, the slave has successfully connected to master m1 and Slave-Application starts to send data to the master. Additionally, the link quality is checked periodically. Checking the link quality is specified in the functions Good_Link_Quality and Bad_Link_Quality in Figure 12b. Herein, Slave Roaming triggers the evaluation request and receives the result from the hardware.

In the first evaluation of test case TestRoaming_noWarning (Figure 11), the Hardware has to be tuned to report a good link quality. Thus, further data can be sent. In the second evaluation, the link quality is determined to be bad. Therefore, a new master is looked up. According to the roaming list, the new master must be m2. A connection request is expected to be sent to m2 by the SUT. As soon as it is observed and reported to the Test-Coordinator, a timer T2 of two seconds is started. This timer assures that when the SUT cannot establish a connection to a master, the SUT chooses a further master and tries to connect to it within two seconds. If it is observed that the SUT requests a connection to the correct master m3, the timer T2 is stopped by the Test-Coordinator. In this test case, the connection is accepted (con_accept) by master m3 and hence confirmed (con_confirm). After the Test-Coordinator noticed the connection to the correct master, it assembles the new roaming list and sends it via the master to the slave. In case that no connection confirmation is received, the default behavior Conf_Default is invoked. Finally, slave and master are disconnected, the guarding timer T1 is stopped and the verdict of this test case is set to pass.

Besides the expected test behavior of test case TestRoaming_NoWarning, default behaviors are specified to catch the observations which lead to a fail or inconclusive verdict. The given test case uses two defaults called Coord_Default and Conf_Default (Figure 13). In UML Testing Profile, test behaviors can be specified by all UML behavioral diagrams, including interaction diagrams, state machines and activity diagrams. Thus, Figure 13 shows how default behaviors can be specified either as sequence diagrams (Figure 13a) or as state machines (Figure 13b).

Coord_Default is an instance-specific default applied to the coordinator. It defines three alternatives. The first two alternatives catch the timeout events of the timers T1 and T2. In both cases, slave and master will be disconnected and the verdict is set to fail. After that, the test component terminates itself. The third alternative catches any other unexpected events. In this case, the verdict is set to inconclusive and the test behavior returns back to the test event which triggered the default.

Conf_Default is an event-specific default attached to the connection confirmation event. In the Test-Coordinator, this default is invoked if either the connection confirmation is not sent from the correct master or another message than the connection confirmation is received. In the first case, the verdict is set to fail and the test component finishes itself. In the latter case, the verdict is set to inconclusive and the test returns to main test behavior.

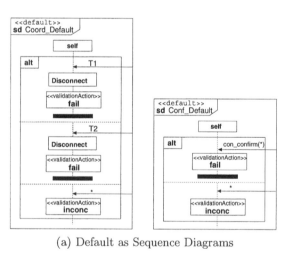

(a) Default as Sequence Diagrams

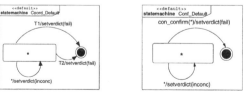

(b) Default as State Machines

Fig. 13. Test Defaults

7   Summary and Outlook

In this paper, we have presented a case study of how to use the newly adopted UML Testing Profile, in which some of the authors were involved. The UML Testing Profile is a UML profile which allows the specification of black-box tests based on UML 2.0. We proposed a methodology of how to derive a test model from an existing design model. Furthermore, we introduced roaming techniques for data transmission using Bluetooth hardware devices and designed an appropriate UML model. As a case study for our UML Testing Profile methodology, we demonstrated its applicability by developing a test model for a Bluetooth roaming model.

Due to missing tool support for the UML version 2.0, we were not able to analyze our models automatically. Our future work will include such a validation. We also plan to investigate the possibilities to generate executable code for both UML 2.0 design and test models. Experience with earlier versions of UML have shown that at least code skeletons can be generated automatically from UML descriptions.

Further study is required to investigate automatic derivation of test models from design model. Additionally, it would be interesting to assess the possibility of hardware test specification using UML Testing Profile.

References

1. J. Rumbaugh, I. Jacobson, and G. Booch, *The Unified Modeling Language Reference Manual*. Addison-Wesley, 1998.
2. http://www.u2-partners.org/.
3. *UML Testing Profile – Request For Proposal*, OMG Document (ad/01-07-08), April 2002.
4. http://www.omg.org/uml.
5. http://www.fokus.fraunhofer.de/u2tp/.
6. I. Schieferdecker, Z. R. Dai, J. Grabowski, and A. Rennoch, "The UML 2.0 Testing Profile and its Relation to TTCN-3," Testing of Communicating Systems – 15th IFIP International Conference, TestCom2003, Sophia Antipolis, France, LNCS 2644, Springer, May 2003.
7. B.Beizer, *Black-Box Testing*. John Wiley & Sons, Inc, 1995.
8. *UML Testing Profile*, Draft Adopted Specification at OMG (ptc/03-07-01), 2003, http://www.omg.org/cgi-bin/doc?ptc/2003-07-01.
9. *Specification of the Bluetooth System (version 1.1)*, Bluetooth Special Interest Group, http://www.bluetooth.com.
10. http://www.iti.uni-luebeck.de/Research/MUC/EKG/.
11. H. Pals, Z. R. Dai, J. Grabowski, and H. Neukirchen, *UML-Based Modeling of Roaming with Bluetooth Devices*, First Hangzhou-Lübeck Conference on Software Engineering (HL-SE'03), 2003.
12. *UML 2.0 Superstructure*, Draft Adopted Specification at OMG (ptc/03-07-06), July 2003.

BCMP Performance Test with TTCN-3 Mobile Node Emulator

Sarolta Dibuz, Tibor Szabó, and Zsolt Torpis

Conformance Laboratory, Ericsson Hungary Ltd.
Laborc 1, HU-1037 Budapest, Hungary
{Sarolta.Dibuz, Tibor.Szabo, Zsolt.Torpis}@eth.ericsson.se

Abstract. In this paper we show guidelines for performance testing through *BRAIN Candidate Mobility Management Protocol (BCMP)*. At first, we investigate the main issues of our tests, then we describe briefly the applied TTCN-3 based distributed parallel test environment. We present the structure of the network to be tested and the Mobile Node Emulator, the main functional element of the performance test. We describe the actual test and the results. Finally, we summarize our experiences and proposals.

1 Introduction

Conformance testing of telecommunication protocols, services and applications has become an unavoidable process within a lifecycle of a product. To achieve high quality one has to ensure that a protocol implementation meets the requirements of the corresponding specification. Objectives, methods and tools of conformance testing are standardized, deeply studied and deployed. The most widely used conformance testing notation is TTCN version 3 [1]. There are some tools available to compile and execute TTCN-3 test suites against protocol implementations.

However, there are non-functional requirements such as performance, quality of service (QoS) and scalability characteristics of an implementation that are out of scope of conformance and functional testing. These requirements are as important as functional requirements. It is often needed to verify that a protocol, an equipment or a network meets non-functional requirements. The goal of performance testing is to ensure that an implementation can operate at a certain performance level. On the other hand, the purpose of scalability testing is to determine whether an application scales for the workload growth.

One of the main differences between conformance and performance testing is the different interpretation of time. Timers in a conformance test ensure that an event occured too early, too late or not at all. In performance testing, one has to establish streams of data, not separated protocol events. Correct timing of the generated load becomes very important.

For performance and scalability testing the conformance of the implementation is assumed. However, since high load may affect correct functionality of the

R. Groz and R.M. Hierons (Eds.): TestCom 2004, LNCS 2978, pp. 50–59, 2004.

implementation, it is necessary to track functional correctness during a performance test [2].

2 Related Work

There are numerous contributions to the field of performance testing with TTCN. PerfTTCN [2] proposes architecture for three types of performance testing: testing for a server, an end-to-end service and a protocol. It introduces foreground testers, which generate test load to the IUT; and background testers, which bring the IUT into a specific load state. PerfTTCN is an extension to TTCN-2. With the proposed new tables it is possible to describe the test configuration, traffic streams, traffic models, measurements, and to give performance constraints. Unfortunately, no known commercial TTCN-2 tool supports PerfTTCN.

Real-time TTCN [3] extends the capability of TTCN-2 to test real-time systems. It defines labels that specify the earliest and latest execution times for statements. It also defines an operational semantics for real-time TTCN by mapping it to timed transition systems.

TimedTTCN-3 [4] is a real-time extension to TTCN-3 that supports the test and measurement of real-time requirements. TimedTTCN-3 introduces absolute time, allows definition of synchronization requirements for test components and provides possibility to specify online and offline evaluation procedures for real-time requirements.

The authors of [5] showed a case study using TTCN-2 for performance test of an HTTP server. They applied the concepts of PerfTTCN, but not the language extensions. Thus, application of a commercial TTCN test executor was possible. The paper shows guidelines to design different parts of testing software (e.g. test port) that have to operate in a performance testing environment and consequently, must have themselves a good performance.

Some papers deal with investigation of BCMP. The most widely known contribution [6] presents the protocol itself and results of simulations performed with ns-2 simulation environment. The goal of simulations was to examine correctness and expected performance of BCMP.

The paper [7] describes a mobile testbed implementation using real network components. [8] concentrates on the scalability aspects of micro-mobility management from a theoretical point of view. Description of implementation of IP micro-mobility protocols and some tests can be found in [9]. Unfortunately, none of the papers above includes performance or scalability test results of networks running BCMP as mobility management protocol.

The main innovation of our measurements is the deployment of a TTCN-3 based parallel testing environment. This environment enables good approximation of real network scenarios while providing comparable results and being extremely flexible and reconfigurable.

3   Requirements on Performance Testing Environment Components

For a functional test of an implementation, in most cases, a few (or a single) test components are enough. However, performance tests may need several parallel components, e.g. foreground and background test components [2], monitor components etc. To control the start of test components a main control utility is needed. The components must have an internal communication protocol and path to communicate with each other and with the main control utility.

3.1   Distributed Parallel Test Environment

The architecture of our test system is based on the TTCN-3 standard [1]. Figure 1 depicts the distributed architecture and its components.

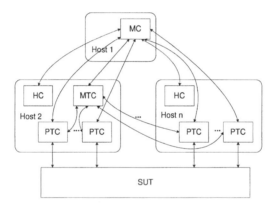

Fig. 1.   Distributed test architecture

The *Main Controller (MC)* creates, starts and terminates the *Main Test Component (MTC)*. MC maintains a control connection with all other components. The *Host Controller (HC)* is responsible for controlling *Parallel Test Components (PTCs)* on a host. There is only one MTC in the whole distributed test system. MTC controls creation, start and termination of PTCs. MTC and PTCs are TTCN-3 test components while MC is a standalone utility.

Connections between different test components can carry protocol data used in testing and control messages between different test components. Connections between an abstract test component (either MTC or PTC) and the real test system interface are called mappings.

In a typical performance test configuration, several (possibly many) PTCs act as background testers, i.e., generate load against the *System Under Test (SUT)* and bring it into a specific load state. Some PTCs act as foreground testers and perform test sequences against the SUT. One of the advantages of TTCN-3 test environment is that backround testers are not implemented as dummy load generators but as test components that can fully track the protocol behaviour.

All of the test components are dynamically reconfigurable, thus enabling adaptation to different test scenarios.

3.2   Critical Performance Problems of the Test System

A performance test system in general, must have better performance than a test system used for functional test only. It has to keep correct timing, packet rate and response time. The test system hardware has to run its own operating system as well. It is essential to track the load on the test system and ensure that enough resources are available during the whole test campaign.

Performance Test Port. The test port connects the abstract test system to the real test system interface. Since a test port is always implementation-dependent, it can not be coded in TTCN-3. One possibility is to write the test port in C++.

The code of the test port should remain small and should not use much CPU power. In many cases it is necessary to simplify an existing test port (that has been used for function testing) to be more efficient [5]. For example, many functions of the test port can possibly be unnecessary for background testers, but fast execution is a critical issue.

Data Definition Modules. Data definition modules that describe *Abstract Service Primitives (ASPs), Protocol Data Units (PDUs)* etc. of the tested protocols can be quite extensive, especially if the test system must cope with multiple protocols or protocol layers at the same time. Large size of modules implies long compilation time. Moreover, that is even more important, a large protocol definition module runs slowly on the test hardware.

Protocol data definitions given in ASN.1 are also problematic: in most cases, these modules are automatically compiled and the encoder/decoder functions are automatically generated. The resulting code has often a suboptimal performance. Consequently, data modules for performance test should be kept as small and simple as possible. One has to consider using manual encoding instead of ASN.1 automatic encoder/decoder functions.

Estimating Performance Limit of Test System. When the load on SUT is increased, the load on test system also increases. If the load (processor or memory utilization, network bandwidth usage) on the test system is too high, it may degrade correct behaviour of the tester. A heavily loaded processor can not keep correct timing, consequently, it can not guarantee the required traffic and can not provide authentic test results.

It is essential to keep workload on test system below its upper bound. To achieve this, we need a method that indicates overloading of the test system.

4   BCMP Performance Test and Experiences

We chose a typical performance test configuration and process to show an example for the considerations mentioned above. In this section we describe the tested system, the objectives and tools of performance test. Finally, we present the results and our experiences.

4.1   System Under Test

The system that we investigated is an IP mobility test network. It consists of mobile IP network elements and test hosts. The network can work with several mobile IP protocols. We investigated *BRAIN Candidate Mobility Management Protocol (BCMP)* [6].

BCMP Network. A BCMP network can be built on top of a legacy IP routed network, running an arbitrary routing protocol. Any number of IP routers may lie between network entities.

Anchor Routers (ANP) maintain a tunnel for each Mobile Node and transmit packets addressed to the Mobile Node toward its current location. ANPs are legacy routers with minimal BCMP specific functionality.

Access routers (AR) serve as attachment points for Mobile Nodes. They are routers at the edge of the network equipped with wireless interface. They manage handovers, maintain and transfer context for each served Mobile Node. ARs also act as packet filters and drop all packets that were not transmitted by/to authorized Mobile Nodes.

Mobile Nodes (MN) represent devices (subscriber's equipment) that wish to access the Internet via the network. They have a wireless interface and the appropriate protocol implementation.

Test Network. The test network is depicted on Fig. 2.

We used three Access Routers (AR1, AR2, AR3) that connect to a single Anchor Router (ANP). Several hundred mobile nodes are necessary for testing the handover performance of the network. Moreover, these mobile nodes must be coordinated and controlled during the execution of tests. It is practically unfeasible to use real mobile terminals with wireless interface for this purpose. Instead, we emulated nodes in TTCN-3 *Mobile Node Emulator (MN Emulator)*. This tool is described in the following subsection.

The MN Emulator software runs on two hosts as a distributed parallel TTCN-3 test environment. The hosts are PCs with P-III 1 GHz processors and 256 MB of memory. We used Linux kernel version 2.4.20 on all PCs (with BCMP features developed at Ericsson). All connections are 100 Mbit Ethernet links.

Since the handover performance of the core BCMP netwok is independent of the physical layer, the wireless connections also can be substituted with Ethernet links.

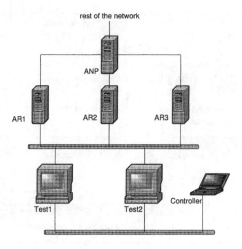

Fig. 2. BCMP test network

Mobile Node Emulator. Figure 3 shows a functional view of MN Emulator.

The Mobile Nodes are represented by Parallel Test Components. The number of PTC instances can be set before the test execution. The behaviour of the mobility protocol is implemented in a protocol module. The tester can specify abstract test events (e.g. login, handover, logout) for each mobile node. Thus, it is possible to use an IP mobility protocol module other than BCMP without changing anything else in the test. This makes comparison of different IP mobility protocols easier.

Each Mobile Node has its own behaviour, message sequence and timer set theoretically independent from the others. However, in a real emulator, parallel test components running on a single-processor machine share the available common resources, e.g. processor and memory capacity. This leaves the problem of synchronization and can lead to undesirable interference that causes false test results (see Sect. 4.2).

Components of the test system communicate with themselves through internal message ports *(Port C, Port D)*. Communication towards the SUT is done through BCMP test port *(Test Port A, Test Port B)*. The BCMP test port is capable to work both with IPv4 and IPv6 network layer. The user plane traffic between mobile nodes is emulated as constant bitrate UDP traffic; i.e., UDP packets are sent out in equal time intervals. Although it is possible to implement a sophisticated traffic model in TTCN-3, in our case it would unacceptably degrade the performance of the test system due to the large number of test components.

The distribution of parallel test components on the two test hosts is done automatically by the TTCN-3 test environment.

The Graphical User Interface (GUI) is used to control execution of the test. In order to reduce load on the test system, it is run on a separate host.

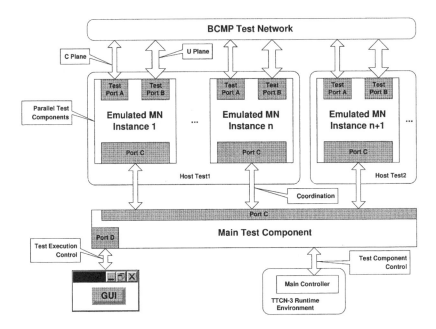

Fig. 3. Mobile Node Emulator – functional view

Test Objectives. The main goal of the test is to investigate handover transaction time (i.e., the length of time interval between the beginning and the successful end of a handover) as a function of varying handoff activity of Mobile Nodes. The handover transaction time influences the number of lost packets during a handover event, thus the quite short handover transaction time is critical from the point of view of a real-time application.

We aimed to produce performance test results that are comparable to other BCMP implementations and different IP micro-mobility protocols. Our tests verify that the BCMP network can scale to handle several hundreds of handover events within a short time. In the following scenario we used 300 emulated Mobile Nodes performing periodic handovers. We measured the processor load on ARs, handover transaction time and message load.

4.2   Test Results

On Fig. 4 the average AR processor load is shown.

Figure 5 shows the average length of a handover (as seen by the MN). It can be seen that below a critical point, increasing number of handovers results in gracefully degrading handover performance (i.e., increasing handover transaction time). Going higher with handover frequency, the load on the AR reaches a critical value resulting in rapidly increasing handover transaction times, which results in very poor handover performance. A preliminary conclusion is that the system sholud be dimensioned such that ARs stay below this critical point.

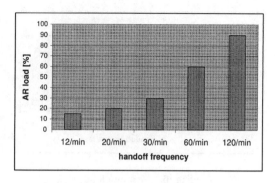

Fig. 4. Access router processor load

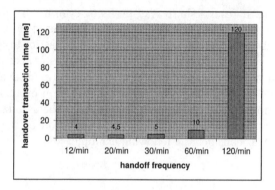

Fig. 5. Handover transaction time

Figure 6 depicts the measured average BCMP message load of the handover activity.

Experiences. During the development of MN Emulator we used some practical tricks that enabled emulation of many nodes with keeping the load on the test system below its upper bound.

If the load on the test host is near to the full utilization of resources (processor and memory usage) then it can be obviously observable through quick decrease of processor idle time and available memory, respectively. We used an other method for observing the reach of load limit of test system. In the log files the actual timestamps of initiated test events are registrated. If these timestamps deviates significantly from the specified event times (a slip comes in the execution) then the system is near to its upper bound of performance and it results incorrect test operation.

It happens often in the test that several MNs have to perform an event (e.g. a handover) at the same time. Obviously, in a one-processor system these events occur not exactly in the same point of time. If we still specify the execution

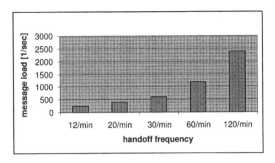

Fig. 6. Message load

for the same time, it results sharp load-peaks or even an overload for the test system. For that reason timing of events to be generated by Mobile Nodes is randomized. A $\Delta\tau$ offset of constant distribution stochastic variable is added to the mean execution time. This way the load on test system can be smoothed.

We observed that sometimes it is not efficient to extensively use the `alt` mechanism of TTCN-3 in the performance-critical main event handler loop of parallel test components. This property comes from the standard TTCN-3 semantics and does not depend on the actual realization of the test execution environment. Let us consider the following example:

```
alt
{
    [] MyPort.receive(template_1) {...}
    [] MyPort.receive(template_2) {...}
    ...
    [] MyPort.receive(template_n) {...}
}
```

When the execution of the test is at an `alt` statement and a message is arrived, in a worst case situation, all n templates must be compared to the message. If a few types of messages are expected to arrive significantly more often than other ones, then it is better to use fewer, more general templates and analyse the incoming message with `if()` conditional operators inside the `alt` construct. Alternatively, use of multiple levels of `alt` statements with less alternatives in the same level also solves the problem. Obviously, the most frequent message should stand on the first place within an `alt`. We can thus save the time of some template matching operations.

It is necessary to use templates as simple as possible for template matching. Outgoing messages should not contain complicated structures, because they slow down coding operations and result huge binary executables. Sometimes this can lead to a difficult design problem.

With the considerations above we achieved that 600 emulated Mobile Nodes can run on the two test hosts without overloading the test system.

5   Conclusions

In this paper we presented a BCMP performance test example focusing on some problems of optimization of the test system. We described the distributed parallel TTCN-3 test system, the investigated test network and the Mobile Node Emulator. Performance test optimization techniques and two methods of observing load limit of the test system were also presented. We showed some results of the measurements and summarized our most important experiences.

Regarding further inverstigations, it would be interesting to study the possibility of using behaviour and traffic models in the emulator instead of simple periodic event generation. Thus, a real scenario could be more precisely approximated. On the other hand, a complicated traffic model results worse performance for the test system. We plan to find a compromise among these requirements.

References

1. ETSI Methods for Testing and Specification, The Testing and Test Control Notation version 3, Part 1: TTCN-3 Core Language. ETSI ES 201 873-1 V2.2.0 (2002-03)
2. Ina Schieferdecker, Bernard Stepien, Axel Rennoch: PerfTTCN, a TTCN Language Extension for Performance Testing. IWTCS 1997, Cheju Island, Korea. Testing of Communicating Systems volume 10, Chapman & Hall.
3. Thomas Walter, Jens Grabowski: Real-Time TTCN for Testing Real-Time and Multimedia Systems. IWTCS 1997, Cheju Island, Korea. Testing of Communicating Systems volume 10, Chapman & Hall.
4. Zhen Ru Dai, Jens Grabowski, Helmut Neukirchen: TimedTTCN-3 – A Real-Time Extension for TTCN-3. The IFIP 14th International Conference on Testing of Communicating Systems, 2002.
5. Roland Gecse, Péter Krémer, János Zoltán Szabó: HTTP Performance Evaluation with TTCN. The IFIP 13th International Conference on Testing of Communicating Systems, Canada, 2000.
6. C. Keszei, N. Georganopoulos, Z. Turányi, A. Valkó: Evaluation of the BRAIN Candidate Mobility Management Protocol. IST Global Summit 2001, Barcelona, September 2001.
7. J.C. Rault, L. Burness, E. García, T. Robles, J. Manner, N. Georganopoulos, P. Ruiz: IP QoS and mobility experimentations within the MIND trial Workpackage. PIMRC2002, Lisbon, Portugal, September 2002 (http://www.lx.it.pt/pimrc2002/)
8. P. Eardley, N. Georganopoulos, M. West: On the Scalability of IP micro mobility management protocols. IEEE Conference on Mobile and Wireless Communication Networks (MCWN2002) Stockholm, Sweden, 9-11 September 2002
9. K. Guillouard, Y. Khouaja, J.C. Rault: Advanced IP mobility management experimentation within a Wireless Access Network WTC2002 Paris, 26th September 2002

FSM Based Interoperability Testing Methods
for Multi Stimuli Model

Khaled El-Fakih[1], Vadim Trenkaev[2], Natalia Spitsyna[2], and Nina Yevtushenko[2]

[1]American University of Sharjah,
PO Box 26666, Sharjah,
United Arab Emirates
kelfakih@aus.ac.ae
[2]Tomsk State University,
36 Lenin str., Tomsk,
634050, Russia
snv@kitidis.tsu.ru,
{vad, yevtushenko}@elefot.tsu.ru

Abstract. In this paper, we propose two fault models and methods for the derivation of interoperability test suites when the system implementation is given in the form of two deterministic communicating finite state machines. A test suite returned by the first method enables us to determine if the implementation is free of livelocks. If the implementation is free of livelocks, the second method returns a test suite that checks if the implementation conforms to the specification. Application examples are used to illustrate the methods.

1 Introduction

The objective of interoperability testing is to assure that two or more protocol implementations can interact and if so whether they behave together as expected [KSK00, VBT01]. As usual, to guarantee the fault coverage we need a formal model of protocol specifications and implementations as well as a formal model of possible faults. One of the widely used formal models for protocol specification and testing is the Finite State Machine (FSM) model. Then, two communicating protocol implementations can be considered as a system of two communicating FSMs (SCFSM). The FSMs communicate asynchronously via bounded internal queues where messages are stored. We consider the case of *multiple stimuli* [SKC02] where two external messages (multiple stimuli input) from the environment can be sent simultaneously to both protocol implementations. We study some properties of a multiple stimuli SCFSM and we use reachability analysis [Wes78, Boc80, BrZa83] to derive the joint behavior of two communicating FSMs.

Often protocol specifications contain optional commands or options that are not specified or parameters that have no restrictions on their implementations. As a corollary, such specifications are not complete and are described by partial FSMs. On

R. Groz and R.M. Hierons (Eds.): TestCom 2004, LNCS 2978, pp. 60-75, 2004.

the other hand, the implementations of these machines are complete and usually tested in isolation using the quasi-equivalence conformance relation. According to this relation, for each defined behavior of a protocol specification the corresponding implementation has to have the same behavior. However, the undefined transitions of the protocol specifications can be completed in different ways by different vendors. This can cause a livelock when an input sequence that traverses undefined transitions is applied to the system implementation. In the first part of the paper, we present a fault model and a method for interoperability testing for livelocks when the system implementation is given in the form of two deterministic communicating finite state machines. A complete test suite detects livelocks (if exist) in any possible system implementation. A livelock is detected by means of a time-out period when traversing a transition that leads to a livelock i.e. a complete test suite has to traverse, for each two possible protocol implementations a transition that can lead to a livelock. Thus, in this case, the considered fault model [STEY03] is different than that usually used in conformance testing. The fault model does not include the specification of the whole system; it only contains the fault domain, i.e. the set of possible protocol implementations. For the compact representation of the fault we use a mutation machine [KPY99].

We note that when an implementation at hand has no livelocks, we are still required to test if it satisfies its specification. Accordingly, in the second part of the paper, we present a related test derivation method. Assuming that the protocol implementations are tested in isolation and found quasi-equivalent to their specification, the test derivation method uses the incremental test derivation methods presented in [EYB02, Elf02] in order to generate tests only for the untested parts of the system implementation. The performed experiments clearly show significant gains in using incremental testing when the tested part of the system implementation consists of up to 80% of the whole implementation.

This paper is organized as follows. Section 2 includes necessary definitions and Section 3 introduces a multiple stimuli model for a system of communicating finite state machines. Section 4 includes a livelock testing method, and Section 5 contains a test derivation method w.r.t. a given specification. Both methods are illustrated using simple application examples. Section 6 concludes the paper.

2   Preliminaries

A *finite state machine* (*FSM*) A is a 5-tuple $\langle S,I,O,h,s_0 \rangle$, where S is a finite nonempty set with s_0 as the initial state; I and O are input and output alphabets; and $h \subseteq S \times I \times O \times S$ is a behavior relation. The behavior relation defines all possible transitions of the machine. Given a current state s_j and input symbol i, a 4-tuple $(s_j,i,o,s_k) \in h$ represents a transition from state s_j under the input i to the next state s_k with the output o, usually written as $s_j \xrightarrow{\ i/o\ } s_k$.

We assume that a FSM A has a *reset capability*, i.e. there is a special reset input "r" that takes the FSM from any state to the initial state. As usually, we assume that each transition with the reset input is correctly implemented, i.e. we do not include the reset input into the input alphabet I.

A transition from a state s_j under input symbol i is called *deterministic* if there exists the only pair (o,s_k) such that $(s_j,i,o,s_k) \in h$. If FSM A has only deterministic transitions then FSM A is said to be *deterministic*; otherwise, A is *non-deterministic*. In the deterministic FSM A instead of behavior relation h we use two functions: *transition function* $\psi: D_A \subseteq S \times I \to S$ and *output function* $\varphi: D_A \subseteq S \times I \to O$ where D_A is called the *specification domain* of the FSM. Therefore, in general, a deterministic FSM is a 7-tuple $\langle S,I,O,\psi,\varphi,D_A,s_0 \rangle$. An FSM is called *Chaos* if it has only chaos transitions, i.e. if $h = S \times I \times O \times S$. When at least one of the sets S, I and O is not a singleton a chaos FSM is non-deterministic.

If for each pair $(s,i) \in S \times I$ there exists $(o,s') \in O \times S$ such that $(s,i,o,s') \in h$ then FSM A is said to be *complete*; otherwise, A is *partial*. For a complete deterministic FSM, the specification domain D_A coincides with the Cartesian product $S \times I$, i.e. a complete deterministic FSM is a 6-tuple $\langle S,I,O,\psi,\varphi,s_0 \rangle$.

FSM $B = \langle S',I,O,g,s_0 \rangle$, $S' \subseteq S$, is a *submachine* of FSM $A = \langle S,I,O,h,s_0 \rangle$ if $S' \subseteq S$ and $g \subseteq h$, i.e. if each transition of FSM B is obtained by fixing an appropriate transition of the FSM A. Given a complete FSM A, we let $Sub(A)$ denote the set of all complete deterministic submachines of A.

In usual way, the behavior relation is extended to input and output sequences. Given state $s \in S$, input sequence $\alpha = i_1 i_2 \ldots i_k \in I^*$ and output sequence $\beta = o_1 o_2 \ldots o_k \in O^*$, the input-output sequence $i_1 o_1 i_2 o_2 \ldots i_k o_k$ is called a *trace of A at state s* if there exists state s' such that $(s,i_1 i_2 \ldots i_k, o_1 o_2 \ldots o_k, s') \in h$, i.e. there exist states $s_1 = s$, s_2, $\ldots$, s_k, $s_{k+1} = s'$ such that $(s_i,i_i,o_i,s_{i+1}) \in h$, $i = 1$, $\ldots$, k. A trace at the initial state is simply called a *trace of A*.

Given deterministic FSMs B and A and states t of FSM B and s of FSM A, state t is *quasi-equivalent* to s, written $t \approx_{quasi} s$, if the set of traces of FSM B at state t contains that of FSM A at state s. If the sets of traces at states t and s coincide, then states t and s are *equivalent*, written $s \cong t$. FSM B is *quasi-equivalent* to A, written $B \approx_{quasi} A$, if the set of traces of FSM B contains that of A. FSMs A and B are *equivalent*, written $A \cong B$, if their sets of traces coincide.

3   Multi Stimuli Model of a System of Communicating Finite State Machines

3.1   A System of Communicating FSMs

Many complex systems are typically specified as a collection of communicating components. We consider here a system that consists of two communicating FSMs (SCFSM) (Fig.1). We let the alphabets $I_1 \cup I_2$ and $O_1 \cup O_2$ represent the externally observable input/output actions (or messages) of the system, while the alphabets E_1 and E_2 represent the internal (hidden) input/output interactions between the two component FSMs. The FSMs communicate asynchronously via bounded internal queues where messages are stored. We consider the case of *multiple stimuli* [KSK02] where simultaneously two external inputs (multiple stimuli input) from the environment can be sent to both component machines. Moreover, in response to an input each component machine can produce a pair of outputs, one to the environment and one to other component machine [TKS03]. We also assume that the system works in a *slow environment* [PYBD96]. This means that the next external input is applied only when the processing of previous external input by the system has been completed, i.e. when the internal queues become empty. Due to this assumption, if the system queues are empty and a multiple stimuli input is applied to the system, each internal queue can get a message. After the processing an internal message by one of the component machines one of the queues will become empty while another message can be added to the input queue of the other component machine. In this case the component machine that has two messages in its input queue processes one of these messages and as a corollary it can produce an input message to the other component machine. Thus, at any time, the length of the input queues does not exceed two.

Under the above assumptions, the collective behavior of the two communicating FSMs can be described by a finite *composed machine* that describes the observable behavior of the system. The composed machine is obtained from a reachability graph [Wes78, BoSu80, BrZa83] that described the collective behavior of the system components in terms of internal and external actions of the system. In the following subsection we give the details of building a reachability graph and a composed machine.

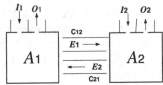

Fig. 1. A system of two communicating finite state machines

We note that after submitting an appropriate external input to the system, i.e. when the input queues are empty, the two component machines can carry on an infinite internal dialogue. In this case we say that the system falls into a livelock. Here, as in the single stimuli mode, a livelock of the system can result in the absence of an external output at least at one external port. Moreover, differently from the single stimuli mode [PYBD96], we also have another type of livelocks that occurs when one of the system components produces an infinite external sequence.

If the system can fall into livelock under an appropriate input sequence then the composed machine enters the designated *Livelock* state with the designated *livelock* output [STEY03]. In this case, the corresponding transition of the composed machine is called *suspicious* and takes the machine to the designated *Livelock* state.

3.2 Reachability Graph and Composed FSM

Formally, we consider a system of two communicating FSMs $A1=\langle Q, I_1 \cup E_2, O_1 \times E_1, h_1, q_0 \rangle$ and $A2=\langle T, I_2 \cup E_1, O_2 \times E_2, h_2, t_0 \rangle$ (Fig. 1) where the channel C12 (C21) is a FIFO queue linking the FSM $A1$ ($A2$) to the FSM $A2$ ($A1$). Thus, the FSM $A1$ has $I_1 \cup E_2$ as the set of inputs and $O_1 \times E_1$ as the set of outputs and the FSM $A2$ has $I_2 \cup E_1$ as the set of inputs and $O_2 \times E_2$ as the set of outputs. The alphabets I_1, I_2 and O_1, O_2 represent the *externally* observable input/output actions of the system, while the alphabets E_1 and E_2 represent the *internal* input/output interactions between the two component machines that are non-observable (hidden). As in [PYBD96] we assume that all the alphabets are pair-wise disjoint.

In order to deal with the situation where a component FSM in response to an input produces only an internal or an external output, we assume that the alphabets O_1, E_1, O_2 and E_2 include the silent message ε. Thus, the output pair $(o,\varepsilon) \in O_1 \times E_1$ corresponds to the situation where $A1$ produces only the external output o to the environment.

To describe the joint behavior of a SCFSM we build a reachability graph G [Wes78, BoSu80, BrZa83]. The reachability graph G is a pair (V,E), where the set V of vertices represents the set of so-called *global states* of the system. The set E of edges represents transitions between global states. A global state of a SCFSM is a 4-tuple (q,t,c_{12},c_{21}) where $q \in Q$, $t \in T$, $c_{12} \in E_1^2$ and $c_{21} \in E_2^2$ are the contents of the internal queues C12 and C21, respectively, where E^2 is the set of all sequences over the alphabet E of length at most two. A global state is called *stable* if all internal queues are empty. Otherwise, it is called *transient*.

Under the above assumptions, a component machine of SCFSM can produce a pair of outputs in response to an input. By this reason, given a stable state and an external input, the system can produce a pair of external output sequences. In case of finite dialogue, the length of these sequences cannot exceed an appropriate integer k. In case of infinite dialogue, the system falls into a livelock, i.e. the system enters the designated *Livelock* state. This happens when at least one component machine of the system does not produce an external output or produces an infinite sequence of external outputs. As usual we assume that a livelock can be detected by means of a timer. In other words, if after an appropriate period of time the system does not produce any external output sequence in at least one of its external ports or it continues producing output actions, then we conclude that the system falls into a livelock.

Given a SCFSM of $A1$ and $A2$, in order to derive the composed machine we construct a reachability graph G that describes the joint behavior of $A1$ and $A2$ under single inputs of the sets I_1 and I_2 and under multi stimuli inputs of the set $I_1 \times I_2$. The externally observable behavior of the SCFSMs, i.e. the composed machine $A1 \lozenge A2$, can be obtained from the reachability graph by hiding all internal actions and pairing inputs with corresponding output sequences of length up to k similar to the single stimuli model [PYBD96]. Each transition of the FSM $A1 \lozenge A2$ has $i_1 i_2 \in I_1 \times I_2$, $i_1 \in I_1$, or $i_2 \in I_2$ as an input label and as an output label it has the designated *livelock* output, in case the transition leads to the designated *Livelock* state, or a pair of finite output sequences (β, γ) of length at most k, where β is defined over the external alphabet O_1 and γ is defined over the external alphabet O_2.

Given a state of the composed machine $A1 \lozenge A2$ and an external (single or multiple stimuli) input, if there exists a path in the reachability graph that starts at the state and includes a cycle with only transient states, then the system falls into *livelock* at the state when the input that labels the head transition of the path is applied. In this case, the composed machine includes a corresponding suspicious transition to the designated *livelock* state labeled with the given input and the designated *livelock* output. Thus, the composed FSM $A1 \lozenge A2$ under a given input either transits to the livelock state producing the livelock output or it transits to another global state producing a pair of finite output sequences.

As an example, consider the FSMs $MM1$ and $MM2$ shown in Figures 2 and 3 below. The sets of external inputs and outputs of $MM1$ are $\{x1, \varepsilon\}$ and $\{y_1, \varepsilon\}$, and the sets of external inputs and outputs of $MM2$ are $\{x_2, x_3, \varepsilon\}$ and $\{y_2, y_3, \varepsilon\}$. The set of internal inputs of $MM1$ (internal outputs of $MM2$) is $\{v_1, v_2, \varepsilon\}$, and the set of internal inputs of $MM2$ (internal outputs of $MM1$) is $\{u_1, \varepsilon\}$. Figure 4 shows a part of the reachability graph of FSMs $MM1$ and $MM2$. For example, from state $1a$ under the input (x_1x_3) the system can reach the stable state $2b$ and produce the output pair $(\varepsilon, y_2 y_2)$ or it can fall into livelock. Thus, in the corresponding composed machine $MM1 \lozenge MM2$, we add an outgoing suspicious transition from state $1a$ to the livelock state labeled with the input/output $(x_1x_3)/Livelock$. Similarly, we include the following suspicious transitions in $MM1 \lozenge MM2$. From state $1b$, transitions $x_1/Livelock$ and $x_2/Livelock$. From state $2b$, transitions $x_2/Livelock$ and $(x_1x_2)/Livelock$. The composed machine $MM1 \lozenge MM2$ is shown in Figure 5.

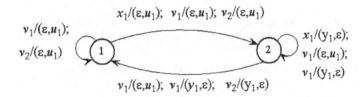

Fig. 2. FSM $MM1$

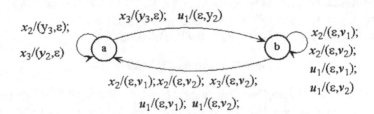

Fig. 3. FSM $MM2$

The composition of two component machines can be partial or complete, deterministic or non-deterministic depending on these machines. Here we note that differently from the single stimuli mode in the multi stimuli mode at each transient state one of the component machines can be faster than the other in producing a response to an applied input or both component machines can produce simultaneously their outputs. However, according to the following proposition, if the component machines are deterministic then their composed machine is also deterministic.

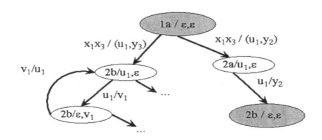

Fig. 4. Part of reachability graph

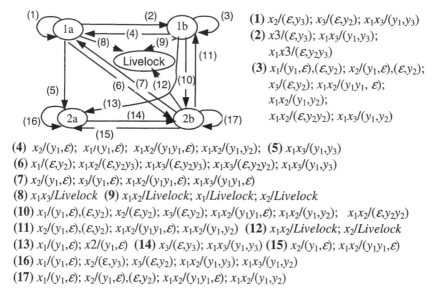

(1) $x_2/(\varepsilon,y_3)$; $x_3/(\varepsilon,y_2)$; $x_1x_3/(y_1,y_3)$
(2) $x3/(\varepsilon,y_3)$; $x_1x_3/(y_1,y_3)$;
    $x_1x3/(\varepsilon,y_2y_3)$
(3) $x_1/(y_1,\varepsilon),(\varepsilon,y_2)$; $x_2/(y_1,\varepsilon),(\varepsilon,y_2)$;
    $x_3/(\varepsilon,y_2)$; $x_1x_2/(y_1y_1,\,\varepsilon)$;
    $x_1x_2/(y_1,y_2)$;
    $x_1x_2/(\varepsilon,y_2y_2)$; $x_1x_3/(y_1,y_2)$

(4) $x_2/(y_1,\varepsilon)$; $x_1/(y_1,\varepsilon)$; $x_1x_2/(y_1y_1,\varepsilon)$; $x_1x_2/(y_1,y_2)$; **(5)** $x_1x_3/(y_1,y_3)$
(6) $x_1/(\varepsilon,y_2)$; $x_1x_2/(\varepsilon,y_2y_3)$; $x_1x_3/(\varepsilon,y_2y_3)$; $x_1x_3/(\varepsilon,y_2y_2)$; $x_1x_3/(y_1,y_3)$
(7) $x_2/(y_1,\varepsilon)$; $x_3/(y_1,\varepsilon)$; $x_1x_2/(y_1y_1,\varepsilon)$; $x_1x_3/(y_1y_1,\varepsilon)$
(8) $x_1x_3/Livelock$ **(9)** $x_1x_2/Livelock$; $x_1/Livelock$; $x_2/Livelock$
(10) $x_1/(y_1,\varepsilon),(\varepsilon,y_2)$; $x_2/(\varepsilon,y_2)$; $x_3/(\varepsilon,y_2)$; $x_1x_2/(y_1y_1,\varepsilon)$; $x_1x_2/(y_1,y_2)$; $x_1x_2/(\varepsilon,y_2y_2)$
(11) $x_2/(y_1,\varepsilon),(\varepsilon,y_2)$; $x_1x_2/(y_1y_1,\varepsilon)$; $x_1x_2/(y_1,y_2)$ **(12)** $x_1x_2/Livelock$; $x_2/Livelock$
(13) $x_1/(y_1,\varepsilon)$; $x2/(y_1,\varepsilon)$ **(14)** $x_3/(\varepsilon,y_3)$; $x_1x_3/(y_1,y_3)$ **(15)** $x_2/(y_1,\varepsilon)$; $x_1x_2/(y_1y_1,\varepsilon)$
(16) $x_1/(y_1,\varepsilon)$; $x_2/(\varepsilon,y_3)$; $x_3/(\varepsilon,y_2)$; $x_1x_2/(y_1,y_3)$; $x_1x_3/(y_1,y_2)$
(17) $x_1/(y_1,\varepsilon)$; $x_2/(y_1,\varepsilon),(\varepsilon,y_2)$; $x_1x_2/(y_1y_1,\varepsilon)$; $x_1x_2/(y_1,y_2)$

Fig. 5. The composed FSM $MM1\lozenge MM2$

Proposition 1. If the component machines $A1$ and $A2$ of a SCFSM are deterministic and the system does not fall into a livelock, then the composed FSM $A1\lozenge A2$ is deterministic.

Proof. Let $(q,t,\varepsilon,\varepsilon)$ be a stable state of the system. Consider the mode "multiple external input", i.e. the case when the composed FSM has an input $i_1i_2\in I_1\times I_2$. The cases with a single stimulus from the environment can be proved in the same way.

Let under the input i_1 and i_2 the FSMs $A1$ and $A2$ at a states q and t produce the output pairs (o_1,e_1) and (o_2,e_2) and enter states q' and t'. Then in the reachability graph there is the transition labeled with $i_1i_2/(o_1,e_1)\&(o_2,e_2)$ from the node $(q,t,\;\varepsilon,\varepsilon)$ to the transient node (q',t',e_1,e_2). Since the FSM $A1$ and the FSM $A2$ communicate asynchronously then there are three cases: one of the FSMs $A1$ or $A2$ starts to work first, or the two FSMs work simultaneously. To prove the statement it is enough to show that in all cases the system enters one and the same state with the same pair of external outputs. Let under the input e_2 the FSM $A1$ at state q' produce the output pair (o_3, e_3) and enter the state q''. Let also under the input e_1 the FSM $A2$ at a state t' produce the output pair (o_4, e_4) and enter the state t''. If FSM $A1$ starts to work first then in the reachability graph there is the transition labeled with $e_2/(o_3, e_3)$ from the state (q', t', e_1, e_2) to the state $(q'', t', e_1 e_3, \varepsilon)$. Now, since the channel queue C21 is empty, the stimulus e_1 is taken from the queue of the channel C12, and FSM $A2$ starts to work, i.e., in the reachability graph there is the transition labeled with $e_1/(o_4, e_4)$ from the node $(q'', t', e_3 e_1, \varepsilon)$ to the node (q'', t'', e_3, e_4). Thus, the system enters the transient state (q'', t'', e_3, e_4) with the external output (o_3, o_4). By direct inspection, one can assure that we have the same next state and the same external output when the FSM $A2$ starts to work first. Let now FSMs $A1$ and $A2$ work simultaneously. Then in the reachability graph there is the transition labeled $e_1 e_2/(o_4, e_4)$ & (o_3, e_3) from the node (q', t', e_1, e_2) to the node (q'', t'', e_3, e_4) and the external output (o_3, o_4).

Thus the reachability graph has three different paths from the node (q', t', e_1, e_2) to the node (q'', t'', e_3, e_4) with the same external output (o_3, o_4), i.e. the composed machine is deterministic.

$\square$

4 Testing Livelocks

We recall that one of the purposes of interoperability testing is to test if the joint behavior of two component implementations has no livelocks. As usual, to guarantee complete fault coverage we need a formal model of possible faults. In general the traditional fault model <specification, conformance relation, fault domain> [PYB96] is used. However, in order to test for livelocks, we do not need the specification of the whole system. Accordingly, in the following we introduce a more general fault model and a method for complete test derivation w.r.t. this model.

4.1 A Fault Model for Livelock Testing

Often protocol specifications contain optional commands or options that are not specified or parameters that have no restrictions on their implementations. As a corollary, such specifications are not complete and are described by partial FSMs. Thus, hereafter, we consider two partial deterministic component specifications $A1$ and $A2$. The implementations of $A1$ and $A2$ are usually tested in isolation using the quasi-equivalence conformance relation. According to this relation, for each defined behavior of $A1$ (or $A2$) the corresponding implementation has to have the same behavior. However, the undefined transitions of $A1$ and $A2$ can be completed in different ways by different vendors. When there are no restrictions imposed, the designers can complete the undefined transitions according to their preferences. This can cause a livelock when an input sequence that traverses undefined transitions is applied to the system implementation.

Formally, we consider two deterministic partial component specifications $A1$ and $A2$ and we assume that their implementations are complete and deterministic. We let

$\mathfrak{R}1$ and $\mathfrak{R}2$ denote the sets of all possible complete deterministic implementations of $A1$ and $A2$. We assume that each machine of the sets $\mathfrak{R}1$ ($\mathfrak{R}2$) is quasi-equivalent to the corresponding partial specification $A1$ ($A2$). An implementation system is the composition of two complete deterministic FSMs of the sets $\mathfrak{R}1$ and $\mathfrak{R}2$, i.e. $\mathfrak{R} = \{Imp1 \Diamond Imp2 \mid Imp1 \in \mathfrak{R}1, Imp2 \in \mathfrak{R}2\}$. Thus, the set $\mathfrak{R}$ is the set of all possible system implementations.

We say that *a test suite is complete* w.r.t. the fault model $<\mathfrak{R}$, livelock-free$>$ if the test suite detects each system implementation that falls into a livelock under some input sequence. Usually a livelock is detected by means of a timer. Therefore, in order to detect a livelock, it is sufficient to traverse a transition of an implementation system that leads to a livelock. In other words, a test suite is complete w.r.t. the fault model $<\mathfrak{R}$, livelock-free$>$ if for each possible system implementation *Imp* of the set $\mathfrak{R}$ that has transitions leading to a livelock, the test suite traverses at least one of these transitions.

A straightforward approach for deriving a complete test suite w.r.t. the fault model $<\mathfrak{R}$, livelock-free$>$ is to explicitly enumerate all possible system implementations and for each implementation with at least one transition leading to a livelock to derive an input sequence that traverses one of these transitions. However, in order to avoid the explicit enumeration of all possible implementation machines, a mutation machine [KPY99] can be used.

The fault domain $\mathfrak{R}j$ of a component machine Aj, $j = 1,2$, can be described by a complete mutation machine MMj. This mutation machine is obtained from Aj by completing its undefined transitions in all possible ways, i.e. for each undefined transition of Aj we add new transitions to all possible states with all possible outputs, or due to the imposed restrictions.

Given a mutation machine MM_j, $j=1,2$, the set of all deterministic submachines of MMj coincides with the set $\mathfrak{R}j$. That is the set $\mathfrak{R}1 = Sub(MM1)$ and the set $\mathfrak{R}2 = Sub(MM2)$. Thus, each possible implementation system is a submachine of the machine $MM \cong MM1 \Diamond MM2$. Accordingly, we can use the fault model $<Sub(MM)$, livelock-free$>$ [STEY03] for livelock testing. In the following subsection we present a method for deriving a complete test suite w.r.t. the model $<Sub(MM)$, livelock-free$>$ without enumerating submachines of the mutation machine MM.

4.2   Test Suite Derivation Method

State s of an FSM A is *reachable* if there exists an input sequence that takes the FSM from the initial state to s. If state s of FSM A is reachable while traversing only deterministic transitions then s is said to be *deterministically reachable*. In this case, we call an input sequence that takes A from the initial state to s while traversing only deterministic transitions a *deterministic transfer* sequence for state s. The set of deterministic transfer sequences for all deterministically reachable states of A is called a *deterministic cover set* of A. Moreover, given the FSM $MM \cong MM1 \Diamond MM2$, we let MM_{NoLTr} denote the submachine obtained from MM by deleting all transitions leading to the *Livelock* state.

In order to derive a complete test suite w.r.t. the fault model $<Sub(MM)$, livelock-free$>$, we consider the following cases.

Extreme Case 1. There are no suspicious transitions in *MM*. That is, the composition of any two complete sub-machines of *MM*1 and *MM*2 does not fall into livelock. In this case, we do not need to test for livelocks.

Extreme Case 2. Each state of the submachine MM_{NoLTr} is reachable via deterministic transitions. In this case, for each outgoing suspicious transition of the state pair *st* of *MM* labeled with the input *x*, we include in the test suite the input sequence $r.\alpha x$ where α is an input sequence that deterministically takes the submachine MM_{NoLTr} from its initial state to the state *st*.

General Case. Generally, not each suspicious transition of the submachine *MM* is deterministically reachable. In this case, we derive a complete test suite as follows.

Algorithm 1. Test Suite Derivation Algorithm

Input: A non-deterministic mutation machine $MM \cong MM1 \Diamond MM2$
Output: A complete test suite w.r.t. the fault model <*Sub(MM)*, livelock-free>

Step 1. Determine the minimal length deterministic cover set *D* of the submachine MM_{NoLTr}, let $m=|D|$. Moreover, let $\alpha_j \in D$ be a deterministic transfer sequence for state s_j.

Step 2. For each deterministically reachable state s_j of MM_{NoLTr} we derive a traversal set $Tr(s_j)$ in the following way. Let α be an input sequence such that the length of α is not greater than $n-m+1$, where *n* is number of states of the FSM *MM*. We include α into $Tr(s_j)$ if there exists an output sequence β of *MM* to α such that the following conditions hold:

- the trace α/β does not traverse twice a state of *MM*,
- α/β does not traverse a deterministically reachable state of MM_{NoLTr},
- the last transition traversed by α/β is suspicious.

Step 3. For each deterministically reachable state s_j of the submachine MM_{NoLTr} we derive the set $E_j = r.\alpha_j.Tr(s_j)$. The test suite is the union of the sets E_j over all deterministically reachable states.

Proposition 2. The test suite returned by Algorithm 1 is complete w.r.t. the fault model <*Sub(MM)*, livelock-free>.

As an example, consider the mutation machine $MM = MM1 \Diamond MM2$ shown in Figure 5. States $1a$ and $2b$ are deterministically reachable from the initial state through the inputs ε and x_1. Thus, we derive the traversal sets for the states $1a$ and $2b$. The input sequences in the traversal set for state $1a$ have to traverse the outgoing suspicious transitions of state $1b$. These are transitions labeled with the inputs x_1, x_2 and (x_1x_2). State $1b$ can be reached from state $1a$ under the inputs x_3 and (x_1x_3). Therefore, $Tr(1a)=\{x_3.x_1, x_3.x_2, x_3.(x_1x_2), (x_1x_3).x_1, (x_1x_3).x_2, (x_1x_3).(x_1x_2)\}$. Moreover, the input sequences of the traversal set for state $2b$ have to traverse the outgoing suspicious transitions of $1b$. In addition, they have to traverse the outgoing suspicious transitions of state $2b$. These are the transitions labeled with the inputs x_2 and (x_1x_2). State $1b$ can be reached from state $2b$ under the inputs x_2 and x_1x_2. Thus, $Tr(2b)=\{x_1, x_2, (x_1x_2)\} \cup \{x_2.x_1, x_2.x_2, x_2.(x_1x_2), (x_1x_2).x_1, (x_1x_2).x_2, (x_1x_2).(x_1x_2)\}$. Therefore, Algorithm 1 returns the complete test suite, $\{r.x_3.x_1, r.x_3.x_2, r.x_3.(x_1x_2), r.(x_1x_3).x_1, r.(x_1x_3).x_2, r.(x_1x_3).(x_1x_2)\} \cup \{r.x_1.x_2, r.x_1.(x_1x_2), r.x_1.x_2.x_1, r.x_1.x_2.x_2, r.x_1.x_2.(x_1x_2), r.x_1.(x_1x_2).x_1, r.x_1.(x_1x_2).x_2, r.x_1.(x_1x_2).(x_1x_2)\}$.

5   Testing w.r.t. Specification

If a system implementation is free of livelocks, we are still required to test if it satisfies the specification. Given the partial specifications $A1$ and $A2$ of the communicating protocol entities and their corresponding implementations $Imp1$ and $Imp2$, we assume that $Imp1$ and $Imp2$ are deterministic, complete, tested in isolation and found quasi-equivalent to $A1$ and $A2$. Thus, we assume that the joint behavior of the complete protocol implementations (i.e. the system implementation) is checked w.r.t. the defined behavior of the partial specifications. Given the specification $Spec$ of the whole system, we are required to determine if $Imp1 \lozenge Imp2 \cong Spec$.

Here we note that $Spec$ of a given SCFSM can be obtained in various ways. For example, $Spec$ can be derived based on our knowledge how the whole SCFSM has to work. In this paper $Spec$ is assumed to be deterministic and complete[1]. However, the components implementations can be completed in different ways by different vendors. Since $Imp1$ and $Imp2$ were tested in isolation and found quasi-equivalent to $A1$ and $A2$, we assume that $Imp1 \lozenge Imp2$ is quasi-equivalent to $Spec$. However, the behavior of the complete implementation machine $Imp1 \lozenge Imp2$ has also to be tested w.r.t. the specification under undefined input sequences. In this case, the incremental testing methods [EYB02, Elf02] are known to return shorter test suites than the W[Chow78], Wp[Fuj91], or HIS[PYLD93] methods. If the fault domain is represented as the set of deterministic submachines of an appropriate mutation machine, then the length of a test suite returned by incremental testing methods is known to essentially depend on the number of deterministic transitions in the mutation machine. By this reason, in this paper, we divide the fault domain into three parts assuming that the implementation of at most one component machine can be faulty or that both component implementations can be faulty. To do this we augment the given partial specification machines $A1$ and $A2$ according to our preference and we obtain $CompA1$ and $CompA2$ as the complete forms of $A1$ and $A2$. In the following two subsections we present a fault model and a test derivation method based on the above assumptions.

5.1   A Fault Model for Testing w.r.t. Specification

Let $Imp1$ and $Imp2$ be two deterministic complete implementations of the partial deterministic protocol specifications $A1$ and $A2$. We recall that $Imp1$ and $Imp2$ are submachines of the mutation machines $MM1$ and $MM2$. In order to determine if the joint behavior of $Imp1$ and $Imp2$, i.e. $Imp1 \lozenge Imp2$, is equivalent to the reference specification $Spec$, we use a traditional fault model $<Spec, \cong, Sub(MM)>$, where the fault domain is the set $Sub(MM)$ of all deterministic submachines of the mutation machine $MM \cong MM1 \lozenge MM2$.

Here we reasonably assume that both implementations can be faulty. A *test suite is complete* w.r.t. the fault model $<Spec, \cong, Sub(MM)>$ if the test suite detects each

---

[1] In the general case an implementation system can be tested w.r.t. the reduction relation since there can occur several options of the behavior under undefined input sequences.

system implementation that is not equivalent to *Spec*. In the following subsection we derive a complete test suite w.r.t. to this fault model.

5.2 Test Derivation Method

In order to generate a complete test suite for the fault model is $<Spec, \cong, Sub(MM)>$, one can use the known W[Chow78], Wp[Fuj91], or HIS[PYLD93] test derivation methods assuming an upper bound m on the number of states of the implementation system is given. This bound can be calculated as the number of states in the composed system $A1 \lozenge A2$. However, these methods generate tests not only for $Sub(MM)$ but also for every possible implementation with up to m states. Thus, we need a more appropriate approach that generate tests for the domain fault domain $Sub(MM)$ taking into account the fact that $Imp1$ and $Imp2$ are tested in isolation and found quasi-equivalent to $A1$ and $A2$, i.e. the machine $Sub(MM)$ has many deterministic transitions. In other words, an approach based on the incremental testing methods presented in [EYB02,Elf02] can be effectively used. These methods generate tests that check the untested parts of an implementation utilizing some information from the tested parts. However, since the lengths of the test suites generated using the incremental methods significantly depend on the number of nondeterministic transitions of MM, which can be too many, we consider three subdomains of the fault domain $Sub(MM)$. Then, we generate tests, using the incremental testing methods, for one subdomain and we reduce, using the reduction algorithm presented in [EPYB03], the other domains based on the expected behavior of the implementation system (or System Under Test (SUT)) to these tests. In other words, we delete from other subdomains nonconforming submachines that are detected with the derived part of a test suite. Particularly, we consider the fault subdomains $Sub(MM1 \lozenge CompA2)$ where $Imp2$ is assumed to be fault free, i.e. $Imp2 \cong CompA2$, and the subdomain $Sub(CompA1 \lozenge MM2)$, where $Imp1$ is assumed to be fault free. We generate incremental tests for the subdomain $Sub(MM1 \lozenge CompA2)$ and we use these tests to reduce the mutation machines MM and $CompA1 \lozenge MM2$ [EPYB03]. Then, we derive tests for the reduced subdomain of $Sub(CompA1 \lozenge MM2)$ and we use these tests to reduce MM. Finally, we generate tests for the fault domain $Sub(MM')$, where MM' is a reduced submachine of the initial mutation machine MM. The details of the method are presented in the algorithm given below.

Here we note that in order to assess the gains of using incremental testing v.s. complete testing of the whole system implementation, we have implemented and experimented with the methods presented in [EYB02]. The experiments show that when the tested part is up to 95% of the whole implementation, on average, the HIS based test suites are 36 times bigger than the corresponding incremental test suites. Moreover, these test suites are on average 11.3, 6.1, and 4.0 times bigger when the tested parts are up to 90%, 85%, and 80% respectively. Moreover, the experiments showed that the ratios of the lengths of the test suites do not significantly depend on the size of specifications.

Algorithm 2. Test Suite Derivation Algorithm

Input: A specification of the whole system *Spec*, partial deterministic components *A*1 and *A*2, and their completed forms *CompA*1 and *CompA*2.

Output: A complete test suite *TS* w.r.t. the fault model <*Spec*, ≅, *Sub(MM)*.

Step 1. Derive *MM*1 and *MM*2 by completing in all possible ways (or due to some preferences) all the undefined transitions of *A*1 and *A*2. Then, derive the mutation machines *MM* ≅ *MM*1◊*MM*2, *MM*1◊*CompA*2, and *CompA*1◊*MM*2.

Step 2. Use an incremental test derivation method for deriving the complete test suite TS_1 w.r.t. the fault model <*Spec*, ≅, *Sub(MM*1◊*CompA*2)>.
Reduce *MM* and *CompA*1◊*MM*2 and obtain *MM'* and *F*2 using TS_1 and the expected output behavior of the SUT to TS_1.

Step 3. Use an incremental test derivation method for deriving the complete test suite TS_2 w.r.t. the fault model <*Spec*, ≅, *Sub(F2)*>.
Reduce *MM'* and obtain *MM"* using TS_2 and the expected output behavior of the SUT to TS_2.

Step 4. Use an incremental test derivation method for deriving the tests suite TS_3 w.r.t. the fault model <*Spec*, ≅, *Sub(MM"))*>.
Output $TS = TS_1 \cup TS_2 \cup TS_3$

Proposition 3. The test suite *TS* generated using Algorithm 2 is complete w.r.t. the fault model <*Spec*, ≅, *Sub(MM)*>.

As an application example, consider the partial deterministic component machines *A*1 and *A*2, shown in Figures 6.1 and 6.2, respectively. The set of external inputs and outputs of *A*1 are $X=\{x_1,\varepsilon\}$ and $Y=\{y_1,\varepsilon\}$. The set of external inputs and outputs of *A*2 are $I=\{i,\ \varepsilon\}$ and $O=\{o,\varepsilon\}$, the set of internal inputs of *A*1 (internal outputs of *A*2) is $V=\{v_1,v_2,\varepsilon\}$, and the set of internal inputs of *A*2 (internal outputs of *A*1) is $U=\{u,\varepsilon\}$. The initial state of *A*1 is the state labeled by "1".

	1	2
x	$1/(\varepsilon, u)$	$2/(y, \varepsilon)$
v_1	$2/(\varepsilon, u)$	
v_2	$1/(y, \varepsilon)/$	$2/(y, \varepsilon)$

	A
i	
u	$a/(o, v_2)$

	1a	2a
x	$1a/(y, o)$	$2a/(y,\varepsilon)$
i	$2a(y, o)$	$1a/(yy, o)$
xi	$2a/(yy, oo)$	$1a/(yyy, o)$

Fig. 6.1. Machine *A*1   **Fig. 6.2.** Machine *A*2   **Fig. 6.3.** The machine *Spec*

	1	2
x	$1/(\varepsilon, u)$	$2/(y, \varepsilon)$
v_1	$2/(\varepsilon, u)$	$1/(y, u)$
v_2	$1/(y, \varepsilon)$	$2/(y, \varepsilon)$

	A
i	$a/(\varepsilon, v_1)$
u	$a/(o, v_2)$

Fig. 7.1. Machine *CompA*1   **Fig. 7.2.** Machine *CompA*2

The specification of the given specification *Spec* is shown in Fig. 6.3 and it has the sequence x as a distinguishing sequence, i.e. the outputs at the states 1*a* and 2*a* of

Spec to *x* are different output pairs (*y*, *o*) and (*y*, *ε*). We assume that the implementations *Imp*1 and *Imp*2 of the *A*1 and *A*2 were tested in isolation and found quasi-equivalent to *A*1 and *A*2, respectively.

	1a	2a
x	1a/(y,o)	2a/(y,ε)
i	2a/(y,o)	1a/(y,ε); 2a/(y,ε); 2a/(y,o); 1a/(yy,o); 2a/(yy,o)
xi	2a/(yy,oo)	1a/(yy,ε); 2a/(yy,ε); 1a/(yyy,o); 2a/(yyy,o); 2a/(yy,o)

Fig. 8.1. Mutation machine *MM*1 ◊*CompA*2

	1a	2a
x	1a/(y,o)	2a/(y,ε)
i	2a/(y,o); 2a/(y,oo); 1a/(y,o); 1a/(y,ε)	1a/(yy,o); 1a/(yy,oo); 2a/(y,ε); 2a/(y,o)
xi	1a/(y,oo); 2a/(yy,oo); 1a/(yy,o); 2a/(yy,ooo); 1a/(yy,oo);	1a/(yyy,o); 1a/(yyy,oo); 2a/(yy,ε); 2a/(yy,o)

Fig. 8.2. Mutation machine *CompA*1◊*MM*2

	1a	2a
x	1a/(y,o)	2a/(y,ε)
i	2a/(y,o); 2a/(y,oo); 1a/(y,o); 1a/(y,ε); 1a/(ε,o);	1a/(yy,o); 1a/(y,oo); 1a/(yy,oo); 1a/(y,o); 1a/(y,ε); 2a/(yy,oo); 2a/(yy,o); 2a/(y,oo); 2a/(y,ε); 2a/(ε,o); 2a/(y,o);
xi	1a/(y,oo); 2a/(yy,oo); 1a/(yy,o); 2a/(yy,ooo); 1a/(yy,oo);	1a/(yyy,o); 1a/(yyy,oo); 1a/(yy,oo); 1a/(yy,o); 1a/(yy,ε); 2a/(yyy,oo); 2a/(yyy,o); 2a/(yy,oo); 2a/(yy,o); 2a/(yy,ε); 2a/(y,o)

Fig. 8.3. Mutation machine *MM* when both implementations can be faulty

In order to test if *Imp*1◊*Imp*2 ≅ *Spec*, we first complete the undefined transitions of *A*1 and *A*2 in all possible ways and we obtain the machines *MM*1 and *MM*2. Then, we derive the mutation machine *MM* ≅ *MM*1◊*MM*2 shown in Fig. 8.3. By direct inspection one can observe that *MM* has no livelocks. We assume that the designers complete the partial specifications *A*1 and *A*2 according to their preferences and obtain the complete deterministic FSMs *CompA*1 and *CompA*2 shown in Figures 7.1 and 7.2, where the added transitions are shown in bold. Moreover, we derive the mutation machines *MM*1◊*CompA*2 and *CompA*1◊*MM*2 shown in Figure 8.1 and 8.2, respectively. All nondeterministic transitions of these mutation machines have to be tested. Afterwards, in **Step 2** of Algorithm 2, we derive the input sequences TS_1 = {*riix*, *ri(x,i)x*} using the incremental methods presented in [EYB02]. Particularly, for the non-deterministic transitions of *MM*1◊*CompA*2, we determine the corresponding transitions in *Spec*. These are transitions, (2a)-*i*/(yy, o)->(1a) and (2a)- (*x*, *i*)/(yyy, o)-> (1a). The characterization set *W* = {*x*} of *Spec* does not traverse these transitions, accordingly, according to the so-called Case-1 of [EYB02], we derive the incremental tests $riix$, $ri(x_i)x$ for testing these transitions. If the SUT is equivalent to *Spec*, the expected behavior of the SUT to the input sequences of TS_1 is $ri/(y, o)i/(yy,o)x/(y,o)$ and $ri/(y, o)$ $(xi)/(yyy,o)x/(y,o)$. Afterwards, using these sequences, we reduce $CompA1\Diamond MM2$ of Fig. 8.2. The reduced machine is that in Fig. 8.2 without underlined transitions. Afterwards, for the untested (i.e. non-deterministic) transitions of $CompA1\Diamond MM2$, we determine the corresponding transitions in *Spec*. This is the transition (1a)-$(x, i)/(yy, oo)$->(2a). In order to test this transition, we apply again the so-called Case-1 of [EYB02] that returns the input sequence $r(x_i)x$, i.e., $TS_2 = \{r(x_i)x\}$. The expected output of a fault-free SUT to $r(x_i)x$ is $r.x_i/(yy, oo).x/(y, \varepsilon)$. Finally, in **Step 3**, using TS_1 and TS_2 and their expected outputs, we reduce the mutation machine *MM*. In this example, TS_1 and TS_2 completely reduce *MM*, i.e., all transitions of *MM* become deterministic and *MM* is equivalent to *Spec* in Fig. 6.3. Thus, we skip **Step 4** and the test suite $TS_1 \cup TS_2$ completely checks if $Imp1\Diamond Imp2 \cong$ *Spec*. The total length of the union of the test suites is 11, while the length of the test suite derived using the W method for the whole specification *Spec* is 18.

6   Conclusion

In this paper, we have proposed two fault models and methods for the derivation of interoperability test suites when the system implementation is given in the form of two deterministic communicating finite state machines. A test suite returned by the first method determines if the implementation is free of livelocks. If the implementation is free of livelocks, the second method returns a test suite that checks if the implementation conforms to the specification.

Acknowledgements. The authors would like to thank Rita Dorofeeva at Tomsk State University for implementing and experimenting with the incremental testing methods. Moreover, the authors from Tomsk State University also acknowledge a partial support from the program "Russian Universities".

References

[BrZa83]   D.Brand and P.Zafiropulo, On communicating finite state machines, J. ACM 30(2), (1983) 323-342.

[BoSu80]   G. v. Bochmann, and C. A. Sunshine, "Formal methods in communication protocol design", *IEEE Trans. on Comm.*, Vol 28, 1980, pp 624-631.

[Chow78]   T. S. Chow, "Test Design Modeled by Finite-State Machines," *IEEE Trans. SE*, vol. 4, no.3, 1978, pp. 178-187.

[Elf02]   K. El-Fakih, Protocol retesting and diagnostic testing methods, Ph.D. Thesis, University of Ottawa, 2002.

[EYB02]   K. El-Fakih, N. Yevtushenko and G.Bochmann, Protocol re-testing methods, Proc. of the IFIP 14th International Conference on Testing of Communicating Systems, 2002, Berlin, Germany, 19-22.

[EPYB03]   K. El-Fakih, S. Prokopenko, N.Yevtushenko, G. Bochmann, Fault diagnosis in extended finite state machines. Proc. of the IFIP 15th International Conference on Testing of Communicating Systems. Lecture Notes in Computer Science 2644, pp. 197-210, 2003.

[Fuj91]   S. Fujiwara, G. v. Bochmann, F. Khendek, M. Amalou, and A. Ghedamsi, "Test Selection Based on Finite State Models," *IEEE Trans. SE*, vol. 17, no. 6, 1991, pp. 591-603.

[KSK00]   S.Kang,, J.Shin, M.Kim, Interoperability Test Suite Derivation for Communication Protocols. Computer Networks, 32 (2000) 347-364.

[KPY99]   I. Koufareva, A. Petrenko, N. Yevtushenko, Test generation driven by user-defined fault models, Proceedings of IFIP TC6 12th International Workkshop on Testing of Communicating Systems, Hungary, 1999. – pp. 215-233.

[PYB96]   A. Petrenko, N. Yevtushenko, G. v. Bochmann. Fault models for testing in context. FORTE'96.

[PYBD96]   A. Petrenko, N. Yevtushenko, G. v. Bochmann, and R. Dssouli, Testing in context: framework and test derivation, Computer communications, Vol. 19, pp. 1236-1249, 1996.

[PYLD93]   A. Petrenko, N. Yevtushenko, A. Lebedev, and A. Das, "Nondeterministic State Machines in Protocol Conformance Testing," *Proc. of the IFIP 6th* IWPTS, France, 1993, pp. 363-378.

[SKC02]   S.Sëol, M.Kim, and S.T.Chanson, Interoperability Test Generation for Communication Protocols based on Multiple Stimuli Principle, Proceedings of the IFIP 14th Inter. Conf. TestCom2002, Berlin, pp.151-169.

[STEY03]   N. Spitsyna , V. Trenkaev, K. El-Fakih, and N. Yevtushenko, FSM based interoperability testing-work in progress, presented as work in progress at FORTE 03, Berlin, Germany, Sept. 2003.

[TKS03]   Trenkaev V., Kim M., and Seol S. Interoperability Testing Based on a Fault Model for a System of Communicating FSMs // Lecture Notes in Computer Science, Vol. 2644: D.Hogrefe, A.Wiles (Eds.), Testing of Communicating Systems, Proceedings, 2003, pp. 226-241

[VBT01]   C. Viho, S.Barbin and L. Tanguy, Towards a formal framework for interoperability testing, Proceedings of the 21st Inter. Conf. FORTE 2001, Korea, pp.51-68.

[West78]   C.H. West, An automated technique of communication protocols validation, IEEE Trans. Comm., 26 (1978) 1271-1275.

On Testing Partially Specified IOTS
through Lossless Queues

Jia Le Huo[1] and Alexandre Petrenko[2]

[1]Department of Electrical and Computer Engineering, McGill University
3480 University Street, Montreal, Quebec, H3A 2A7, Canada
Jiale@macs.ece.mcgill.ca
[2]CRIM, Centre de recherche informatique de Montréal
550 Sherbrooke Street West, Suite 100, Montreal, Quebec, H3A 1B9, Canada
Petrenko@crim.ca

Abstract. In this paper, we discuss how to test partially specified IOTS through lossless queues. A liberal assumption is made of the IOTS model by allowing both blocked and unspecified input actions. For testing IOTS through unbounded queues, we demonstrate that test cases can directly be derived from the specification when the transition coverage criterion is used, and we provide two test derivation algorithms, for fully specified and partially specified IOTS, respectively. Applying the derived tests to test IOTS through bounded queues is also discussed.

1   Introduction

Transition systems with concurrent input/output behavior are usually modeled by input/output transition systems (IOTS). Here, we explore how to test IOTS through queues with the following scenario of system communication in mind. As shown in Fig. 1, L_1 and L_2 are two message-passing systems. Output actions of L_1 are stored in the input queue of L_2, and, if the input queue is not empty, L_2 can read an input action and make a transition according to the action read. The communication from L_2 to L_1 is symmetrically configured. This scenario is common in communicating systems.

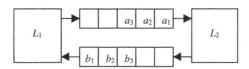

Fig. 1. The communication between two message-passing systems. L_1 and L_2 "read" input actions from their input queues and "write" output actions into the output queues

We notice that, in this scenario, either system can block its own input actions by not reading the input queue; the output actions of the other system, however, are not blocked, but stored in the queues. Therefore, the systems do not have to be receptive to input actions in every state, whereas their output actions are never blocked. Queues

R. Groz and R.M. Hierons (Eds.): TestCom 2004, LNCS 2978, pp. 76–94, 2004.
© IFIP 2004

in this scenario store actions for a later consumption and, thus, are called *lossless queues*.

A system that can block input actions is usually rendered as an IOTS with input actions missing in some states. The system's behavior in these states is fully specified. In particular, the system decides not to read input actions from the input queue.

Input actions could also be missing due to underspecification. The missing actions are "don't cares", i.e., the consequence of the actions is not specified, so that any behavior of the IOTS's implementations after the actions is acceptable.

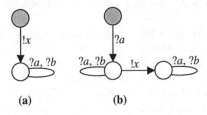

(a)   (b)

Fig. 2. Difference between two types of missing input actions in IOTS. For the IOTS in the figure, the input actions (decorated with ?) are a and b, the output action (decorated with !) is x, and the starting states are shaded by grey: (a) the missing input actions are blocked; (b) the missing input action b is unspecified

Fig. 2 illustrates the difference between these two types of missing input actions. In Fig. 2(a), the starting state has no transition on any input action. For a system with input queue, this means that, in this state, the IOTS does not read any input action from its input queue, so input actions are blocked. In Fig. 2(b), on the other hand, input action a is specified in the starting state, but input action b is not. Since it is hard to imagine that the IOTS can read only input action a, but not action b, without knowing which action is in the input queue, the missing action b is understood as unspecified. Implementations of this IOTS can behave arbitrarily after reading b in the starting state.

We say that an action is *enabled* in a state if the corresponding transition on the action starting from the state is defined. An IOTS is *input-enabled* if all input actions are enabled in every state. Moreover, an IOTS is *fully specified* if, in each state, either all input actions are enabled or no input action is enabled; otherwise, the IOTS is *partially specified*. Input-enabled IOTS are fully specified, but fully specified IOTS may have missing input actions and, therefore, need not be input-enabled.

In this paper, specifications can be partially specified, whereas implementations must be fully specified, but not necessarily input-enabled.

A model closely related to IOTS, called input/output automata (IOA), is first formalized in [7], among others. The difference between the two models is marginal, at least from the viewpoint of testing. In [7], it is stated that an IOA "generates output and internal actions autonomously". A system modeled by IOA, therefore, cannot have its output blocked by other systems. Non-blocking of output is ensured by requiring that IOA be input-enabled.

Although there is some research done for IOTS-based testing (for references, see, e.g., [3], [9], [10]), none of them, in our opinion, provides a satisfactory answer to testing IOTS in the aforementioned scenario.

Testing based on the IOTS model is explored in [12], among others, which establishes the so-called **ioco** testing framework. In that framework, a tester and an implementation under test (IUT) communicate synchronously: testers are modeled by labeled transition systems (LTS), and implementations are modeled by input-enabled IOTS. Because of synchronous composition, testers of the **ioco** framework can block the output actions of IUT, violating the assumption that "output actions can never be blocked by the environment" [p. 106, 12]. Also because of synchronous communication, when applying the **ioco** framework to test IOTS through queues, one has to compose IOTS with queues, which is not realistic if the queues have unbounded capacity.

The **ioco** testing framework is further elaborated for multi-channel IOTS (MIOTS) in [5]. In that paper, in each state of an implementation, either all input actions of a communication channel are enabled or they are all blocked. Similar to the approach in [12], output actions of IUT can be blocked. Moreover, testers are empowered with the ability to observe refusal of input or output by IUT. While it is indeed possible to detect absence of output (quiescence) by using a proper timer, it is unclear how refusal of input can be observed in an arbitrary system.

Testing IOA systems with synchronous communication is also studied in [11], where it is assumed that testers, instead of blocking output, can observe input/output conflict with IUT. In that paper, however, both specifications and implementations must be input-enabled.

Testing IOTS through queues with unbounded capacity is first explored in [13] and [14], where both specifications and implementations can block input actions. However, the proposed approach relies on explicitly composing IOTS with infinite state queue contexts, so it is not clear how this approach could be implemented in practice.

Testing IOTS through unbounded queues is also considered in [6], where a stamping mechanism is proposed to order the output actions with respect to the input actions, while quiescence is ignored. A stamping process observes and records local actions of IUT, so it is not always realistic to assume that such a process is available.

Testing IOTS through bounded queues is explored in [8], which only considers input-enabled specifications. However, the queue model used in that paper is different from the one used here. In [8], it is assumed that queues feed input actions to IOTS, which leads to the requirement that both testers and IUT must be input-enabled to avoid blocking the output of queues. In the communication scenario of Fig. 1, we assume that contents of queues are read by IOTS, so testers and IUT can block input actions. Examples of the queue model assumed in [8] are shift registers, whereas examples of the queue model assumed in this paper are message queues.

This paper studies how to test IOTS through lossless queues. Unlike previous work, we make a liberal assumption about the system model, namely, the specification of a system can have both blocked and unspecified input actions. We believe that such a model is closer to real system specifications than other models known to us.

A "naïve" test derivation algorithm would derive tests from the composition of such a specification IOTS and its input/output queues. Computing the composition is usually not viable, when the queues have unbounded capacity, or faces the state explosion problem, when the queues have bounded capacity. Moreover, there is no guarantee that a test case derived by this approach will observe the queues' capacities because the information of capacities is lost in the composition.

Here, we derive tests directly from a specification, not from its composition with queues. The derived tests aim at covering transitions of the specification. For testing IOTS through unbounded queues, the resulting test cases traverse only specified transitions, whereas in the case of bounded queues, the test cases also obey the bound of queues.

The paper is organized as follows. We provide some preliminaries of the paper in Section 2. Section 3 introduces the testing architecture. Section 4 discusses how to test fully specified IOTS through unbounded queues, building the basis for testing partially specified IOTS through unbounded queues in Section 5. Sections 4 and 5 provide two test derivation algorithms with the transition coverage criterion in mind. Section 6 briefly discusses testing IOTS through bounded queues. Conclusions are provided in Section 7.

2 Preliminaries

Here, we use a definition of input/output transition systems (IOTS) that is similar to the one of input/output automata (IOA) in [7]. Formally, an *input/output transition system* is a 5-tuple $L = <S, I, O, \lambda, S_0>$, where

- S is a countable (not necessarily finite) set of states;
- I and O are finite sets of input and output action types, respectively, which satisfy the condition $I \cap O = \varnothing$;
- $\lambda \subseteq S \times (I \cup O \cup \{\tau\}) \times S$ is a transition relation, where $\tau \notin I \cup O$ is the internal action type;
- $S_0 \subseteq S$ is a non-empty, finite set of initial states.

After [12], we only consider strongly converging specifications and implementations, i.e., systems that contain no cycle of internal transitions. We use $IOTS(I, O)$ to represent the set of all IOTS with input set I and output set O.

For IOTS $L = <S, I, O, \lambda, S_0>$, we use $init(s)$ to denote the set of actions enabled in state $s \in S$, i.e., $init(s) = \{a \in (I \cup O \cup \{\tau\}) \mid \exists s_1 \in S \text{ s.t. } ((s, a, s_1) \in \lambda)\}$. L is *input-enabled* if all input actions are enabled in each state, i.e., $I \subseteq init(s)$ for each $s \in S$; L is *fully specified* if either all input actions are enabled or no input action is enabled in each state, i.e., either $I \subseteq init(s)$ or $I \cap init(s) = \varnothing$ for each $s \in S$. If L is not fully specified, it is *partially specified*. State $s \in S$ is called *stable* if no output or internal actions are enabled in s: $init(s) \cap (O \cup \{\tau\}) = \varnothing$. State $s \in S$ with no action enabled, i.e., $init(s) = \varnothing$, is called a *deadlock* state. L *deadlocks* if there is a deadlock state reachable from a starting state.

With multiple initial states, internal transitions, and a transition relation (not a function), the IOTS considered in this paper are non-deterministic and, thus, can model a wide range of systems on various levels of abstraction. On the other hand, we call an IOTS *deterministic* if it has a single initial state, contains no internal transitions, and the transition relation is a function, i.e., $(s, a, s_1), (s, a, s_2) \in \lambda$ for $a \in I \cup O$ implies $s_1 = s_2$.

The projection operator $\downarrow A$ projects action sequences onto the alphabet $A \subseteq I \cup O$. Let ε denote the empty sequence of actions, $\varepsilon_{\downarrow A} = \varepsilon$. For $u \in (I \cup O \cup \{\tau\})^*$ and $a \in I \cup O \cup \{\tau\}$, $(ua)_{\downarrow A} = u_{\downarrow A}a$ if $a \in A$; otherwise, $(ua)_{\downarrow A} = u_{\downarrow A}$. A sequence $u \in (I \cup O)^*$ is called a *trace* of IOTS L in state $s \in S$ if there exist actions $a_1, \ldots, a_k \in I \cup O \cup \{\tau\}$, such that $u = (a_1 \ldots a_k)_{\downarrow(I \cup O)}$, and states $s_1, \ldots, s_{k+1} \in S$, such that $(s_i, a_i, s_{i+1}) \in \lambda$ for all $i = 1, \ldots, k - 1$ and $s_1 = s$. L *executes* trace u if L makes a sequence of transitions from its starting state and the corresponding action sequence projected onto $I \cup O$ is u. We use *traces*(s) to denote the set of traces of L in state s, and sometimes, by using L to refer to the set of L's initial states, we use *traces*(L) to denote the union of traces in L's initial states. State $s \in S$ with a sequence $b_1b_2 \ldots b_k \in O^*$ such that $(b_1b_2 \ldots b_k)^* \subseteq$ *traces*(s) is called an *oscillating* state. L *oscillates* if there is an oscillating state reachable from a starting state.

IOTS L is called *input-progressive* if it neither oscillates nor deadlocks. If L is input-progressive, it must consume an input action to make a transition in less than $|S|$ steps, where $|S|$ is L's number of states.

Following [13] and [12], we refer to a trace that takes IOTS L from state $s \in S$ to a stable state as a *quiescent trace* in s, and we use *qtraces*(s) to denote the set of all quiescent traces in s. Similar to the case of traces, *qtraces*(L) denotes the union of the quiescent traces in L's initial states. Traces and quiescent traces can be used to distinguish non-deterministic systems, whereas traces alone are sufficient to distinguish deterministic systems.

We use a usual operator **after**. For IOTS L, L-**after**-U denotes the set of states that are reachable by L when it executes the traces in the set U.

We use suspension traces to refer to sequences of quiescent traces executable by an IOTS. As usual ([12]), the symbol δ indicates quiescence, i.e., the absence of output and internal actions in a system. To explicitly represent quiescence in IOTS L, we add self-looping δ transitions to the stable states of L, similar to [12]. The augmented IOTS is denoted as L_δ, where the δ actions are treated as output actions. For state s of L, we define a *suspension trace* in s to be a trace of L_δ in s. We use *straces*(L) to denote the set of all suspension traces of L in the initial states. *straces*(L) is a superset of traces and quiescent traces augmented with intermediate quiescence.

Composition of IOTS formalizes the interaction of several systems. Here, we use the traditional parallel composition $\|$ of labeled transition systems (LTS), i.e., transition systems that do not distinguish input from output.

Formally, for IOTS $L_1 = <S, I_1, O_1, \lambda_1, S_0>$ and $L_2 = <T, I_2, O_2, \lambda_2, T_0>$ such that $O_1 \cap O_2 = \varnothing$, the *parallel composition* $L_1 \| L_2$ is the IOTS $<R, (I_1 \cup I_2) \setminus (O_1 \cup O_2), O_1 \cup O_2, \lambda, S_0 \times T_0>$, where the set of states $R \subseteq S \times T$ and the transition relation λ are the smallest sets obtained by applying the following inference rules:

- $S_0 \times T_0 \subseteq R$;
- if $a \in (I_1 \cup O_1) \cap (I_2 \cup O_2)$, $(s_1, a, s_2) \in \lambda_1$, and $(t_1, a, t_2) \in \lambda_2$, then $s_2t_2 \in R$ and $(s_1t_1, a, s_2t_2) \in \lambda$;
- if $a \in \{\tau\} \cup (I_1 \cup O_1) \setminus (I_2 \cup O_2)$ and $(s_1, a, s_2) \in \lambda_1$, then $s_2t_1 \in R$ and $(s_1t_1, a, s_2t_1) \in \lambda$;
- if $a \in \{\tau\} \cup (I_2 \cup O_2) \setminus (I_1 \cup O_1)$ and $(t_1, a, t_2) \in \lambda_2$, then $s_1t_2 \in R$ and $(s_1t_1, a, s_1t_2) \in \lambda$.

Sometimes, we have to transform a partially specified IOTS to a fully specified one by completing the former's input transitions, so we use a completion operator similar to [6]. For IOTS $L = <S, I, O, \lambda, S_0>$, operator $Comp: IOTS(I, O) \rightarrow IOTS(I, O)$ is defined as $Comp(L) = <S \cup \{s_L^t\}, I, O, \lambda_c, S_0>$ where s_L^t is a trap state and λ_c is defined as $\lambda \cup \{(s, a, s_L^t) \mid init(s) \cap I \neq \emptyset, a \in I \setminus init(s)\} \cup \{(s_L^t, b, s_L^t) \mid b \in I \cup O\}$. Notice that, unlike the operator in [6], $Comp(L)$ is a fully specified IOTS, not input-enabled, because the states, where all input actions are blocked, have no input enabled in $Comp(L)$.

3   Testing Architecture with Lossless Queues

When testing a communicating system, we assume the closed system shown in Fig. 1. The tester and the implementation under test (IUT) are the end systems of the queues. Both systems, along with the queues, are modeled by IOTS. The interaction between the components in the closed system is described by their parallel composition.

The IUT Imp belongs to $IOTS(I, O)$ and the tester $Test$ belongs to $IOTS(O \cup \{\delta\}, I)$, where symbol δ denotes the detection of quiescence, i.e., output queue of Imp is empty. The input actions of Imp correspond to the output actions of $Test$, and vice versa. When seen in the closed system, the action types of Imp, $Test$, the input queue Q_I, and the output queue Q_O are assigned according to Fig. 3, to avoid using the same action types at different interfaces.

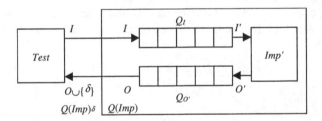

Fig. 3. The input and output action types of the components in the testing architecture: $Test \in IOTS(O \cup \{\delta\}, I)$, $Imp' \in IOTS(I', O')$, $Q_I \in IOTS(I, I')$, and $Q_{O'} \in IOTS(O', O)$

In the closed system, the actions of Imp are relabeled by $'$. Formally, operator $'$ is defined on actions: $(a)' = a'$, and $(a')' = a$. We lift the operator to sets of actions, traces, and IOTS: for action set A, $A' = \{a' \mid a \in A\}$; for traces, $'$ is recursively defined as $\varepsilon' = \varepsilon$ and $(ua)' = u'a'$ for trace u and action a; for IOTS $L \in IOTS(I, O)$, L' belongs to $IOTS(I', O')$ and is derived from L by relabeling each action $a \in I \cup O$ to a'. Imp in the closed system is relabeled by $'$.

For the queues, each input action a (or a') corresponds to an output action a' (or a). We define the queue model with the $'$ operator. Formally, an *unbounded queue with input set A*, Q_A, is a deterministic IOTS $<S_A, A, A', \lambda_A, \{\varepsilon\}>$, where the state set $S_A = A^*$ and the transition relation $\lambda_A = \{(u, a, ua) \mid u, ua \in S_A\} \cup \{(av, a', v) \mid av, v \in S_A\}$.

By definition, Q_A is input-enabled and has infinitely many states, so it is "unbounded". As an example, Fig. 4 shows an unbounded queue $Q_{\{a\}}$ with a single input action a.

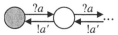

Fig. 4. An unbounded queue with a single input action a

As seen in Fig. 3, the input queue is Q_I, and the output queue is $Q_{O'}$ (notice the property of the ' operator: $a'' = a$). The behavior of the closed system shown in Fig. 3 can be described by the IOTS $Test \parallel (Q_I \parallel Imp' \parallel Q_{O'})_\delta$ where L_δ is IOTS L augmented by adding self-looping δ transitions (see Section 2).

Imp composed with its input/output queues can be described by the operator $Q(\ )$. For $L \in IOTS(I, O)$, $Q(L) = hide(I' \cup O')(Q_I \parallel L' \parallel Q_{O'})$, where operator $hide(A)(\ )$ relabels transitions of an IOTS with actions in A to internal action τ. $Q(L)$ is similar to the queue operator as in [13] and [14]. From the tester's point of view, the observable behavior of the closed system shown in Fig. 3 can be described by $Test \parallel Q(Imp)_\delta$ since the actions in $I' \cup O'$ are not observable.

Some properties are usually assumed for IOTS in a composition, e.g., input-enabledness [7] and full compatibility [8]. Here, we state a compatibility condition for each interface in the closed system shown in Fig. 3.

For $Test$ and Imp, output actions are usually under their total control, so the output actions of $Test$ and Imp have to be accepted immediately by $Q(Imp)_\delta$ and $Q_{O'}$, respectively.

Definition 1. Let $L_1 = \langle S, I_1, O_1, \lambda_1, S_0 \rangle$ and $L_2 = \langle T, I_2, O_2, \lambda_2, T_0 \rangle$, L_1 is *output compatible* with L_2 if, for any state st of $L_1 \parallel L_2$ and any action $a \in O_1 \cap I_2$, $a \in init(s)$ implies $a \in init(t)$.

If L_1 is output compatible with L_2, the output of L_1 is not blocked by L_2 in the composition. L_1 is output compatible with L_2 if L_2 is input-enabled, but the condition is not necessary. In Fig. 3, $Test$ is output compatible with $Q(Imp)_\delta$ and Imp is output compatible with $Q_{O'}$, because the queues are input-enabled (and therefore, $Q(Imp)_\delta$ is input-enabled).

On the other hand, requiring the queues in the testing architecture (Fig. 3) to be output compatible with the tester or IUT (as in [8]) is too strong for the closed system with lossless queues. Here, output actions of queues can be stored for a later consumption. This means that an input queue can be composed with a system without being output compatible with the system. Such a queue is a storage media that does not lose data not requested immediately, such as message queues, so it is *lossless*. A queue that is not output compatible with the system must be lossless. In [8], on the contrary, a queue is a media that only transfers data, but does not keep it, such as shift registers, so that some data might be lost if the system at the end of the queue is not receptive to the queue's output.

We require that, before executing a test case, $Q(Imp)$ must be properly initialized, i.e., Imp, Q_I, and Q_O must be in (one of) their initial states, respectively. The requirement can be met with the following three assumptions. First, we can reset Imp reliably. Second, the input queue Q_I, which is usually under the control of Imp, is reset reliably to an empty queue when Imp is reset. Third, the tester only assigns the verdict **pass** after emptying the output queue Q_O, which is usually under the tester's control. On the other hand, if the verdict **fail** is assigned, Imp is immediately rejected, so there is no need to execute another test case.

Instead of assuming that we can clear the output queue before executing a test case, we make the last assumption to prevent the situation where an IUT can produce a wrong output after the tester reaches the verdict **pass**. This assumption immediately excludes specifications that oscillate from further consideration, but still leaves us with a wide class of specifications. Moreover, we require that specifications do not have deadlock states, which are usually used to model system breakdown triggered by unspecified behavior or implementation faults. Therefore, we only consider in the paper input-progressive specifications, which do not oscillate or deadlock by definition.

We find it convenient to use the delay operator as defined in [1] to describe the behavior of $Q(L)$. Delay operators are a subset of so-called semi-commutation functions (see [4]). Intuitively, an IUT's output actions can be delayed from the viewpoint of a tester; whereas the tester's output actions (i.e., the IUT's input actions) can be delayed from the viewpoint of the IUT. The delay operation expresses the effect of queues on traces.

For a sequence set (language) $E \subseteq A^*$, a subalphabet $A_1 \subseteq A$, operator $delay[A_1]$: $2^{A^*} \to 2^{A^*}$ calculates the smallest superlanguage of E such that for $u, v \in A^*$, any $a \in A \setminus A_1$ and $a_1 \in A_1$:

- $E \subseteq delay[A_1](E)$ and
- $ua_1av \in delay[A_1](E)$ implies $uaa_1v \in delay[A_1](E)$.

According to the definition, $delay[A_1](E)$ derives a language from E by shifting symbols in A_1 towards the end of each word in E while keeping the relative order of symbols in A_1 and $A \setminus A_1$, respectively.

From the viewpoint of a tester, the traces and quiescent traces of an input-progressive IOTS $L = \langle S, I, O, \lambda, S_0 \rangle$ in a queue context are $traces(Q(L)) = pref(delay[O](traces(L)))$, where $pref(U)$ is the prefix closure of trace set U, and $qtraces(Q(L)) = delay[O](qtraces(L))$, respectively.

On the other hand, after a trace u is executed by the tester, L can execute any trace in $delay[I](uO^*) \cap traces(L)$. Since L is input-progressive, each input action can cause at most $|S| - 1$ output actions, so u can cause at most $l(u) = |u_{\downarrow_I}| \times (|S| - 1) - |u_{\downarrow_O}|$ additional output actions in L. Therefore, the corresponding traces executable by L can be refined as $delay[I](uO^{l(u)}) \cap traces(L)$, where A^n is the sublanguage of A^* with at most n symbols in each word. Finally, when a quiescent trace u is executed by $Q(L)$, L executes any quiescent trace in $delay[I](u) \cap qtraces(L)$.

In the following, we use the variable $Spec$ along with Imp. $Spec$ and Imp represent the specification and implementation of a system, respectively, that belong to $IOTS(I, O)$ and have finite number of states.

4   Testing Fully Specified IOTS through Unbounded Queues

We assume in this section that *Spec* is fully specified and input-progressive, whereas *Imp* is fully specified. Neither *Spec* nor *Imp* has to be input-enabled. In Section 5, we will lax the restriction on fully specified *Spec*.

There are a couple of conformance relations that can be formulated between *Spec* and *Imp* in a context with unbounded queues, for example, see [13], [6], and [8]. We briefly introduce them as follows.

Definition 2. For *Spec*, *Imp* $\in$ *IOTS(I, O)*,

- *Imp* is *queue-context trace included* into *Spec* if $traces(Q(Imp)) \subseteq traces(Q(Spec))$;
- *Imp* is *queue-context quiescent trace included* into *Spec* if $traces(Q(Imp)) \subseteq traces(Q(Spec))$ and $qtraces(Q(Imp)) \subseteq qtraces(Q(Spec))$;
- *Imp* is *queue-context suspension trace included* into *Spec* if $straces(Q(Imp)) \subseteq straces(Q(Spec))$.

Queue-context trace inclusion relation is similar to the $\leq_{trQ}$ relation in [13]. In [6], the trace inclusion relation is used. Queue-context quiescent trace inclusion relation is similar to the $\leq_{Q}$ relation in [13]. Finally, the suspension trace inclusion relation is used in the **ioco** testing framework [12], and the queued testing framework [8] uses the queued suspension trace inclusion relation.

Since $Q(L)$ usually has infinitely many states, its trace set may not be regular. In [13], an attempt is made to use so-called tracks to characterize the traces and quiescent traces of $Q(Spec)$ and $Q(Imp)$. However, [13] only proves that tracks are finite if the specification has finite behavior, i.e., with finitely many traces and quiescent traces. It is not known whether tracks are regular for (finite state) specifications with infinite behavior, so it is not clear how the track characterization can be applied to these specifications.

In the following, we restrict ourselves to the case of the queue-context quiescent trace inclusion relation and derive tests directly from the original specification alone according to the transition coverage criterion. The results for other relations can be similarly formulated.

We first define a test case with respect to the set of traces of $Q(Spec)$ that we want to verify in $Q(Imp)$ (test purposes) using the chosen conformance relation. As usual, we require that a test case has finite behavior and is deterministic. The latter means that in each state of the test case, either only one input action to *Imp* is enabled, or all output actions of *Imp* (including quiescence, which indicates that the output queue of *Imp* is empty) are enabled, except for deadlock states, where the test case terminates and the verdicts are assigned. Therefore, the structure of a test case should be a tree, which branches only when output actions of the IUT are read from the queue. The verdicts are assigned in the following way. As assumed in Section 3, **pass** verdicts are only assigned after the tester observes quiescence, i.e., only when the tester emptied the output queue of the IUT. On the other hand, verdict **fail** is assigned when wrong output or premature quiescence is observed. In particular, $delay[I](\beta O^{I(\beta)}) \cap traces(Spec)$ contains all traces that can be executed by *Spec* after the tester executes β and the input queue Q_i is empty. If the intersection is empty, verdict **fail** is assigned to the tester state corresponding to the observation of β. Similarly, $delay[I](\{\beta\}) \cap$

qtraces(Spec) contains all quiescent traces that can be executed by *Spec* after the tester executes β and observes quiescence of $Q(Spec)$. Therefore, we assign **fail** if the intersection is empty or **pass** otherwise.

Definition 3. For *Spec* $\in$ *IOTS(I, O)*,

1. An *output-branching trace tree* (OBTT) of *Spec* is a finite set of traces $U \subseteq$ *traces(Q(Spec))* that satisfies the following conditions: for $\forall$ u_1, $u_2 \in U$, there exist v, w_1, $w_2 \in (I \cup O)^*$ and b_1, $b_2 \in O$ ($b_1 \neq b_2$) such that $u_1 = vb_1w_1$ and $u_2 = vb_2w_2$.

2. For OBTT U of *Spec*, a *test case* $T(U)$ with respect to the queue-context quiescent trace inclusion relation is a deterministic IOTS $T(U) = <S_t \cup \{\textbf{pass}, \textbf{fail}\}, O \cup \{\delta\}, I, \lambda_t, \{\varepsilon\}>$, where the state set S_t and the transition relation λ_t are the smallest sets derived by the following inference rules:
    *   *pref(U)* $\subseteq S_t \subseteq$ *traces(Q(Spec))*;
    *   for β, $\beta a \in$ *pref(U)*, where $a \in I$, $(\beta, a, \beta a) \in \lambda_t$;
    *   for $\beta \in S_t$, where there is no $a \in I$ such that $\beta a \in$ *pref(U)*,
        *   for $b \in O$, $(\beta, b, \textbf{fail}) \in \lambda_t$ if $delay[I](\beta b O^{I(\beta b)}) \cap$ *traces(Spec)* = $\varnothing$; otherwise, $\beta b \in S_t$ and $(\beta, b, \beta b) \in \lambda_t$;
        * $(\beta, \delta, \textbf{fail}) \in \lambda_t$ if $delay[I](\{\beta\}) \cap$ *qtraces(Spec)* = $\varnothing$; otherwise, $(\beta, \delta, \textbf{pass}) \in \lambda_t$.

3. The *test length* of a test case $T(U)$ is the length of the longest input sequences that the tester has to apply, i.e., $\textbf{max}\{|u\downarrow_I| \mid u \in traces(T(U))\}$.

4. A *test suite* is a set of test cases.

The number of expected output actions is finite because *Spec* is input-progressive; moreover, test case has no cycles. Therefore, a test case has finite behavior.

We have the following proposition claiming the soundness of the test cases.

Proposition 1. For *Spec*, *Imp* $\in$ *IOTS(I, O)*, if *Imp* is *queue-context quiescent trace included* into *Spec*, then for any test case $T(U)$ of *Spec* as in Definition 3, no state of $T(U) \parallel Q(Imp)_\delta$ contains **fail** as a substate.

One possible way to define an output-branching trace tree is covering a transition of *Spec*. Transition coverage is a widely used criterion in software testing. In protocol testing, covering a given transition is also a typical test purpose.

A trace $u \in$ *traces(L)* *covers* a transition (s_1, a, s_2) of $L \in$ *IOTS(I, O)* if there exist $\beta \in$ *pref(u)* and, if $a \in (I \cup O)$, $\beta a \in$ *pref(u)* such that $s_1 \in L$-**after**-β. A test case $T(U)$ *covers* a transition (s_1, a, s_2) of *Spec* if there is a trace u in the composition $T(U) \parallel (Q_I \parallel Spec' \parallel Q_O)_\delta$ such that $u\downarrow_{I \cup O}$ covers (s_1, a', s_2) of *Spec'*. According to the discussion in Section 3, a test case $T(U)$ covers a transition of *Spec* if and only if there exists a trace $v \in delay[I](traces(T(U))O^*)$ covering the transition of *Spec*. A test suite is a *transition cover test* of *Spec* if each transition (s_1, a, s_2) of *Spec* is covered by at least one test case in the suite.

Notice that, due to limited control, a test case covering a transition cannot guarantee that the transition is actually executed in any test run. We can only assume that if the test case is executed a sufficient number of times, the transition will eventually be executed. This is a so-called fairness or *all-the-weather* assumption.

The following proposition states that it is sufficient to look into the traces of *Spec*, not the traces of *Q(Spec)*, to derive a transition cover test.

Proposition 2. For $Spec = <S, I, O, \lambda, S_0>$, a transition (s_1, a, s_2), and a test case $T(U_1)$, where $U_1 \subseteq traces(Q(Spec))$, that covers the transition, there exists a test case $T(U_2)$, where $U_2 \subseteq traces(Spec)$, that also covers the transition; moreover, the test length of $T(U_2)$ does not exceed that of $T(U_1)$.

Proof: According to the definition of a test case covering a transition of *Spec*, there is a trace u of $T(U_1) \parallel (Q_I \parallel Spec' \parallel Q_0)_\delta$ such that $u_{\downarrow_{I \cup O'}}$ covers transition (s_1, a', s_2) of *Spec'*. Therefore, $(u_{\downarrow_{I \cup O'}})'$ is a trace of *Spec* and covers (s_1, a, s_2). Let $U_2 = \{(u_{\downarrow_{I \cup O'}})'\}$ (a singleton) and $T(U_2)$ be the test case for the OBTT U_2. $T(U_2)$ is a test case covering (s_1, a, s_2) because $a_1a_1'a_2a_2'a_3a_3'...$, where $a_1a_2a_3... = (u_{\downarrow_{I \cup O'}})'$, is a trace of $T(U_1) \parallel (Q_I \parallel Spec' \parallel Q_0)_\delta$ and $(a_1a_1'a_2a_2'a_3a_3'...)_{\downarrow_{I \cup O'}} = a_1'a_2'a_3'... = u_{\downarrow_{I \cup O'}}$ covers (s_1, a', s_2).

Moreover, if $T(U_1)$ executes $u_{\downarrow_{I \cup O}}$, the traces executable by *Spec* is a subset of $pref(delay[I](u_{\downarrow_{I \cup O}}O^*))$, so $(u_{\downarrow_{I \cup O}})' \in pref(delay[I](u_{\downarrow_{I \cup O}}O^*))$ $((u_{\downarrow_{I \cup O}})'$ is a trace of *Spec*). Thus, $T(U_2)$'s test length $|(u_{\downarrow_{I \cup O}})'_\downarrow|$ is equal to or less than $|(u_{\downarrow_{I \cup O}})_\downarrow|$. Since $u_{\downarrow_{I \cup O}}$ is a trace executable by $T(U_1)$, the test length of $T(U_2)$ does not exceed that of $T(U_1)$. QED

Intuitively, if a tester $T(U)$ can execute a trace u of *Spec*, then it is possible that the trace u' is executed by *Spec'* in the closed system $T(U) \parallel (Q_I \parallel Spec' \parallel Q_0)_\delta$. As a result, $T(U)$ covers all transitions of *Spec* that are covered by u in *Spec*.

According to Proposition 2, to derive a test suite that is a transition cover test of *Spec*, we only have to find a set of traces that cover every transition of *Spec*. Since the trace set is based on a regular language, i.e., *traces(Spec)*, there is an algorithm to derive such a set. Here, we propose an algorithm to derive a transition cover test with the shortest (in terms of the test length) test cases.

Procedure 1. To derive a transition cover test for *Spec*
  Input: $Spec = <S, I, O, \lambda, S_0>$
  Output: A transition cover test of *Spec* $\{T(U_1), T(U_2), ...\}$
  Step 1: Let $U = \emptyset$, $V = O^{|S|-1} \cap traces(Spec)$. While *Spec* has a transition not covered by traces in U, do:
      Step 1.1: for each $v \in V$:
          add v to U if v covers a transition that is not covered by any trace in U;
      Step 1.2: let $V = VIO^{|S|-1} \cap traces(Spec)$;
  end of the while-loop in Step 1.
  Step 2: For each $u \in U$
      delete u from U if $u \in pref(U \setminus \{u\})$.
  Step 3: Let $i = 1$. While $U \neq \emptyset$, do:
      Step 3.1: let $U_i = U$;
      Step 3.2: for each pair of traces β, $\beta a \in pref(U_i)$ such that $a \in I$, let $U_i = U_i \setminus \beta(I \cup O \setminus \{a\})(I \cup O)^*$;
      Step 3.3: let $U = U \setminus U_i$ and $i = i + 1$;
  end of the while-loop in Step 3.
  Step 4: Use Definition 3 to build test cases $T(U_1)$, $T(U_2)$, ..., and return the test suite $\{T(U_1), T(U_2), ...\}$.

Step 1 of Procedure 1 implements a breadth-first search for the traces covering transitions of *Spec* with the shortest input projections. The resulting traces are stored in the set *U*. Step 2 deletes the traces that are prefixes of other traces in *U*. Step 3 groups traces in *U* to derive the output-branching trace trees, since we need two different test cases for two traces in *U* that have a common prefix followed by two different actions, at least one of which is an input action. Step 4 builds test cases according to the trace trees.

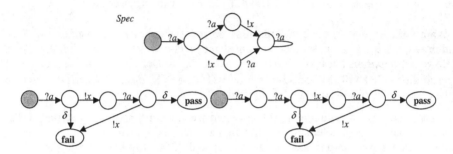

Fig. 5. A specification IOTS and a transition cover test for it

Example 1. Fig. 5 shows a specification and a transition cover test derived by Procedure 1. After Step 1 is applied, *U* could be {*a, ax, aa, aax, axa, aaxa*}. After Step 2, traces *a, ax, aa,* and *aax* are deleted from *U* because *a, ax* ∈ *axa* and *aa, aax* ∈ *aaxa*, respectively. Step 3 separates *axa* and *aaxa* into two different output branching trace trees, and Step 4 builds the test cases as shown in the figure.

Notice that, due to the fact that the order of traces examined in Step 1.1 is not fixed, other transition cover tests could also be derived by the procedure. For example, we could have *U* = {*a, ax, axa, aa, aax, axaa*} after Step 1 and, accordingly, *U* = {*aax, axaa*} after Step 2. The largest test length of the test cases (three) is not influenced, however, by this non-deterministic choice of traces.

In each step of Procedure 1, set *U* has at most $|\lambda|$ traces, each with the input projection of at most $|S|$ actions, where $|\lambda|$ and $|S|$ are the number of transitions and the number of states in *Spec*, respectively. The reason is that any transition of *Spec* can be covered by a trace of at most $|S|$ actions, and each trace in *U* covers at least one new transition. Therefore, Procedure 1 stops in finite steps for a finite state *Spec*, so the procedure is an algorithm that derives a test suite with at most $|\lambda|$ test cases, whose test lengths are at most $|S|$.

5   Testing Partially Specified IOTS through Unbounded Queues

In this section, we assume that *Spec* is partially specified and input-progressive, whereas *Imp* is fully specified.

For partially specified IOTS, we might have some unexpected results when the test cases by Definition 3 are executed.

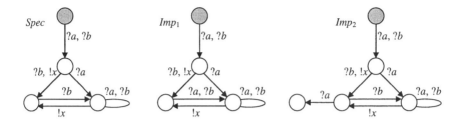

Fig. 6. A partially specified IOTS *Spec* and two implementations

Example 2. In Fig. 6, since the transition on input action a is not specified in *Spec* after sequence ax, Imp_1 should be considered a correct implementation for *Spec*. However, Imp_1 fails a test with trace aax. According to Definition 3, the test case will reach the verdict **fail** if trace $aaxx$ is observed. However, $aaxx \in delay[O](axax)$, so the trace can be observed when testing Imp_1.

There are several solutions to this problem when testing partially specified IOTS, one of which is to complete the specification and let any implementation pass a test if unspecified input actions are executed ([6] and [2]). However, when the closed system of our testing architecture is considered (Fig. 3), this solution may cause some problems.

Example 3. In Fig. 6, Imp_2 should also be a correct implementation of *Spec*. When a test case with trace $aaxbx$ is executed, Imp_2 may execute the trace axa. This trace leads Imp_2 to a deadlock state, where input action b is blocked. According to Definition 3, the tester observes premature quiescence: $aaxb\delta$.

The problem in Example 3 is inherent to the solution of completing the specification because the intuition behind the completion operation is that all input actions should be accepted by the IUT, which is not the case if we consider systems that can refuse to read their input actions from queues. Intuitively, the problem can be solved by restraining the tester from applying any input that might not be specified in *Spec*. As a result, some transitions may not be testable, in other words, covered by the resulting test cases.

To avoid executing unspecified input actions of *Spec*, traces covering the transitions to the trap state s'_{Spec} of *Comp(Spec)* should be excluded from consideration. If s'_{Spec} is reached, there is no need to further test *Spec* as its behavior might not be specified.

A state of $Q(Comp(L))$ is an *exception state* if it has the trap state s'_L as a substate. We define the set of all exception states of $Q(Comp(L))$ as $S_E(L)$. The *exception trace set* of $Q(Comp(L))$ is defined as $etraces(L) = \{u \in traces(Q(Comp(L))) \mid Q(Comp(L))$-$after$-$u \cap S_E(L) \neq \varnothing\}$. The *exception suspension trace set* of $Q(Comp(L))$ is defined as $estraces(L) = \{u \in (I \cup O \cup \{\delta\})^* \mid \exists v \in pref(u) \cap straces(Q(Comp(L)))$ s.t. $Q(Comp(L))$-$after$-$v \cap S_E(L) \neq \varnothing\}$. Due to the definition of operator *Comp*, $estraces(L)$ contains sequences that are not in $straces(Q(Comp(L)))$, but their prefixes are in $straces(Q(Comp(L)))$ and lead $Q(Comp(L))$ to some exception states.

The conformance relations introduced in Section 4 are rewritten below to account for partially specified *Spec*:

Definition 4. For *Spec, Imp* ∈ *IOTS*(*I, O*),

- *Imp* is *queue-context trace included* into *Spec* if *traces*($Q(Imp)$) \ *etraces*(*Spec*) ⊆ *traces*($Q(Comp(Spec))$) \ *etraces*(*Spec*);
- *Imp* is *queue-context quiescent trace included* into *Spec* if *traces*($Q(Imp)$) \ *etraces*(*Spec*) ⊆ *traces*($Q(Comp(Spec))$) \ *etraces*(*Spec*) and *qtraces*($Q(Imp)$) \ *etraces*(*Spec*) ⊆ *qtraces*($Q(Comp(Spec))$) \ *etraces*(*Spec*);
- *Imp* is *queue-context suspension trace included* into *Spec* if *straces*($Q(Imp)$) \ *estraces*(*Spec*) ⊆ *straces*($Q(Comp(Spec))$) \ *estraces*(*Spec*).

When *Spec* is fully specified, Definition 4 reduces to Definition 2. In Definition 4, the exclusion of *Spec*'s exception sets eliminates all unspecified behavior, so that the rest of *Imp* should be specified by *Spec*. Based on this discussion, we refine the definition of output-branching trace trees.

Definition 5. For *Spec* ∈ *IOTS*(*I, O*), an *output-branching trace tree* of *Spec* is a finite set of traces U ⊆ *traces*($Q(Spec)$) \ *etraces*(*Spec*) that satisfies the following conditions: for ∀ u_1, u_2 ∈ U, there exist v, w_1, w_2 ∈ $(I \cup O)^*$ and b_1, b_2 ∈ O ($b_1 \neq b_2$) such that $u_1 = vb_1w_1$ and $u_2 = vb_2w_2$.

At the same time, Definition 3 still applies to test cases for partially specified IOTS.

Similar to Section 4, we want to derive a transition cover test of *Spec* with respect to the queue-context quiescent trace inclusion relation. The definitions of a trace and test case covering a transition of *Spec* remain the same as in Section 4. The definition of transition cover test, on the other hand, should take into account exception traces. Formally, a transition of *Spec* is *coverable* if there is a test case that covers the transition. A test suite is a *transition cover test* of *Spec* if each coverable transition of *Spec* is covered by at least one test case in the suite.

The following statement is the generalization of Proposition 2 to the case of partially specified *Spec*.

Proposition 3. For *Spec* = <*S, I, O,* λ*, S_0*>, a coverable transition (s_1, a, s_2), and a test case $T(U_1)$, where U_1 ⊆ *traces*($Q(Spec)$) \ *etraces*(*Spec*), that covers the transition, there exists a test case $T(U_2)$, where U_2 ⊆ *traces*(*Spec*), that also covers the transition; moreover, the test length of $T(U_2)$ does not exceed that of $T(U_1)$.

Proof: According to the definition of a test case covering a transition of *Spec*, there is a trace u of $T(U_1) \parallel (Q_I \parallel Spec' \parallel Q_O)_\delta$ such that $u_{\downarrow_{I \cup O'}}$ covers transition (s_1, a', s_2) of *Spec'*. Similar to the proof of Proposition 2, we let $U_2 = \{(u_{\downarrow_{I \cup O'}})'\}$, and prove that $T(U_2)$ is a test case covering (s_1, a, s_2), and the test length of $T(U_2)$ does not exceed that of $T(U_1)$. The only difference from that proof is that we now have to prove $(u_{\downarrow_{I \cup O'}})' \notin$ *etraces*(*Spec*) so that U_2 is an OBTT according to Definition 5.

The states reachable by *Spec*, after the tester executes a trace v and the input queue is empty, is *Comp*(*Spec*)-**after**-*delay*[I](vO^*) (see Section 3), so checking whether $v \in$ *etraces*(*Spec*) is equivalent to checking whether the trap state $s'_{Spec} \in$ *Comp*(*Spec*)-**after**-*delay*[I](vO^*).

Suppose $(u_{\downarrow_{I \cup O'}})' \in$ *etraces*(*Spec*), then $s'_{Spec} \in$ *Comp*(*Spec*)-**after**-*delay*[I](($u_{\downarrow_{I \cup O'}})'O^*$), which implies that $s'_{Spec} \in$ *Comp*(*Spec*)-**after**-*delay*[I]($u_{\downarrow_{I \cup O'}}O^*$) (because $(u_{\downarrow_{I \cup O'}})' \in$ *pref*(*delay*[I]($u_{\downarrow_{I \cup O'}}O^*$))), which in turn implies that $u_{\downarrow_{I \cup O}} \in$

etraces(*Spec*). This result, however, contradicts the fact that $u\downarrow_{I\cup O} \in pref(U_1) \subseteq$ *traces*(*Spec*) \ *etraces*(*Spec*). Therefore, $(u\downarrow_{I\cup O_0})' \notin etraces(Spec)$. QED

Attempts to generalize Procedure 1 to the case of partially specified *Spec* faces the problem that it is unknown how to determine which transitions of *Spec* are coverable because *etraces*(*Spec*) is not regular.

Here, we take a pragmatic approach by restricting the test length of the test cases, which allows us to determine which transitions are coverable with the given constraint. Formally, a transition of *Spec* is *k-coverable* if there is a test case $T(U)$ with test length k that covers the transition. We can verify that if a transition is k-1 coverable, it is k-coverable. A test suite is a *transition k-cover test* if all *k-coverable* transitions are covered by at least one test case in the suite.

Given a bound k, we can now generalize Procedure 1 to derive a transition k-cover test for a partially specified *Spec*. Intuitively, this can be done by examining traces of *Spec* incrementally to derive the test cases whose test lengths are not larger than k. When examining trace $va \in traces(Spec)$, where $a \in I$, we have to verify whether va belongs to *etraces*(*Spec*). Similar to the proof of Proposition 3, checking whether $va \in etraces(Spec)$ is equivalent to checking whether $s'_{Spec} \in Comp(Spec)$-**after-***delay*[I]($vaO^{l(va)}$). Since $vaO^{l(va)}$ is a finite set, *delay*[I]($vaO^{l(va)}$) is a finite set, too. The problem of verifying whether $va \in etraces(Spec)$ is, therefore, decidable.

Based on the discussions above, we have the following algorithm.

Procedure 2. To derive a transition k-cover test for *Spec*

> **Input:** *Spec* $\in$ *IOTS*(I, O) and bound k
> **Output:** A transition k-cover test of *Spec* {$T(U_1)$, $T(U_2)$, …}
> **Step 1:** Let $U = \varnothing$, $V = O^{|S|-1} \cap traces(Spec)$, $i = 0$. While *Spec* has a transition not covered by traces in U and $i \leq k$, do:
>> **Step 1.1:** for each $v \in V$
>>> add v to U if v covers a transition that is not covered by any trace in U;
>> **Step 1.2:** let $V = VIO^{|S|-1} \cap traces(Spec)$, for $v \in V$:
>>> delete v from V if $s'_{Spec} \in Comp(Spec)$-**after-***delay*[I]($vO^{l(v)}$);
>> **Step 1.3:** $i = i + 1$;
> end of the while-loop in Step 1.
> **Step 2:** For each $u \in U$
>> delete u from U if $u \in pref(U \setminus \{u\})$.
> **Step 3:** Let $i = 1$. While $U \neq \varnothing$, do:
>> **Step 3.1:** let $U_i = U$.
>> **Step 3.2:** for each pair of traces β, $\beta a \in pref(U_i)$ such that $a \in I$, let $U_i = U_i \setminus \beta(I \cup O \setminus \{a\})(I \cup O)^*$;
>> **Step 3.3:** let $U = U \setminus U_i$ and $i = i + 1$;
> end of the while-loop in Step 3.
> **Step 4:** Use Definition 3 to build test cases $T(U_1)$, $T(U_2)$, … , and return the test suite {$T(U_1)$, $T(U_2)$,…}.

Step 1 of Procedure 2 is different from that of Procedure 1: it stops when the bound k is reached and checks whether a trace in set V belongs to *etraces*(*Spec*).

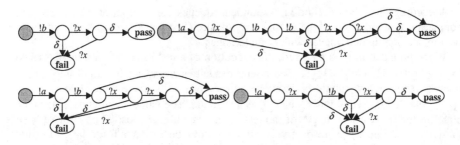

Fig. 7. A transition cover test for the *Spec* in Fig. 7

Example 5. Fig. 7 shows a transition 3-cover test derived by Procedure 2 for the *Spec* in Fig. 6. All transitions on action *a*, except the one from the starting state, are not covered by this suite. However, it can be proved that these transitions on *a* are, in fact, not coverable, so the obtained test suite is a transition cover test for the *Spec*.

To obtain the test suite in Fig. 7, $U = \{a, ax, b, ab, axb, axbx, axbb\}$ after Step 1, and $U = \{b, ab, axbx, axbb\}$ after Step 2.

6   Testing IOTS through Bounded Queues

The test suites derived by Procedures 1 and 2 have finitely many test cases, and each test case, by definition, has finite behavior. Therefore, once a test suite is constructed, we can calculate the capacity of the queues used when a conforming implementation of an input-progressive specification is tested. This suggests that bounded queues (i.e., queues with bounded capacity) can be used in the testing architecture (Fig. 3) for a given test suite. Intuitively, this can be done by requiring that the queue capacities be large enough so that the queues do not overflow when a conforming IUT is tested. Since we assume that *Spec* is input-progressive, there is a lower bound of the queue capacities to meet the condition. When the output queue overflows, on the other hand, we are sure that a non-conforming IUT is tested.

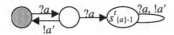

Fig. 8. A bounded queue with capacity 1 and a single input action *a*

We start with the definition of bounded queues. Formally, a *bounded queue with input set A and capacity n*, $Q_{A\text{-}n}$, is a deterministic IOTS $<S_{A\text{-}n} \cup \{s'_{A\text{-}n}\}, A, A', \lambda_{A\text{-}n}, \{\varepsilon\}>$, where the set $S_{A\text{-}n} = \{u \in A^* \mid |u| \leq n\}$, and the transition relation $\lambda_{A\text{-}n} = \{(u, a, ua) \mid u, ua \in S_{A\text{-}n}\} \cup \{(av, a', v) \mid av, v \in S_{A\text{-}n}\} \cup \{(u, a, s'_{A\text{-}n}) \mid u \in S_{A\text{-}n}, |u| = n, \text{ and } a \in A\} \cup \{(s'_{A\text{-}n}, a, s'_{A\text{-}n}) \mid a \in A \cup A'\}$. The trap state $s'_{A\text{-}n}$ once reached indicates that the queue overflows. Fig. 8 shows an example of a bounded queue, $Q_{\{a\}\text{-}1}$.

According to the definition, bounded queues are input-enabled, so the compatibility conditions of the testing architecture (Section 3) are not violated when we replace unbounded queues with bounded ones.

When bounded queues are used, the execution of a test case *Test* can be described by *Test* $\|$ $(Q_{l\text{-}n}$ $\|$ *Imp'* $\|$ $Q_{O'\text{-}m})_\delta$. The queue capacities n and m, for input and output queues, respectively, should be large enough to ensure that there is no state of *Test* $\|$ $(Q_{l\text{-}n}$ $\|$ *Spec'* $\|$ $Q_{O'\text{-}m})_\delta$ that has $s'_{l\text{-}n}$ or $s'_{O'\text{-}m}$ as a substate. The value n can always be taken equal to the longest test length of the test cases, which is at most $|S|$ or k for fully or partially specified *Spec*, respectively, and m could be estimated similarly. Further reducing the estimated value of n and m is an optimization problem and is not discussed here due to the lack of space.

7   Conclusion

In this paper, we discussed how to derive tests when testing (not necessarily input-enabled) IOTS through lossless queues with the intention to cover each transition of a non-deterministic specification. We introduced the testing architecture, along with the compatibility condition at each interface. Although the traces of IOTS composed with a pair of unbounded queues are usually not regular, we demonstrated that the transition cover test can be derived from a regular language, namely, the trace set of the specification. We first considered testing fully specified IOTS and formalized the basic ideas of the test derivation algorithm. Treating partially specified IOTS, where coverability of transitions is still an open problem, we took a pragmatic approach by restricting the test length of test cases. Based on the test suites derived for testing IOTS through unbounded queues, we discussed how to use bounded queues in the testing architecture, which makes our method more practical.

Our work differs from previous work by distinguishing between blocked and unspecified input actions, which brings our model closer to the real-world designs of communicating systems. IOTS in this paper can have states that block input actions, where the system does not read its input queue. Unspecified input actions are treated as "don't care" situation in the specification, so our test derivation method does not require fully specified designs.

An important contribution of this paper is that we use a widely used (transition) coverage criterion to derive a finite test suite directly from a specification. This allows us to avoid either explicitly composing the specification with unbounded queues (as in [14]) or devising IUT with a local observer (as in [6]).

Concerning future work, it is interesting to explore how to determine whether a transition of a partially specified IOTS is coverable, so that we could estimate the bound k for which a transition k-cover test is a transition cover test. Moreover, it is still unknown, when testing IOTS through unbounded queues, whether there is an algorithm to derive test cases based on some fault models. Also, we only demonstrated how to derive transition cover tests for the queue-context quiescent trace inclusion relation. It would be interesting to derive tests for more stringent conformance relations, e.g., queue-context suspension trace inclusion. A foreseeable difficulty of this work is that intermediate quiescence of a system is not always observable through the queue contexts. Some other conformance relations could be tested by exploiting the ability to observe overflow of bounded queues. Consider two single-state IOTS, where both states are stable. One IOTS is input-enabled, whereas the other deadlocks. They are not distinguishable according to the conformance relations in this paper. In fact, they cannot be distinguished when tested through unbounded queues. On the other hand, if a bounded input queue is used with the IOTS that deadlocks, the queue could eventually overflow, so the deadlocking IOTS is distinguishable from the input-enabled one. Last, but not least, although the test cases derived by Procedures 1 and 2 are the shortest in terms of test lengths, the number of test cases is not the smallest. Some test cases are redundant because the transitions that they cover are covered by other test cases. Further reducing the number of test cases is an optimization problem still under investigation.

Acknowledgement. This work was in part supported by the NSERC discovery grant OGP0194381.

References

1. Balemi, S.: Control of Discrete Event Systems: Theory and Application. Ph.D. thesis, Swiss Federal Inst. of Technology, Zurich, Switzerland (1992)
2. van der Bijl, M., Rensink, A., Tretmans, J.: Compositional Testing with IOCO. In: Proc. 3rd Intl. Workshop on Formal Approaches to Testing of Software, FATES 2003. Canada (2003)
3. Brinksma, E., Tretmans, J.: Testing Transition Systems: An Annotated Bibliography. In: Cassez, F., Jard, C., Rozoy, B., Ryan, M. (eds.): Modeling and Verification of Parallel Processes. Lecture Notes in Computer Science, Vol. 2067. Springer-Verlag, Berlin Heidelberg New York (2001)
4. Clerbout, M., Latteux, M., Roos, Y.: Semi-Commutations. In: Diekert, V., Rozenberg, G. (Eds.): The Book of Traces. World Scientific (1995)
5. Herrink, L., Tretmans, J.: Refusal Testing for Classes of Transition Systems with Inputs and Outputs. In: Mizuno, T., Shiratori, N., Higashino, T., Togashi, A. (Eds.): Formal Description Techniques and Protocol Specification, Testing and Verification. Chapman & Hill (1997)
6. Jard, C., Jéron, T., Tanguy, L., Viho, C.: Remote Testing Can be as Powerful as Local Testing. In: The Proceedings of the IFIP Joint International Conference, Methods for Protocol Engineering and Distributed Systems, FORTE XII/PSTV XIX. China (1999)
7. Lynch, N., Tuttle, M. R.: An Introduction to Input/Output Automata. In: CWI Quarterly, Vol. 2, No. 3 (1989)
8. Petrenko, A., Yevtushenko, N., Huo, J. L.: Testing Transition Systems with Input and Output Testers. In: Proc. IFIP 15th Int. Conf. Testing of Communicating Systems. TestCom'2003, France. Lecture Notes in Computer Science, Vol. 2644. Springer-Verlag, Berlin Heidelberg New York (2003)
9. Phalippou, M.: Executable Testers. In: The Proceedings of the IFIP Sixth International Workshop on Protocol Test Systems, IWPTS'93. France (1993)
10. Segala, R.: Quiescence, Fairness, Testing and the Notion of Implementation. In: The Proceedings of CONCUR'93. Lecture Notes in Computer Science, Vol. 715. Springer-Verlag, Berlin Heidelberg New York (1993)
11. Tan, Q. M., Petrenko, A.: Test Generation for Specifications Modeled by Input/Output Automata. In: The Proceedings of the IFIP 11th International Workshop on Testing of Communicating Systems, IWTCS'98. Russia (1998)

12. Tretmans, J.: Test Generation with Inputs, Outputs and Repetitive Quiescence. In: Software-Concepts and Tools, Vol. 17, Issue 3 (1996)
13. Tretmans, J., Verhaard, L.: A Queue Model Relating Synchronous and Asynchronous Communication. In Linn, R. J., Jr., Üyar, M. Ü. Eds.: Protocol Specification, Testing and Verification, XII. Elsevier Science Publishers B. V. (North-Holland) (1992)
14. Verhaard, L., Tretmans, J., Kim, P., Brinksma, E.: On Asynchronous Testing. In: The Proceedings of the IFIP 5th International Workshop on Protocol Test Systems, IWPTS'92. Canada (1992)

Testing Multi Input/Output Transition System with All-Observer[*]

Zhongjie Li, Jianping Wu, and Xia Yin

Department of Computer Science and Technology, Tsinghua University,
Beijing 100084, P.R.China
{lzj, yxia}@csnet1.cs.tsinghua.edu.cn
jianping@cernet.edu.cn

Abstract. Multi input/output transition system (MIOTS) models the interface distribution of a system by partitioning its inputs and outputs into channels. The MIOTS refusal testing theory has been based on singular observers. Such an observer is useful for eliminating nondeterminism in the testing process, but also contributes to the large size of the test suites. We propose an alternative type of observers: all-observer, which can observe all the output channels simultaneously, and help to reduce a test suite effectively. An algorithm is presented to generate an all-observer test suite from the specification. The derived test suite is sound for all MIOTS systems, and complete for a class of MIOTS systems that are common in practice. We also discuss the problem of factorized all-observer test generation. Our work complements the MIOTS refusal testing with singular observers.

1 Introduction

Conformance testing is an operational way to check the correctness of a system implementation by means of experimenting. Tests are applied to the implementation, and based on observations made during the execution of the tests, a verdict about the correctness of the implementation is given. In formal conformance testing it is assumed that we have a formal specification, and implementations whose behavior is also formally modeled but not apriori known. Labeled Transition System (LTS) is a well-known model [1,2] for describing processes. LTS does not distinguish between the initiative of actions, which is not very realistic. So input/output transition system (IOTS) was proposed to model the more common communication via actions that are initiated by the system (output), and initiated by the environment (input) [3]. The IOTS model has no consideration for the distribution of communication interfaces between the system and the environment. To overcome this deficiency, [4] proposed a new model called multi input/output transition system (MIOTS), which partitions the inputs and outputs into different channels reflecting the locations where actions occur.

---

[*] This work was supported by the 973 project No.2003CB314801 and NSFC project No.90104002, No.60102009

R. Groz and R.M. Hierons (Eds.): TestCom 2004, LNCS 2978, pp. 95–111, 2004.

For MIOTS implementations, the conformance to an LTS specification is defined as the implementation relation *multi input/output refusal preorder* $\leq_{mior}$. **mioco**$_{\mathcal{F}}$ is a generalization of $\leq_{mior}$, which requires that all responses an implementation can perform after every trace in the set of traces $\mathcal{F}$ are allowed by the specification. Testing for **mioco**$_{\mathcal{F}}$ consists of serial compositions of providing a single input action at some input channel and detection of its acceptance or rejection, and observing some output channel and detection of the occurrence or absence of outputs produced at this channel. Such tests are modeled by *singular observers*. After each trace in $\mathcal{F}$, an individual test is needed for checking each output channel to see if the implementation behaves correctly at this channel. This method avoids the nondeterministic outputs of the implementation at different channels, and also allows for stronger testing power in general. However, it also contributes to the large size of the derived test suite, which means big time expense in test generation as well as in test execution.

Just like singular observers, all-observer is a special class of MIOTS that can observe all the output channels simultaneously. We present in this paper a test generation algorithm. For a specification with respect to **mioco**$_{\mathcal{F}}$, the algorithm generates an all-observer test suite, which is smaller than the singular observer test suite, sound for all MIOTS systems, and complete for special MIOTS systems (which are common in practice, e.g. queue systems).

Factorized test generation [5] is a technique that aims to avoid the generation of tests for a complicated correctness criterion directly from a large specification. In [5], for a specification s and **mioco**$_{\mathcal{F}}$, **mioco**$_{\mathcal{F}}$ is decomposed into **mioco**$_{\{\sigma\}}(\forall \sigma \in \mathcal{F})$. Then for each trace, a selection process is applied to obtain a reduced-size specification. This decomposition is very inefficient, especially when $\mathcal{F}$ contains a lot of traces. So we propose an improved $\mathcal{F}$-partition method, which groups all the traces having the same selection process in one set, and thus makes the test generation more efficient. It is shown that this optimization is necessary for the factorized all-observer test generation.

This paper is organized as follows. Sect. 2 reviews the preliminaries of the refusal testing theory for MIOTS. Sect. 3 describes our work on the all-observer test generation. Sect. 4 discusses the factorized test generation in all-observer based testing. Concluding remarks and future works are presented in sect. 5.

2   Refusal Testing for MIOTS

Definition 1. *A (labeled) transition system over L is a quadruple $\langle S, L, \rightarrow, s_0 \rangle$ where S is a (countable) set of states, L is a (countable) set of observable actions, $\rightarrow \subseteq S \times L \times S$ is a set of transitions, and $s_0 \in S$ is the initial state.*

We denote the class of all transition systems over L by $\mathcal{LTS}(L)$. The observable behavior of a transition system is expressed using sequences consisting of actions and sets of refused actions, i.e., sequences in $(L \cup P(L))^*$ ($P(L)$ is the power-set of L). Such sequences are called *failure traces*, comparable to *traces* (those in L^*). A *refusal transition* is defined as a self-loop transition in the form

$s \xrightarrow{A} s'$ where $A \subseteq L$ is called *a refusal* of s, meaning that the system is unable to perform any action in A from state s.

Definition 2. *Let* $p \in \mathcal{LTS}(L)$, *then*

1. $init(p) =_{def} \{\alpha \in L | \exists p' : p \xrightarrow{\alpha} p'\}$
2. $der(p) =_{def} \{p' | \exists \sigma \in (L \cup P(L))^* : p \xrightarrow{\sigma} p'\}$
3. $ftraces(p) =_{def} \{\sigma \in (L \cup P(L))^* : p \xrightarrow{\sigma}\}$
4. $pref(\sigma_2) = \{\sigma_1 | \exists \sigma' : \sigma_1 \cdot \sigma' = \sigma_2 \text{ and } \sigma_1, \sigma_2, \sigma' \in (L \cup P(L))^*\}$
5. P **after** $\sigma =_{def} \{p' | \exists p \in P : p \xrightarrow{\sigma} p'\}$
6. p *is deterministic iff* $\forall \sigma \in L^* : |\{p\} \text{ after } \sigma| \leq 1$
7. p *is output-finite if there is a natural number* N *s.t.* $\forall p' \in der(p)$, *the set* $X = \{\sigma_u \in (L_U)^* | p' \xrightarrow{\sigma_u}\}$ *is finite and* $\forall \sigma_u \in X : |\sigma_u| \leq N$, *where* L_U *is the set of output actions.*

Definition 3. *A multi input/output transition system* p *over partitioning* $\mathcal{L}_I = \{L_I^1, \ldots, L_I^n\}$ *of* L_I *and partitioning* $\mathcal{L}_U = \{L_U^1, \ldots, L_U^m\}$ *of* L_U *is a transition system with inputs and outputs,* $p \in \mathcal{LTS}(L_I \cup L_U)$, *such that for all* $L_I^j \in \mathcal{L}_I$, $\forall p' \in der(p)$, *if* $\exists a \in L_I^j : p' \xrightarrow{a}$ *then* $\forall b \in L_I^j : p' \xrightarrow{b}$. *The universe of multi input/output transition systems over* $\mathcal{L}_I$ *and* $\mathcal{L}_U$ *is denoted by* $\mathcal{MIOTS}(\mathcal{L}_I, \mathcal{L}_U)$.

Refusal testing [6] is a kind of such implementation relation where experiments are not only able to detect whether actions can occur, but also able to detect whether actions can fail, i.e. refused by the system. In MIOTS refusal testing [4], special action labels $\theta_i^j (j = 1, \ldots, n)$ are added to observe the inability of the implementation to accept an input action in channel L_I^j (input suspension, denoted by ξ^j), and $\theta_u^k (k = 1, \ldots, m)$ are added to observe the inability to produce outputs in channel L_U^k (output suspension, denoted by δ^k). Let $\Theta = \{\theta_i^1, \ldots, \theta_i^n, \theta_u^1, \ldots, \theta_u^m\}$ denote all the suspension detection labels. Then, implementations that are modeled as members of $\mathcal{MIOTS}(\mathcal{L}_I, \mathcal{L}_U)$ are observed by observers modeled in $\mathcal{MIOTS}(\mathcal{L}_U^\theta, \mathcal{L}_I^\theta)$ where $\mathcal{L}_I^\theta = \{L_I^1 \cup \{\theta_i^1\}, \ldots, L_I^n \cup \{\theta_i^n\}\}$, $\mathcal{L}_U^\theta = \{L_U^1 \cup \{\theta_u^1\}, \ldots, L_U^m \cup \{\theta_u^m\}\}$. Communication between observer and system is modeled by the parallel composition operator $\|$. Observations that can be made by an observer u interacting with p by means of $\|$ now may consist these suspension detection actions: $obs(u, p) =_{def} \{\sigma \in (L \cup \Theta)^* | (u \| p) \xrightarrow{\sigma}\}$.

Singular observers are a special class of MIOTS observers. They consist of finite, serial compositions of providing a single input action at some channel L_I^j and detection of its acceptance or rejection, and observing some channel L_U^k and detection of the occurrence or absence of outputs produced at this channel. The set of all singular observers over $\mathcal{L}_I$ and $\mathcal{L}_U$ is denoted by $\mathcal{SOBS}(\mathcal{L}_U^\theta, \mathcal{L}_I^\theta)$.

In correspondence with the observations defined on $(L_I \cup L_U \cup \Theta)^*$, we define the suspension traces of p to be its failure traces restricted to $(L_I \cup L_U \cup \mathcal{L}_I \cup \mathcal{L}_U)^*$: $straces(p) =_{def} ftraces(p) \cap (L_I \cup L_U \cup \mathcal{L}_I \cup \mathcal{L}_U)^*$. Responses of the implementation after a specific suspension trace that can be observed by singular observers are collected into the set *out*.

$$out(p \textbf{ after } \sigma) =_{def} \{x \in L_U | \exists p' : p \xrightarrow{\sigma} p' \xrightarrow{x}\}$$
$$\cup \quad \{\xi^j | 1 \leq j \leq n, \exists p' : p \xrightarrow{\sigma} p' \text{ and } init(p') \cap L_I^j = \emptyset\}$$
$$\cup \quad \{\delta^k | 1 \leq k \leq m, \exists p' : p \xrightarrow{\sigma} p' \text{ and } init(p') \cap L_U^k = \emptyset\}$$

Definition 4 (multi input/output refusal preorder).
$i \in \mathcal{MIOTS}(\mathcal{L}_I, \mathcal{L}_U)$ and $s \in \mathcal{LTS}(L_I \cup L_U)$, then

$$i \leq_{mior} s =_{def} \forall u \in \mathcal{SOBS}(\mathcal{L}_U^\theta, \mathcal{L}_I^\theta) : obs(u, i) \subseteq obs(u, s).$$

[4] has proved that $i \leq_{mior} s$ iff $\forall \sigma \in (L_I \cup L_U \cup \mathcal{L}_I \cup \mathcal{L}_U)^* : out(i \textbf{ after } \sigma) \subseteq out(s \textbf{ after } \sigma)$. Checking this *out* inclusion condition for all the suspension traces is too time consuming in practice. Therefore, [4] further generalizes this condition to an arbitrary (and possible finite) set $\mathcal{F} \subseteq (L_I \cup L_U \cup \mathcal{L}_I \cup \mathcal{L}_U)^*$, and define a corresponding implementation relation **mioco$_\mathcal{F}$**:

Definition 5. i **mioco$_\mathcal{F}$** $s =_{def} \forall \sigma \in \mathcal{F} : out(i \textbf{ after } \sigma) \subseteq out(s \textbf{ after } \sigma)$.

3   All-Observer Testing for MIOTS

3.1   All-Observer

The all-observer is also a special class of MIOTS observers. Besides providing input actions and observing single-channel outputs or suspensions, they are additionally equipped with an all-output-channel observing mode: observing all the m output channels ($L_U^k, k = 1, \ldots, m$) and detection of an output at some channel, or no output at all. This collective output suspension is denoted by a special label δ (called all-channel output suspension, meaning the refusal of L_U), which can be detected by the all-observer using the label $\theta_u : \theta_u =_{def} \langle \theta_u^1, \ldots, \theta_u^m \rangle$. The set Θ denotes the set of all the suspension detection labels: $\Theta = \{\theta_i^1, \ldots, \theta_i^n, \theta_u^1, \ldots, \theta_u^m, \theta_u\}$, and let $\Psi = \{\xi^1, \ldots, \xi^n, \delta_1, \ldots, \delta^m, \delta\}$ denote the counterpart suspension actions of the system. Other notations follow those in Sect. 2.

Definition 6. *An all-observer u over $\mathcal{L}_I$ and $\mathcal{L}_U$ is a finite, deterministic MIOTS $u \in \mathcal{MIOTS}(\mathcal{L}_U^\theta, \mathcal{L}_I^\theta)$ such that*

$$\forall u' \in der(u) : init(u') = \emptyset \text{ or } init(u') = L_U \cup \{\theta_u\}$$
$$\text{or } init(u') = \{a, \theta_i^j\} \text{ for some } j \in \{1, \ldots, n\} \text{ and } a \in L_I^j$$
$$\text{or } init(u') = L_U^k \cup \{\theta_u^k\} \text{ for some } k \in \{1, \ldots, m\}$$

the set of all-observer over $\mathcal{L}_I$ and $\mathcal{L}_U$ is denoted by $\mathcal{AOBS}(\mathcal{L}_U^\theta, \mathcal{L}_I^\theta)$.

Definition 7. *Communication between all-observer and system is modeled by the operator $\| : \mathcal{MIOTS}(\mathcal{L}_U^\theta, \mathcal{L}_I^\theta) \times \mathcal{LTS}(L_I \cup L_U) \to \mathcal{LTS}(L_I \cup L_U \cup \Theta)$, defined by the following inference rules:*

$$\frac{u \xrightarrow{a} u', p \xrightarrow{a} p'}{u \| p \xrightarrow{a} u' \| p'} (a \in L_I \cup L_U) \qquad \frac{u \xrightarrow{\theta_i^j} u', init(p) \cap L_I^j = \emptyset}{u \| p \xrightarrow{\theta_i^j} u' \| p} (j \in \{1, \ldots, n\})$$

$$\frac{u \xrightarrow{\theta_u} u', init(p) \cap L_U = \emptyset}{u \| p \xrightarrow{\theta_u} u' \| p} \qquad \frac{u \xrightarrow{\theta_u^k} u', init(p) \cap L_U^k = \emptyset}{u \| p \xrightarrow{\theta_u^k} u' \| p} (k \in \{1, \ldots, m\})$$

Definition 8. *An all-observer test* $t \in \mathcal{AOBS}(\mathcal{L}_U^\theta, \mathcal{L}_I^\theta)$ *such that* $\forall t' \in der(t)$:

$$init(t') = \emptyset \qquad \textit{iff} \qquad t' = \textbf{pass or } t' = \textbf{fail}$$

where **pass** *and* **fail** *are verdicts that indicate the (in)correctness of implementation i when running t against i.*

A test suite is sound if it never rejects correct implementations, and a test suite is exhaustive if each incorrect implementation always fails this test suite. In practice test suites are required to be sound, but not necessarily exhaustive. A test suite is called complete if it is both sound and exhaustive. [4] presents a test generation algorithm that produces complete $\mathcal{SOBS}$ test suites for specifications with respect to **mioco**$_\mathcal{F}$. The $\mathcal{SOBS}$ test suite generated by the algorithm tends to be very large because the necessity to check each output channel after each $\sigma \in \mathcal{F}$ using a separate test. Our goal is: for given **mioco**$_\mathcal{F}$ and specification s, to replace the complete $\mathcal{SOBS}$ test suite with an $\mathcal{AOBS}$ test suite, which has a smaller size, and preserves the soundness unconditionally, and preserves the completeness conditionally. We presents an all-observer test generation algorithm in the next section. It is modified from the singular-observer algorithm with two changes: one, merging test purposes by checking more traces in one test case; two, observing all the output channels simultaneously after performing each trace in $\mathcal{F}$ using one test, instead of checking the output channels one by one using m tests. The two changes all help to reduce the size of a test suite.

3.2   Test Generation

Let $p \in \mathcal{MIOTS}(\mathcal{L}_I, \mathcal{L}_U)$, abbreviate "$p$ **after** σ" to "$p-\sigma$", and define $out_2(p-\sigma)$ to be the union of $out(p-\sigma)$ and the possible all-channel output suspension δ: $out_2(p-\sigma) =_{def} out(p-\sigma) \cup \{\delta | \exists p' \in p-\sigma : init(p') \cap L_U = \emptyset\}$. In addition, we define the out set of a state set P to be: $out(P) =_{def} \{out(p-\epsilon)|p \in P\}$. We denote with $\bar{\sigma}$ the trace σ where each occurrence of a refusal action ξ^j, δ or δ^k is replaced by its detection label θ_i^j, θ_u or θ_u^k, and vice versa.

The $\mathcal{AOBS}$ test generation algorithm is shown as follows. The rationale behind is that it constructs tests that check the condition set forth in Def. 5: $out(i-\sigma) \subseteq out(s-\sigma)$ for each $\sigma \in \mathcal{F}$.

Algorithm 1
input: $s = \langle S, L_I \cup L_U, \rightarrow, s_0 \rangle, \mathcal{F} \subseteq (L_I \cup L_U \cup \mathcal{L}_I \cup \mathcal{L}_U)^*$
output: test case $t_{\mathcal{F},S}$
initial value: $\mathcal{S} = \{s_0\}$ after ε
Apply one of the following non-deterministic choices recursively.

1. if $\mathcal{F} = \emptyset$ then $t_{\mathcal{F},S} :=$ **pass**

2. take some $L_I^j \in \mathcal{L}_I$ and $a \in L_I^j$, such that $\mathcal{F}' = \{\sigma | a \cdot \sigma \in \mathcal{F}\} \neq \emptyset$ and $\mathcal{S}' = \mathcal{S}$ **after** a, then

$$t_{\mathcal{F},S} := a; t_{\mathcal{F}',S'} + \begin{cases} \theta_i^j; \textbf{fail} & \xi^j \notin out(\mathcal{S}) \text{ and } \epsilon \in \mathcal{F} \\ \theta_i^j; \textbf{pass} & \textit{otherwise} \end{cases}$$

3. take some $L_I^j \in \mathcal{L}_I$ such that $\mathcal{F}' = \{\sigma|\xi^j \cdot \sigma \in \mathcal{F}\} \neq \emptyset, \mathcal{S}' = (\mathcal{S} \text{ after } \xi^j)$, then

$$t_{\mathcal{F},\mathcal{S}} := a; \textbf{pass} + \theta_i^j; t_{\mathcal{F}',\mathcal{S}'} \quad (a \text{ is any input in } L_I^j)$$

4. observe on all the output channels

$$t_{\mathcal{F},\mathcal{S}} := \begin{aligned} & \sum\{x; \textbf{fail} \mid x \notin out(\mathcal{S}), \epsilon \in \mathcal{F}\} \\ + & \sum\{x; \textbf{pass} \mid x \notin out(\mathcal{S}), \epsilon \notin \mathcal{F}\} \\ + & \sum\{x; t_{\mathcal{F}',\mathcal{S}'} \mid x \in out(\mathcal{S}), \mathcal{F}' = \{\sigma|x \cdot \sigma \in \mathcal{F}\}, \mathcal{S}' = \mathcal{S} \text{ after } x\} \\ + & \begin{cases} \theta_u; \textbf{fail} & \text{if } \epsilon \in \mathcal{F} \text{ and } \exists k \in \{1,\dots,m\}, \delta^k \notin out(\mathcal{S}) \\ \theta_u; \textbf{pass} & \text{otherwise} \end{cases} \end{aligned}$$

where $x \in L_U$

5. take some $L_U^k \in \mathcal{L}_U$, if $\mathcal{F}' = \{\sigma|\delta^k \cdot \sigma \in \mathcal{F}\} \neq \emptyset$ and $\mathcal{S}' = \mathcal{S} \text{ after } \delta^k$, then

$$t_{\mathcal{F},\mathcal{S}} := \sum\{x; \textbf{fail} \mid x \notin out(\mathcal{S}), \epsilon \in \mathcal{F}\} + \sum\{x; \textbf{pass} \mid otherwise\} + \theta_u^k; t_{\mathcal{F}',\mathcal{S}'}$$

where $x \in L_U^k$ □

Step 1 assigns **pass** in case no trace in $\mathcal{F}$ is performed. Step 2 and 3 each supplies an input to the implementation at some channel L_I^j and continues if the implementation is able to accept or refuse this input, respectively. Step 4 awaits an output action at any output channel or observes an all-channel output suspension. Step 5 awaits a single-channel output suspension to test deeper. For each response that is unspecified by the specification, a **fail** verdict is given. In particular, when θ_u is observed but there exists an output channel that should not suspend at the current states (i.e., $\delta^k \notin out(\mathcal{S})$), a **fail** verdict should be made. With this strategy, it is apparent that an all-observer test cannot detect unspecified single-channel output suspension, because the suspension will be screened by an output at another channel that is also under observation in the all-output-channel observing mode. This limitation makes Algorithm 1 unable to generate an exhaustive test suite. We will give a demonstration and discuss this problem in Sect. 3.4. Fig. 1 compares $\mathcal{AOBS}$ with $\mathcal{SOBS}$ tests in the way they check the output behavior of the implementation after performing σ. An $\mathcal{SOBS}$ test suite uses m tests: $t_1, \dots, t_m$, each for one output channel. These tests are substituted in the $\mathcal{AOBS}$ test suite by only one test t as shown in Fig. 1b, where x_k generally refers to any $x \in L_U^k$.

3.3   Soundness

Proposition 1. *Let* $p \in \mathcal{MIOTS}(\mathcal{L}_I, \mathcal{L}_U)$, *then* $\delta \in out_2(p - \sigma)$ *implies* $\delta^k \in out(p - \sigma), k = 1, \dots, m$.

Tests generated by Algorithm 1 in Sect. 3.2 check all and only the traces in $\mathcal{F}$ to see if the *out*-inclusion condition holds. There are five types of observations: (1) input action $a \in L_I^j$, (2) input suspension ξ^j, (3) output action $y \in L_U^k$, (4) single-channel output suspension δ^k, (5) all-channel output suspension δ. Only three of them (2, 3, 5) may be associated with verdicts. **fail** verdicts are only given for unspecified output or input and output suspension, which all mean non-conformance, so the $\mathcal{AOBS}$ tests generated by Algorithm 1 must be sound.

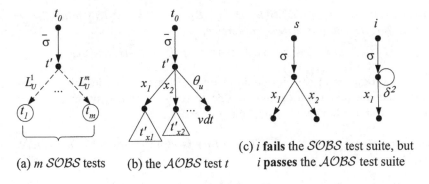

(a) m $\mathcal{SOBS}$ tests   (b) the $\mathcal{AOBS}$ test t

(c) i **fails** the $\mathcal{SOBS}$ test suite, but i **passes** the $\mathcal{AOBS}$ test suite

Fig. 1. testing σ for output: $\mathcal{SOBS}$ vs. $\mathcal{AOBS}$ tests

Proposition 2. *Let* $s \in \mathcal{LTS}(L_I, L_U)$, $\mathcal{F} \subseteq (L_I \cup L_U \cup \mathcal{L}_I \cup \mathcal{L}_U)^*$, *then the* $\mathcal{AOBS}$ *test suite generated by Algorithm 1 is sound for* s *w.r.t.* **mioco**$_\mathcal{F}$.

Algorithm 1 generates sound but not exhaustive test suites. See Fig. 1c for an example, suppose x_1 and x_2 respectively belong to L_U^1 and L_U^2 of a specification s and $\mathcal{F} = \{\sigma\}$, the implementation i will fail the $\mathcal{SOBS}$ tests because it has an unspecified output suspension (δ^2, as shown by the self-loop transition) after performing σ. This error, however, will not be disclosed by the $\mathcal{AOBS}$ tests generated by Algorithm 1, because the output-checking test always stops with a **pass** verdict after the action x_1. This example shows that the all-observer generally have a weaker testing power than singular observers. The exhaustiveness can only be preserved conditionally, as is shown in the next section.

3.4   Completeness

In this section, we discuss the problem of generating complete all-observer test suites. We show that this is possible for a special class of MIOTS in case $\mathcal{F}$ satisfies a given condition.

Definition 9. *Let* $s \in \mathcal{LTS}(L_I, L_U)$, $L_\theta = L_I \cup L_U \cup \mathcal{L}_I \cup \mathcal{L}_U$, *strace-reordering is a relation defined on* $(L_\theta)^*$, $\sim \subseteq (L_\theta)^* \times (L_\theta)^*$:

$$\forall \sigma_1, \sigma_2 \in (L_\theta)^*, \sigma_1 \sim \sigma_2 =_{def} \sigma_1 \lceil (L_I \cup \mathcal{L}_I \cup L_U^k \cup \{L_U^k\}) = \sigma_2 \lceil (L_I \cup \mathcal{L}_I \cup L_U^k \cup \{L_U^k\}), k = 1, \dots, m$$

where $\sigma \lceil A$ *is the projection of* σ *on the action set* A, *resulting in a trace consisting of only actions in* A *with their original order.*

If $\sigma_1 \sim \sigma_2$, we say σ_2 is an *strace-reordering* of σ_1. For example, use a, b for inputs, and x, y, z for outputs at different channels, then $(a \cdot x_1 \cdot x_2 \cdot y \cdot \delta^2 \cdot z \cdot b \cdot x \cdot y) \sim (a \cdot y \cdot x_1 \cdot \delta^2 \cdot z \cdot x_2 \cdot b \cdot y \cdot x)$. $\sim$ is an equivalence relation on $(L_\theta)^*$. A real background of this relation is the queue systems [7].

Definition 10. Let $p \in \mathcal{LTS}(L_I \cup L_U), \mathcal{L}_I = \{L_I^1, \ldots, L_I^n\}$ and $\mathcal{L}_U = \{L_U^1, \ldots, L_U^m\}$, we say p is strace-reorderable, if

$$\forall \sigma_1, \sigma_2 \in (L_\theta)^* \text{ and } \sigma_1 \sim \sigma_2: \sigma_1 \in straces(p) \text{ iff } \sigma_2 \in straces(p)$$

Queue systems is an intuitionistic example of strace-reorderable systems, but note that not all the strace-reorderable systems are queue systems. Strace-reorderable systems have two important properties.

Proposition 3. Suppose $p \in \mathcal{LTS}(L_I \cup L_U)$ is strace-reorderable, $\sigma \in (L_\theta)^*$, $x \in L_U^{k'}$, $k \neq k'$, then

1. $\delta^k \notin out(p - \sigma)$ implies $\delta^k \notin out(p - \sigma \cdot x)$

2. $\forall p', p \xrightarrow{\sigma} p' : (p' \xrightarrow{\delta^k} \text{ and } p' \xrightarrow{x}) \text{ implies } \delta^k \in out(p - \sigma \cdot x)$

Proof.

1. (by contradiction) $\delta^k \in out(p - \sigma \cdot x)$ implies $p \xrightarrow{\sigma \cdot x \cdot \delta^k}$, in turn implies $p \xrightarrow{\sigma \cdot \delta^k \cdot x}$ because p is strace-reorderable and $\sigma \cdot x \cdot \delta^k \sim \sigma \cdot \delta^k \cdot x$. Then we have $\delta^k \in out(p - \sigma)$, so a contradiction.

2. We first show that $p \xrightarrow{\sigma} p' : (p' \xrightarrow{\delta^k} \text{ and } p' \xrightarrow{x} p'') \text{ implies } p'' \xrightarrow{\delta^k}$. Otherwise, suppose $\exists y \in L_U^k : p'' \xrightarrow{y}$, then $p \xrightarrow{\sigma \cdot \delta^k \cdot x \cdot y}$. Because p is strace-reorderable and also $\sigma \cdot \delta^k \cdot x \cdot y \sim \sigma \cdot \delta^k \cdot y \cdot x$, we will have $p \xrightarrow{\sigma \cdot \delta^k \cdot y \cdot x}$, which is impossible by the definition of δ^k. From $p'' \xrightarrow{\delta^k}$ we have $\delta^k \in out(p - \sigma \cdot x)$. $\square$

The first statement means that, if p does not suspend on the channel L_U^k after a trace σ, it will not either after the trace $\sigma \cdot x$ where x belongs to a different output channel. The second statement comes from the fact that, if p cannot produce any output at the channel L_U^k in a state p', it cannot either after a further output action x at a different channel. These properties characterize the independence of the output behaviors occurring at different channels of a strace-reorderable system.

Definition 11. $s \in \mathcal{LTS}(L_I, L_U)$, $\mathcal{F} \subseteq (L_I \cup L_U \cup \mathcal{L}_I \cup \mathcal{L}_U)^*$, for $\forall k \in \{1, \ldots, m\}$, the boolean predicate $keep_{\mathcal{F}}(\delta^k)$ is true if

$$\forall \sigma \in \mathcal{F} \text{ and } \delta^k \notin out(s - \sigma), \forall y \in L_U \backslash L_U^k : y \in out(s - \sigma) \text{ implies } \sigma \cdot y \in \mathcal{F}$$

"$L_U \backslash L_U^k$" is the difference between L_U and L_U^k. In case s is output-finite (cf. Def. 2.7), from a finite set $\mathcal{F}$, we can always derive a finite set $\mathcal{F}'$ that satisfies $\forall k \in \{1, \ldots, m\} : keep_{\mathcal{F}'}(\delta^k)$. One of such sets is $\mathcal{F}_0 = \mathcal{F} \cup \{\sigma \cdot \sigma_u \in straces(s) | \sigma \in \mathcal{F}, \sigma_u \in (L_U)^*\}$. This expansion is necessary for the purpose of detecting unspecified single-channel output suspension δ^k, as explained later.

On the contrary, a system that is not output-finite may produce infinite output sequences (and possible with infinite length) in some state. We exclude such systems in the discussion of completeness and assume that specifications are output-finite. However, we do not require this for implementations; an implementation may produce endless outputs (e.g. on entering an error state). Some straightforward properties of $keep_{\mathcal{F}}(\delta^k)$ are summarized below.

Proposition 4. *Let* $s \in \mathcal{LTS}(L_I \cup L_U), \sigma \in (L_\theta)^*, \forall k (k = 1, \ldots, m)$

1. $\delta^k \in out(s - \sigma)$ *implies* $keep_{\{\sigma\}}(\delta^k)$

2. *if* $\delta^k \notin out(s - \sigma)$ *and* $\neg \exists y \in L_U \setminus L_U^k$ *s.t.* $y \in out(s - \sigma)$, *then* $keep_{\{\sigma\}}(\delta^k)$

3. $keep_{\{\sigma\}}(\delta^k)(\forall \sigma \in \mathcal{F})$ *implies* $keep_{\mathcal{F}}(\delta^k)$

Proposition 5. *Let* $s \in \mathcal{LTS}(L_I \cup L_U)$, $i \in \mathcal{MIOTS}(\mathcal{L}_I, \mathcal{L}_U)$, s *and* i *are all strace-reorderable, and* s *is ouput-finite,* $\mathcal{F} \subseteq (L_\theta)^*$ *and satisfies* $keep_{\mathcal{F}}(\delta^k)(k = 1, \ldots, m)$, T *is the* $\mathcal{AOBS}$ *test suite generated by Algorithm 1, then* T *is exhaustive for* s *w.r.t.* **mioco**$_{\mathcal{F}}$.

Proof. We have to prove: $\forall i \in \mathcal{MIOTS}(\mathcal{L}_I, \mathcal{L}_U) : \neg(i \ \textbf{mioco}_{\mathcal{F}} \ s)$ implies $(i \ \textbf{fails} \ T)$, this equals to proving:

$$\text{``}\exists \sigma \in \mathcal{F} : out(i - \sigma) \nsubseteq out(s - \sigma)\text{''} \quad \text{implies} \quad \text{``}\exists t \in T : i \ \textbf{fails} \ t\text{''} \qquad (\#)$$

If $\exists \sigma \in \mathcal{F}$ s.t. $out(i - \sigma) \nsubseteq out(s - \sigma)$, at least one of the following three cases must hold according to the definition of out:

case1. $\exists \xi^j : \xi^j \in out(i - \sigma)$ but $\xi^j \notin out(s - \sigma)$. Let t be the test checking the input at L_I^j after σ, then $\xi^j \in out(i - \sigma)$ implies $\exists i' : i \xrightarrow{\sigma} i' \xrightarrow{\xi^j} i'$. According to Algorithm 1 step 2, since $\xi^j \notin out(s - \sigma)$, we have $(t \xrightarrow{\bar{\sigma}} t' \xrightarrow{\theta_i^j} \textbf{fail})$. So $\exists i' : t \| i \xrightarrow{\bar{\sigma}} t' \| i' \xrightarrow{\theta_i^j} \textbf{fail} \| i'$, this means $i \ \textbf{fails} \ t$. $(\#)$ holds.

case2. $\exists y \in L_U^k : y \in out(i - \sigma)$ but $y \notin out(s - \sigma)$. Similar reasoning leads to $(\#)$.

case3. $\exists \delta^k : \delta^k \in out(i - \sigma)$ but $\delta^k \notin out(s - \sigma)$. Let t be the test checking the output in L_U after σ, then we have three facts (as are illustrated in Fig. 2):

I. $\delta^k \notin out(s - \sigma)$;   II. $\delta^k \in out(i - \sigma)$;   III. the test $t: t \xrightarrow{\bar{\sigma}} t' \xrightarrow{\theta_u^k} \textbf{fail}$

Next we consider two cases about i and prove that "$i \ \textbf{fails} \ t$" always holds.

(1) The implementation i can suspend simultaneously at all the output channels, i.e., $\delta \in out_2(i - \sigma)$, then $\exists i' : i \xrightarrow{\sigma} i' \xrightarrow{\delta} i'$. So from III: $\exists i'$ and t' s.t. $t \| i \xrightarrow{\bar{\sigma}} t' \| i' \xrightarrow{\theta_u^k} \textbf{fail} \| i'$, then $i \ \textbf{fails} \ t$.

(2) i cannot suspend at all the output channels, i.e., i must produce an output at some channel after performing σ:

$$\forall i', (i \xrightarrow{\sigma} i' \xrightarrow{\delta^k}) \text{ implies } (\exists k' \neq k \text{ and } y \in L_U^{k'} : i' \xrightarrow{y})$$

From II, we know $\exists i' : i \xrightarrow{\sigma} i' \xrightarrow{\delta^k} i'$, so $\exists k' \neq k$ and $y \in L_U^{k'} : i' \xrightarrow{y}$ ....IV.

(2.1) If $y \notin out(s - \sigma)$, it can be proved $i \ \textbf{fails} \ t$, similar to above case2.

(2.2) Else $y \in out(s - \sigma)$, then from the fact I and the assumption that $\mathcal{F}$ satisfies $keep_{\mathcal{F}}(\delta^k)(k = 1, \ldots, m)$, we have $\sigma \cdot y \in \mathcal{F}$.

By Algorithm 1, the $\mathcal{AOBS}$ test t must have a y transition after $\bar{\sigma} : t' \xrightarrow{y}$, as shown in Fig. 2.

Let $\sigma' = \sigma \cdot y$, we have the following facts resembling I, II and III:

I'. $\delta^k \notin out(s - \sigma')$ (By I and Proposition 3.1)

II'. $\delta^k \in out(i - \sigma')$ (By $i \xrightarrow{\sigma} i' \xrightarrow{\delta^k} i'$, IV and Proposition 3.2)

III'. the $\mathcal{AOBS}$ test t: $t \xrightarrow{\bar{\sigma} \cdot y} t'' \xrightarrow{\theta_u}$ **fail** (By I' and Algorithm 1)

Similar to the proof in (1) and (2) we may further grow the $\mathcal{AOBS}$ test t as: $t \xrightarrow{\bar{\sigma}'} t'' \xrightarrow{y'}$ where $k'' \neq k$ and $y' \in L_U^{k''}$, as shown in Fig. 2c.

For $\sigma'' = \sigma' \cdot y'$, continue with the proof like that for (1) and (2). Under the assumption that s is output-finite, the process must end at a trace $\sigma^0 \in \mathcal{F}$: $\sigma^0 = \sigma \cdot y \cdot y' \cdot \ldots$, where $y, y', \ldots$ are outputs at channels other than L_U^k. Then we have:

-I- $\delta^k \notin out(s - \sigma^0)$;   -II- $\delta^k \in out(i - \sigma^0)$;   -III- $t_0 \xrightarrow{\bar{\sigma^0}} t^0 \xrightarrow{\theta_u}$ **fail**

And one of the following two conditions must be true:

end-condition1: $\delta \in out_2(i - \sigma^0)$. Then by -III-: i **fails** t.

end-condition2: $\exists k^0 \neq k$ and $y^0 \in L_U^{k^0} : y^0 \in out(i - \sigma^0)$ but $y^0 \notin out(s - \sigma^0)$. Then t: $t^0 \xrightarrow{y^0}$ **fail**, and so i **fails** t.

Now, it can be concluded by case1 to case3 that: $\forall \sigma \in \mathcal{F}$, $out(i - \sigma) \not\subseteq out(s - \sigma)$ implies $\exists t \in T : i$ **fails** t, (#) always holds. $\qquad \square$

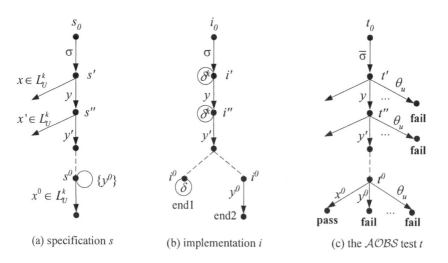

(a) specification s (b) implementation i (c) the $\mathcal{AOBS}$ test t

Fig. 2. growing of the $\mathcal{AOBS}$ test

The key in the proof is that, an unspecified single-channel output suspension, screened by a series of outputs at other channels, will manifest itself eventually when all the allowed outputs (they are finite, because the specification s is output-finite) at the interfering channels of the implementation have been produced and then only "unspecified" output or all-output-channel suspension can be produced by the implementation (these two cases both result in a **fail** verdict). Proposition 5 gives the sufficient condition to achieve this effect: to preserve single-channel output suspension through interfering outputs, the specification and implementation must be strace-reorderable; to detect the suspension eventually, all the allowed outputs at other channels must be further checked, which is guaranteed if $\mathcal{F}$ satisfies the *keep* condition.

Theorem 1. *Let* $s \in \mathcal{LTS}(L_I \cup L_U)$, $i \in \mathcal{MIOTS}(\mathcal{L}_I, \mathcal{L}_U)$, s *and* i *are all strace-reorderable, and* s *is ouput-finite,* $\mathcal{F} \subseteq (L_\theta)^*$ *and satisfies* $keep_{\mathcal{F}}(\delta^k)(k = 1, \ldots, m)$, T *is the* $\mathcal{AOBS}$ *test suite generated by Algorithm 1, then* T *is complete for* s *w.r.t.* **mioco**$_{\mathcal{F}}$.

This theorem is obvious from Propositions 2 and 5. By now, we have achieved the second goal set in Sect. 3.1. The exhaustiveness of all-observer tests is accomplished by making stronger test assumptions about the models of both specifications and implementations. This technique has often been used for test selection, or test-suite size reduction [8]. In practice, queue systems are strace-reorderable and often output-finite. Therefore, the all-observer test generation has promising application values.

3.5   Examples

In this section, we use some examples to illustrate the all-observer test generation algorithm.

Example 1. Figure 3a shows an strace-reorderable and output-finite specification $q \in \mathcal{MIOTS}(\mathcal{L}_I^\theta = \{\{a, \xi\}\}, \mathcal{L}_U^\theta = \{\{x, \delta^1\}, \{y, \delta^2\}\})$. After the input action a, q either produces x, or produces y, or produces x and y in an arbitrary order. τ denotes an internal action. Let $\mathcal{F} = \{a, a \cdot x, a \cdot y, a \cdot x \cdot y, a \cdot y \cdot x\}$. The $\mathcal{AOBS}$ and $\mathcal{SOBS}$ test suites generated by Algorithm 1 and the algorithm in [4] (after merging relevant tests) respectively are shown in Fig. 3b and Fig. 3c. Only output-checking tests are listed for comparison. The $\mathcal{SOBS}$ test suite contains six tests $t_1 \sim t_6$ (e.g. t_3 checks the output at the channel L_U^1 both after the trace a and after $a \cdot x \cdot y$, and also the output at the channel L_U^2 after $a \cdot x$). Since $\forall \sigma \in \mathcal{F} : \delta^k \in out(s - \sigma), keep_{\mathcal{F}}(\delta^k)(k = 1, \ldots, m)$ holds (by Propositions 4.1 and 4.3), by Theorem 1 we know that the $\mathcal{AOBS}$ test suite is complete. It contains only one test, but is testingly equivalent to the six $\mathcal{SOBS}$ tests.

Example 2. Also for q in Example 1, now let $\mathcal{F} = \{a, a \cdot \delta^1, a \cdot \delta^2\}$, the $\mathcal{SOBS}$ and $\mathcal{AOBS}$ test suites are shown in Fig. 3d. It can be verified that $\mathcal{F}$ satisfies $keep_{\mathcal{F}}(\delta^k)$ for each k in $\{1, \ldots, m\}$. First, we have $\delta^k \in out(s - a)$ for $k = 1, 2$, so $keep_{\{a\}}(\delta^k)$. Then, although $\delta^2 \notin out(s - a \cdot \delta^1)$, there isn't any $z \in L_U \backslash L_U^2 : z \in out(s - a \cdot \delta^1)$; by Proposition 4.2 we have $keep_{\{a \cdot \delta^1\}}(\delta^2)$. Also, by the fact

$\delta^1 \in out(s - a \cdot \delta^1)$ and Proposition 4.1 we know $keep_{\{a \cdot \delta^1\}}(\delta^1)$. Similar arguments hold for $keep_{\{a \cdot \delta^2\}}(\delta^1)$ and $keep_{\{a \cdot \delta^2\}}(\delta^2)$. Therefore by Theorem 1 the $\mathcal{AOBS}$ test suite is complete. It contains three tests with the same testing power as the four $\mathcal{SOBS}$ tests (which are left to readers and not shown in Fig. 3). Furthermore, execution of t_1' always results in **pass** verdict and thereby can be removed.

We have illustrated Algorithm 1 by two examples where each $\mathcal{F}$ satisfies the exhaustiveness-preserving condition. In case $\mathcal{F}$ does not satisfy this condition, we must first expand it to get one that does. At the same time, we will obtain a stronger conformance relation than the original **mioco**$_{\mathcal{F}}$.

4   Factorized All-Observer Test Generation

4.1   Factorized Test Generation

Definition 12. *The universe of selection processes over L_I is defined by*

$\mathcal{SLTS}(L_I) =_{def} \{p \in \mathcal{LTS}(L_I) | p \text{ is deterministic}\}$

Let $s \in \mathcal{LTS}(L_I \cup L_U)$ and $q \in \mathcal{SLTS}(L_I)$, then the transition system $s\|_{L_I} q \in \mathcal{SLTS}(L_I \cup L_U)$ is defined by the following inference rules.

$$\frac{s \xrightarrow{a} s', q \xrightarrow{a} q'}{s\|_{L_I} q \xrightarrow{a} s'\|_{L_I} q'}(a \in L_I) \qquad \frac{s \xrightarrow{x} s'}{s\|_{L_I} q \xrightarrow{x} s'\|_{L_I} q}(x \in L_U)$$

For a very large specification s, selection process q can be used to isolate a smaller specification $s\|_{L_I} q$ that contains only the responses to the input sequences specified in q, but discards all responses to other input sequences. The operator $\|_{L_I}$ imitates the synchronous communication operator $\|$ but only synchronizes input actions. $s\|_{L_I} q$ can be seen as the projected specification of s onto q.

[5] gives the soundness-preserving condition for the factorized test generation. For $s \in \mathcal{LTS}(L_I \cup L_U), q \in \mathcal{LTS}(L_I)$ and $\mathcal{F} \subseteq (L_I \cup L_U \cup \mathcal{L}_I \cup \mathcal{L}_U)^*$, if q satisfies the condition "$\mathcal{F}\lceil L_I \subseteq traces(q)$"($\mathcal{F}\lceil L_I =_{def} \{\sigma\lceil L_I | \sigma \in \mathcal{F}\}$), then a sound test suite of $s\|_{L_I} q$ with respect to **mioco**$_{\mathcal{F}}$ is also sound for s with respect to **mioco**$_{\mathcal{F}}$. [5] also gives the completeness-preserving condition for the factorized test generation. A boolean predicate is defined as $accept_q(\sigma) =_{def}$

$\forall \sigma' \in pref(\sigma), \exists q'(q \xrightarrow{\sigma'} q') : q' \xrightarrow{a} (\forall a \in L_I)$. If q satisfies the condition "$\forall \sigma \in \mathcal{F} : accept_q(\sigma\lceil L_I)$", then a complete test suite of $s\|_{L_I} q$ with respect to **mioco**$_{\mathcal{F}}$ is also complete for s with respect to **mioco**$_{\mathcal{F}}$.

Another problem in test generation for **mioco**$_{\mathcal{F}}$ is that $\mathcal{F}$ may contain many traces, which means both time and space challenging to test generation tools. A feasible way is to decompose the correct criterion **mioco**$_{\mathcal{F}}$ into smaller ones.

Proposition 6.

1. $\mathbf{mioco}_{\mathcal{F}} = \bigcap_{\sigma \in \mathcal{F}} \mathbf{mioco}_{\{\sigma\}}$
2. $\mathbf{mioco}_{\mathcal{F}} = \mathbf{mioco}_{\mathcal{F}_1} \cap \mathbf{mioco}_{\mathcal{F}_2} \cap \ldots \cap \mathbf{mioco}_{\mathcal{F}_n}$ $(\mathcal{F} = \mathcal{F}_1 \cup \mathcal{F}_2 \cup \ldots \cup \mathcal{F}_n)$

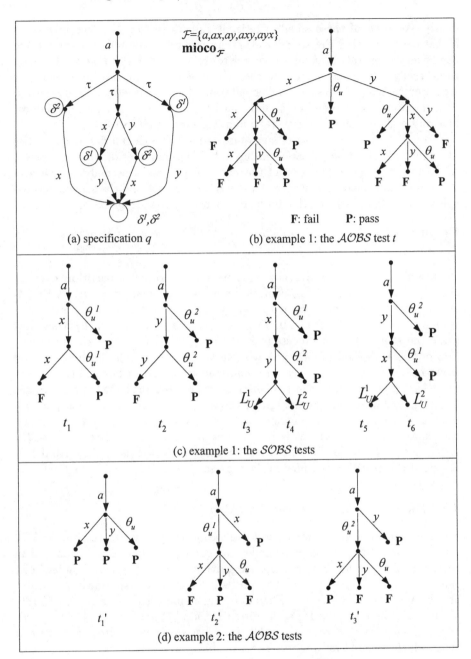

(a) specification q

(b) example 1: the $\mathcal{AOBS}$ test t

F: fail   P: pass

(c) example 1: the $\mathcal{SOBS}$ tests

(d) example 2: the $\mathcal{AOBS}$ tests

Fig. 3. All-observer test generation

By Proposition 6.1, **mioco**$_{\mathcal{F}}$ can be splitted into a set of smaller relations **mioco**$_{\{\sigma\}}(\sigma \in \mathcal{F})$ for which the correctness check may be performed independently. For each of these small criteria, it suffices to take a selection process q that satisfies either the soundness-preserving or the completeness-preserving condition to generate a (sound or complete) test suite for $s\|_{L_I}q$ and $\mathbf{mioco}_{\{\sigma\}}$, respectively. These test suites are then combined into one test suite, which is sound or complete in testing implementations for its $\mathbf{mioco}_{\mathcal{F}}$-relation with s. This method was proposed in [5] and called factorized test generation. The test generation algorithm is the one in [4] and it generates $\mathcal{SOBS}$ tests.

To partition $\mathcal{F}$ into a set of singletons reduces the calculation complexities at furthest, but it is very inefficient due to the large number of traces contained in $\mathcal{F}$: an individual application of the selection process is needed for each σ in $\mathcal{F}$, even for the traces sharing the same selection process and the same projected specification. To overcome this problem, we need a coarser partitioning of $\mathcal{F}$.

Definition 13. *Let* $\sigma, \sigma' \in (L_I \cup L_U \cup \mathcal{L}_I \cup \mathcal{L}_U)^*$, *we say* σ *is affinal to* σ' *if:* $\sigma\lceil L_I = \sigma'\lceil L_I$, *denoted by:* $\sigma \perp \sigma'$.

affinal ($\perp$) is an equivalence relation and $\mathcal{F}$ forms a partition over $\perp$: $\mathcal{F}_\perp = \{\mathcal{F}_1, \mathcal{F}_2, \ldots, \mathcal{F}_h\}$. $\mathcal{F}_i\lceil L_I$ contains only one trace, denoted as σ_i. By Proposition 6.2, we know that $\mathbf{mioco}_{\mathcal{F}}$ can be decomposed into a set of criteria $\mathbf{mioco}_{\mathcal{F}_i}(i = 1, \ldots, h)$. Traces in $\mathcal{F}_i$ have the same projection on L_I; thus they share the same selection process (e.g. $stick(\sigma_i)$ or $fan(\sigma_i)$, two kinds of selection processes defined in [5]). Now we generate a test suite for each $s\|_{L_I}q_i$ and $\mathbf{mioco}_{\mathcal{F}_i}$ for $i = 1, \ldots, h$, where q_i is constructed in line with σ_i. This improvement can greatly reduce the frequency of calculating projected specifications. Furthermore, such trace grouping helps to merge test cases that check the failure traces having common prefixes, and to reduce the size of the final composed test suite. This improvement is just an optimization for the factorized $\mathcal{SOBS}$ test generation, but for factorized $\mathcal{AOBS}$ test generation using Algorithm 1, it is indeed necessary, as we show in the next section.

4.2 Factorized All-Observer Test Generation

Using Algorithm 1 for factorized test generation we get $\mathcal{AOBS}$ test suites. Will they still be sound or complete under the respective condition established in Sect. 4.1? Proposition 2 shows that Algorithm 1 generates sound $\mathcal{AOBS}$ test suites for general MIOTS systems; so does it for projected specifications, which are certainly MIOTS systems. Therefore, Algorithm 1 can be used to generate a sound $\mathcal{AOBS}$ test suite for each $\mathbf{mioco}_{\mathcal{F}_i}$ and $s\|_{L_I}q_i$ ($\mathcal{F}_i \in \mathcal{F}_\perp, i = 1, \ldots, h$), where q_i satisfies $\sigma_i \in traces(q_i)$. All these test suites are united into one test suite, which is sound for s with respect to $\mathbf{mioco}_{\mathcal{F}}$.

Proposition 5 specifies the requirements imposed on the specification s, the implementation i and $\mathcal{F}$ for Algorithm 1 to generate an exhaustive $\mathcal{AOBS}$ test suite for s with respect to $\mathbf{mioco}_{\mathcal{F}}$. To apply this proposition to factorized $\mathcal{AOBS}$ test generation, we must prove that these requirements are still satisfied by both the projected specifications and $\mathcal{F}_i$ in the smaller criterion $\mathbf{mioco}_{\mathcal{F}_i}$. Ideally, all of the following three guesses should true:

guess1. the projected specifications $s\|_{L_I}q_i$ are output-finite

guess2. the projected specifications $s\|_{L_I}q_i$ are strace-reorderable

guess3. for each $\mathcal{F}_i \in \mathcal{F}_\perp$ and the projected specification $s\|_{L_I}q_i$: $keep_{\mathcal{F}_i}(\delta^k)(k = 1, \ldots, m)$

It is obvious that guess1 is true if the specification s is output-finite, because any selection process only "copies" the original outputs but never adds. However, guess2 is not hinted by the assumption that s is strace-reorderable. Nevertheless, if q satisfies $accept_q(\sigma\lceil L_I)$, $s\|_{L_I}q_i$ will have properties similar to Proposition 3.

Proposition 7. Let $s \in \mathcal{LTS}(L_I \cup L_U)$ be strace-reorderable, $q \in \mathcal{SLTS}(L_I)$, $p \equiv s\|_{L_I}q$, $x \in L_U^{k'}$, $k \neq k'$. For $\forall \sigma \in (L_\theta)^*$, if $accept_q(\sigma\lceil L_I)$, then

1. $\delta^k \notin out(p - \sigma)$ implies $\delta^k \notin out(p - \sigma \cdot x)$

2. $\forall p', p \xrightarrow{\sigma} p' : (p' \xrightarrow{\delta^k} and\ p' \xrightarrow{x})$ implies $\delta^k \in out(p - \sigma \cdot x)$

This proposition can be proved using the fact that $accept_q(\sigma\lceil L_I)$ implies $out(s - \sigma) = out(p - \sigma)$ and $out(s - \sigma \cdot x) = out(p - \sigma \cdot x)$ (note that $\sigma \perp \sigma \cdot x$, so $accept_q(\sigma \cdot x\lceil L_I)$. Then $\delta^k \notin out(p - \sigma)$ implies $\delta^k \notin out(s - \sigma)$. From Proposition 3 and the assumption s is strace-reorderable, we have $\delta^k \notin out(s - \sigma \cdot x)$, so also $\delta^k \notin out(p - \sigma \cdot x)$. Similar reasoning leads to part 2 of the proposition. These properties of $s\|_{L_I}q$ expressed by Proposition 7 are really what matter in the proof of exhaustiveness of the $\mathcal{AOBS}$ test suites in Proposition 5. It doesn't matter that $s\|_{L_I}q$ is not strace-reorderable.

Proposition 8. Let $s \in \mathcal{LTS}(L_I \cup L_U), q \in \mathcal{SLTS}(L_I), \mathcal{F} \subseteq (L_\theta)^*$ and $\forall \sigma \in \mathcal{F}$: $accept_q(\sigma\lceil L_I), p \equiv s\|_{L_I}q$. Then for each k in $\{1, \ldots, m\}$: "$keep_{\mathcal{F}}(\delta^k)$ holds for s" iff "$keep_{\mathcal{F}}(\delta^k)$ holds for p".

Proposition 9. Let $s \in \mathcal{LTS}(L_I \cup L_U)$, and $\mathcal{F}_\perp = \{\mathcal{F}_1, \mathcal{F}_2, \ldots, \mathcal{F}_h\}$. If $\mathcal{F}$ satisfies $keep_{\mathcal{F}}(\delta^k)$ for s, $\mathcal{F}_i$ will also satisfy $keep_{\mathcal{F}_i}(\delta^k)$ for s:

$$\forall \delta^k (k = 1, \ldots, m) : keep_{\mathcal{F}}(\delta^k)\ implies\ keep_{\mathcal{F}_i}(\delta^k)(i = 1, \ldots, h)$$

Proposition 9 can be proved easily using Def. 11 and the fact $\sigma \perp \sigma \cdot y$. It means that the predicate $keep_{\mathcal{F}_i}(\delta^k)$ is preserved in the affinal partition of $\mathcal{F}$. Proposition 8 can be proved using Def. 11 and the equation $out(s - \sigma) = out(p - \sigma)$. It means that the predicate is preserved in the projected specification. From these two propositions, it can be concluded: given that $\mathcal{F}$ satisfies $keep_{\mathcal{F}}(\delta^k)$ for s, we have $\forall \mathcal{F}_i \in \mathcal{F}_\perp : keep_{\mathcal{F}_i}(\delta^k)(k = 1, \ldots, m)$ hold for each projected specification $s\|_{L_I}q_i$. q_i is the selection process satisfying $accept_{q_i}(\sigma_i\lceil L_I)$ where $\mathcal{F}_i\lceil L_I = \sigma_i$. This is guess3. Now, completely analogous to the process of proving Proposition 5, it can be shown that Algorithm 1 generates a complete $\mathcal{AOBS}$ test suite for each of the projected specification $s\|_{L_I}q_i$ with respect to the corresponding decomposed criterion **mioco**$_{\mathcal{F}_i}$, if only the original requirements imposed on the specifications s, the implementation i and the set of failure traces $\mathcal{F}$ are satisfied, and also a selection process q_i complying with the completeness-preserving condition is used. Combining this result with the fact that **mioco**$_{\mathcal{F}}$ can be decomposed according to the affinal partition of $\mathcal{F}$, we get Theorem 2.

Theorem 2. *Let* $s \in \mathcal{LTS}(L_I \cup L_U)$, $i \in \mathcal{MIOTS}(\mathcal{L}_I, \mathcal{L}_U)$, s *and* i *are all strace-reorderable, and* s *is ouput-finite,* $\mathcal{F} \subseteq (L_\theta)^*$ *and satisfies* $keep_\mathcal{F}(\delta^k)(k = 1, \dots, m)$. $\mathcal{F}_\perp = \{\mathcal{F}_1, \mathcal{F}_2, \dots, \mathcal{F}_h\}, \mathcal{F}_i \lceil L_I = \{\sigma_i\}$. *For* $i = 1, \dots, h$, *let* $q_i \in \mathcal{SLTS}(L_I)$ *and satisfies* $accept_{q_i}(\sigma_i)$, *let* $p_i \equiv s \|_{L_I} q_i$, *and* $T_{\mathcal{F}_i}(p_i)$ *is the* $\mathcal{AOBS}$ *test suite generated by Algorithm 1 for* p_i *w.r.t.* $\mathbf{mioco}_{\mathcal{F}_i}$, *Then*

$$\bigcup_{\mathcal{F}_i \in \mathcal{F}_\perp} T_{\mathcal{F}_i}(p_i) \text{ is complete for } s \text{ w.r.t. } \mathbf{mioco}_\mathcal{F}.$$

Consequently, for strace-reorderable specifications and implementations, if the specification is output-finite, Algorithm 1 can be used for the factorized generation of complete $\mathcal{AOBS}$ test suites, following the same rule that governs the factorized generation of $\mathcal{SOBS}$ tests. Thus a single framework exists for the factorized generation of both singular-observer and all-observer tests.

5   Conclusions and Future Work

In this paper we present a new method of testing MIOTS, viz. with a kind of observers called all-observer. The all-observer is superior to singular observers in the sense that they can observe the responses of the implementation at all the output channels simultaneously in a testing process. As a result, a test suite consisting of all-observer tests is often much smaller than the one consisting of singular observer tests. This means time-savings in both test generation and test execution. However, the discriminating power of all-observer is generally weaker than that of singular observers, because it may fail to capture the unspecified single-channel output suspensions. We give a test generation algorithm to derive all-observer tests for a specification s with respect to the relation $\mathbf{mioco}_\mathcal{F}$. The algorithm can generate a sound test suite for any MIOTS systems, but can only generate a complete test suite for a subset of the MIOTS systems: *strace-reorderable*, which characterizes the independence of the output behaviors occurring at different channels, and *output-finite*, which is only required for the specification but not for the implementation.

We then studied the problem of factorized all-observer test generation. For the decomposition of the correctness criterion, an optimized $\mathcal{F}$-partition technique is proposed to take advantage of the fact that many traces in $\mathcal{F}$ may share the same selection process. For the reduction of the specification, it is proved that the soundness and completeness conditions in factorized singular-observer test generation are also valid for the factorized all-observer test generation.

In theory, the all-observer complements the singular observers in testing MIOTS. In practice, queue systems is a possible domain applying the all-observer testing. Finally, in case an MIOTS is strace-reorderable, the trace set $\mathcal{F}$ may be reduced according to the strace-reordering relation without weakening the correct criterion. This is to be studied in future.

References

1. R. De Nicola and M.C.B. Hennessy. Testing equivalences for processes. Theoretical Computer Science, 34:83–133, 1984.
2. R. De Nicola. Extensional equivalences for transition systems. Acta Informatica, 24:211–237, 1987.
3. J. Tretmans. Test generation with inputs, outputs and repetitive quiescence. Software — Concepts and Tools, 17(3):103–120, 1996.
4. L. Heerink and J. Tretmans. Refusal testing for classes of transition systems with inputs and outputs. In FORTE X/PSTV XVII'97, pp. 23–38. 1997.
5. E. Brinksma, L. Heerink, and J. Tretmans. Factorized test generation for multi-input/output transition systems. TestCom'98. pp. 67–82. 1998.
6. I. Phillips. Refusal testing. Theoretical Computer Science, 50(2):241–284, 1987.
7. J. Tretmans, L. Verhaard. A queue model relating synchronous and asynchronous communication. In PSTV'92, pp. 131–145. 1992.
8. J. Tretmans. A formal approach to conformance testing. In Sixth International Workshop on Protocol Test Systems, pp. 257–276. 1994.

Soip over Satellite Testing – TIM Experience

Giulio Maggiore[1], Letterio Pirrone[2], Gaethan Donlap Kouang[2],
Federico Piovan[3], and Biagio Ricco Galluzzo[3]

[1]TIM,
via del Giorgione 159, 00147 Roma
gmaggiore@mail.tim.it
[2]EUTELSAT,
lpirrone@eutelsat.fr, gdonlap@eutelsat.fr
[3]Telecom Italia Lab,
via Reiss Romoli 274, 10148 Torino,
federico.piovan@tilab.com, biagio.ricco@tilab.com

Abstract. In the present Mobile Telecommunications scenario, the transmission of SS7 signalling on traditional TDM circuits is evolving to a SS7 over IP network (SoIP) solution, due to the continuous efficiency research in optimizing transmission and to the continuous goal of cost reduction. Some operators are using SoIP network in a national environment, while international SoIP networks are going to be deployed in a few years. Since transmissions over satellite may represent a fast way to deploy an international Backbone, TIM performed a trial in cooperation with TILAB, using Cisco Signalling Gateways and EUTELSAT satellite network. This paper describes the most significant results obtained by this experience, with respect to two critical aspects of satellite connection: the Transmission Delay and the Bandwidth Availability. Satellite delay put in evidence some practical limitations for the current Cisco release (called MB9), if compared with the traditional terrestrial Backbone; a special upgraded release (MB9-SAT) resolved them, but dynamic allocation of bandwidth asked for a detailed investigation on configuration criteria, in order to avoid system congestion. Both releases have been tested also with a delay-line simulator, to examine their performances on traffic management with delay varying between 0 and 700 ms. These activities drove us to outline an operative reference model, useful to understand network behavior under different conditions and to configure its fundamental parameters.

Glossary

B_{ETH}:	Signalling on Ethernet traffic Band
B_{IN}:	Traffic Band injected into IP Network
$B_{IN, max}$:	Maximum threshold of B_{IN} before congestion
B_S:	Total Satellite Band
B_{SS7}:	Signalling traffic Band
ΔB:	Increase of Signalling traffic band
CWND:	Congestion Window
DAMA:	Dynamic Assignment Multiple Access

R. Groz and R.M. Hierons (Eds.): TestCom 2004, LNCS 2978, pp. 112–127, 2004.
© IFIP 2004

DPC:	Destination Point Code
EUTELSAT:	Satellite Communications company
GTT:	Global Title Translation
IETF:	Internet Engineering Task Force
IP:	Internet Protocol
M2PA:	MTP2 user Peer-to-peer Adaptation layer
MSU :	Message Signalling Unit
MTP2:	Message Transfer Part 2
MTP3:	Message Transfer Part 3
N_A:	SCTP Associations' Number
OSI:	Open System Interconnection
PAMA:	Permanent Assignment Multiple Access
RTT:	Round Trip Time
SIGTRAN :	Signalling Transport
SCCP:	Signlling Connection Control Part
SCTP:	Stream Control Transmission Protocol
SG:	Signaling Gateway
SoIP :	Signalling SS7 over Internet Protocol
SS7:	Signalling System n.7
T_{ACK} / T_{ALL}:	ACKnowledge / ALLocation Time
TCP:	Transport Control Protocol
TDM:	Time Division Multiplexing
TDMA:	Time Division Multiple Access
TILAB:	Telecom Italia LABoratories
TIM:	Telecom Italia Mobile S.p.A.
TT:	Traffic Terminal
VLAN:	Virtual Local Area Network
WAN:	Wide Area Network

1   Introduction

Satellite communication represents the pioneering stage of telecommunication network in those parts of the world not covered by transmissions infrastructures: it allows a fast deployment of a telecommunication network, giving access to those services typically provided by the wire line and wireless terrestrial networks.

The paper presents some results of SoIP over satellite testing, implemented with CISCO Signalling Gateways, at first equipped with release MB9, then with a special release for "SoIP over satellite" called MB9-SAT. Both of them have been tested also with a delay-line simulator, in order to examine their performances under different delay conditions. Results and observations lead to outline an operative reference model, mainly aimed to guide in the configuration of fundamental transport parameters.

2   Soip over Satellite Testing

The acronym SoIP (Signalling SS7 over IP) can be referred to every system dealing with transport of signalling messages over an IP network.

Signalling Gateways (SG) allow SS7 messages to be transported on IP networks, according to the architectural model proposed by SigTran (IETF Working Group). Usually they are composed of several modules, each of them performing the major functionalities, as shown in Figure 1:

- the line interfaces, that set up the signalling circuits front-end, realizing the interworking function of MTP2 layer messages;
- the central processor, that performs MTP3 and SCCP layers, managing the connection;
- the IP Fast Ethernet Interfaces, that perform system connections to IP backbone.

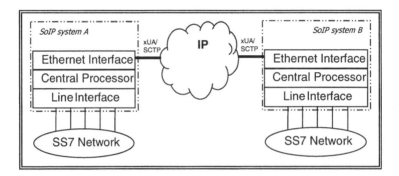

Fig. 1. SoIP System general architecture

Concerning with IP transport, the protocol stack defined by SigTran specifies the replacement of the TCP protocol (layer 4 of OSI reference model) with the new SCTP protocol [1]. The TCP is designed in order to ensure the transfer of long files without the control of the transit time; instead, the SCTP is designed in order to satisfy the timing requirements of the signalling by containing transit delays. Interworking functions between SS7 and IP protocols rely on an adaptation layer, positioned between transport and application layers, which performs adaptation at SS7 layer 2, or 3 and higher, according to manufacturer's strategies [2], [3], [4].

2.1   Testing Architecture

The system under test is composed by the following basic equipments (see Fig. 2):

- SS7 Traffic Simulator, used as load generator, to send and receive the signalling protocols messages. It is able to generate Message Signalling Unit (MSU) of different length (60, 120 and 270 Bytes length are commonly used) and with two types of SS7 routing (via DPC in MTP level or GTT in SCCP level). The Traffic Simulator has a 30 Signalling Links limit capacity, each link able to transport up to 64 Kb/s, so that 30 Erlang bi-directional is the maximum traffic load.
- Signalling Gateways (A and B) are Cisco ITP7500, transporting SS7 layer 3 (MTP3) on SCTP through the adaptation layer M2PA [5], while IP network layer is transferred through a Fast Ethernet.

SG's performances on IP terrestrial backbone have already been estimated in latest trials, where each SG was able to get over 0.98 – 1 Erlang per link on 30 connected Signalling Link, varying MSU's length.

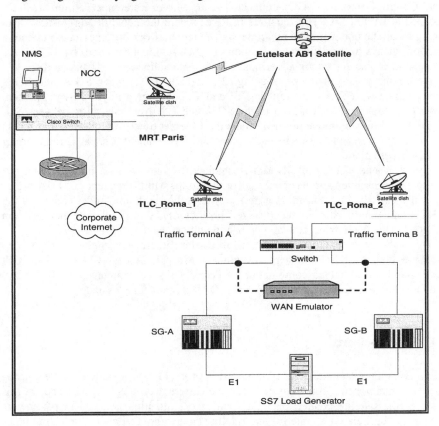

Fig. 2. SoIP over Satellite Testing Architecture

- Traffic Terminal: interface device between Ethernet and Satellite networks, described in paragraph 2.2.
- WAN Emulator: device emulating a Wide Area Network (WAN), whose basic features are fully configurable, such as network bandwidth, packet delay time, packet loss rate, packet's priority, etc. etc. Along the trial it was used only as a delay-line simulator, to allow a detailed performance measurement on delay variation.

2.2   Satellite Connection

EUTELSAT provides the space segment and the satellite connectivity by Linkway Platform from ViaSat Inc., a pay-per-use satellite communication system based on Traffic Terminals: these devices can transport multiple protocols traffic (IP, ATM, Frame Relay, ISDN and Signaling System 7) through a native 10BaseT Ethernet connection to the terrestrial networking equipment, manage the IP routing table and assign dynamical satellite bandwidth as needed.

Remote configuration and control of the entire network are carried out by the Network Control Computer (NCC), connected to the Master Reference Terminal (MRT), installed at EUTELSAT Headquarters in Paris, where the network administrator can configure all the parameters in real time: a complete network becomes a cost-effective solution, thanks to the efficient utilization of space segment resources by TDMA access and their sharing among all terminals by dynamic allocation of bandwidth.

As for the testing network (see Fig. 2), Signalling Gateways SG-A and SG-B communicate with Traffic Terminals TT1 and TT2 through a Layer-2 Switch, where two VLANs separate the traffic between SG-A and TT1 from the traffic between SG-B and TT2: Linkway modems encapsulate the Ethernet traffic into the satellite access protocol and transmit bursts to each other on a Permanent Virtual Circuit, using TDMA access mode.

The requested satellite bandwidth is obtained by two carriers, both of them dynamically accessible from terminals, according to the Multi Frequency TDMA protocol (only one terminal transmitting on a carrier at the same time under control of the MRT); taking into account the protocol headers and the guard time between the TDMA bursts, the maximum available bandwidth per carrier is 2320 Kbps.

This value represents the maximum full duplex Ethernet throughput on satellite, available both as full Permanent Assignment Multiple Access (PAMA, i.e. 2048 Kb/s) Band and as mixed combination of Permanently Assignment (i.e. 1024 Kb/s) and Dynamic Assignment Multiple Access (DAMA, exceeding) Band.

2.3   Test Typologies

It's in common experience that IP transport is prone to delays, which can be emphasized by interworking functions between the different protocols in use and, in this case, by the satellite connection: that's why more attention is asked to parameters such as packet delay, loss rate [6] and satellite bandwidth availability in testing innovative signalling transport systems.

In fact, performance testing has the purpose to evaluate the traffic level (in terms of Loss Rate and Transit Delay) that can be handled respecting SS7 standard specifications, while varying MSU length, SS7 routing (via DPC in MTP level or GTT in SCCP level) and the bandwidth allocation on the satellite network.

The trial's main target was to evaluate critical impacts of the satellite connection usage on the whole system, as introduced in the following paragraph.

2.4   Critical Aspects

The satellite connection introduces two critical aspects on the system: the Transmission Delay and the Bandwidth Availability.

A traditional SoIP system introduces a 20-40 ms delay due to processing on single SGs, which complies with acknowledges timers of SS7 messages. Now, satellite connection introduces 640-680 ms Round Trip Time (RTT), that means the entire system's RTT will be about 700 ms: it's necessary to evaluate the impact of Transmission Delay on the SS7 messages time-outs and on the SCTP retransmission timers [7], [8], [9].

Satellite bandwidth can be assigned in two different ways: PAMA Band is permanently assigned on satellite, whereas DAMA Band is assigned on demand and if available, according to a specific negotiating algorithm, with configurable allocation/de-allocation speeds. When using PAMA Band, the satellite connection affects entire system only by introducing its nominal delay; when using DAMA Band it's necessary to estimate the negotiating algorithm incidence on entire system delay and on possible SG congestions.

3   Main Results

3.1   Transmit Delay Effects

In order to investigate the transmit delay effects on satellite link (about 700 ms RTT), system equipments have been configured as follows:

- Satellite band: PAMA Band at 2048 Kb/s with about 150 Kb/s DAMA Band, so that there is no bottleneck on this side;
- Signalling Gateway: IOS in Release MB9 and one SCTP association, with Congestion Window (CWND) growing from initial value to 64000 Bytes (maximum value), as configured by manufacturer.

CWND is one of the SCTP variables regulating the transmission rate, as focused later on.

Two are the anomalous consequences we observe:

1) when generated traffic stays between 400 and 850 Kb/s in Ethernet Band, there is a transient congestion up to 70 s (loss rate 40-70%);
2) when traffic exceeds 850 Kb/s, congestion lasts for more than 240 s.

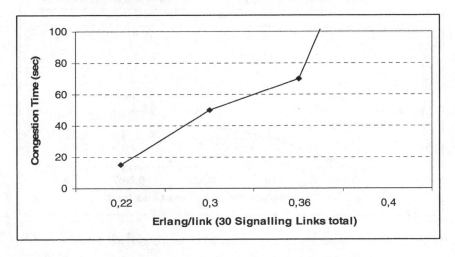

Fig. 3. Congestion Time vs. Erlang/link (Rel. MB9)

Figure 3 shows how congestion duration increase with generated SS7 traffic: when load generator works at 0.36 Erlang/link, there is a transient congestion of about 70 s that limits Transmitted Band to 300 Kb/s, even if generated band is about 1020 Kb/s. This is connected with CWND rising from initial value to the needed level.

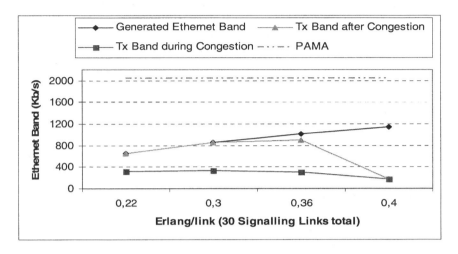

Fig. 4. Generated and Transmitted Ethernet Band vs. Erlang/link (Rel. MB9)

In Figure 4 there's an example of how Transmitted Band vary with generated SS7 traffic (both during and after congestion): when traffic is 0.36 Erlang/link, Transmitted Band is 300 Kb/s during 70 s of transient congestion and rises to 900 Kb/s after it, even if generated band is about 1020 Kb/s.

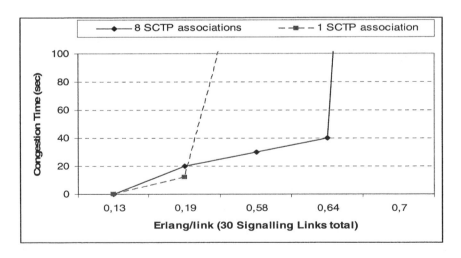

Fig. 5. Congestion Time vs. Erlang/link (8 associations, Rel. MB9)

To improve such a limited performance, the simplest step is activating more than one SCTP associations, even if it implies that occupied Ethernet band increases, SS7 traffic being equal, according to number of activated and then used associations.

Moreover uniform distribution of SS7 traffic among all SCTP associations is not granted, because SG strictly divides messages according to their Signalling Link Code, when in-sequence delivery is required: thus, the SS7 interface configuration (link-sets amount and dimension) could influence packet distribution and congestion conditions as well.

Setting Association number $N_A=8$ (maximum link-sets dimension) obtains a little improvement on critical behaviour, without totally solving it (see Figures 5 and 6): the initial congestion is shorter in time and lower in percentage (duration 20-40 s, loss rate 5-20 %), and it becomes a continuous state after a higher threshold (while generated traffic doesn't exceed 1900 Kb/s, equal to 0.64 Kb/s in this case), but it is still unacceptable, bringing forward that N_A is not decisive.

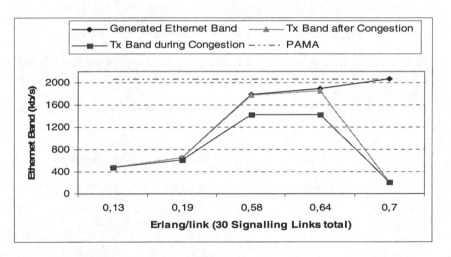

Fig. 6. Generated and Transmitted Ethernet Band vs. Erlang/link (8 associations, Rel. MB9)

For a further examination of the single SCTP association behavior varying RTT, we replace the satellite connection with a WAN Emulator and increase RTT value on this instrument: congestion happens when RTT exceeds 600 ms, with loss rate growing with RTT itself, independently from MSU length (60 or 270 Bytes) and SS7 routing (DPC or GTT), as shown in Figure 7.

This result confirms RTT on satellite link is so high that the amount of data waiting for acknowledge (called OUTSTAND) reaches CWND Maximum Value too fast, driving the system to a congestion state: that's why the configuration of the single association shall be modified in terms of SCTP parameters.

In order to make them accessible to operator, manufacturer modifies SG Operative System (special Release MB9-SAT), suggesting values in brackets: Initial CWND Size (384000), Retransmit CWND Rate (0, SCTP Fast Restart), Fast CWND Rate (0), Transmission Queue Depth (8000); besides, CWND never grows over its initial value.

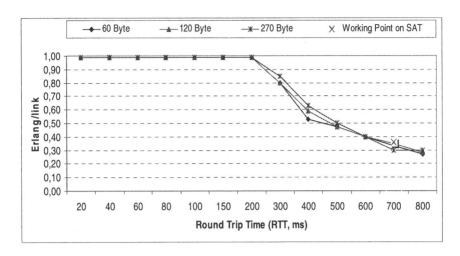

Fig. 7. Traffic Limitation vs. RTT (1 association, Rel. MB9)

Experimental checking with WAN Emulator shows complete absence of congestion through only one SCTP association, even when SS7 traffic rises suddenly to 30 Erlang (see Figure 8).

After this updating, we can proceed to evaluate bandwidth availability effects, coming back to satellite connection.

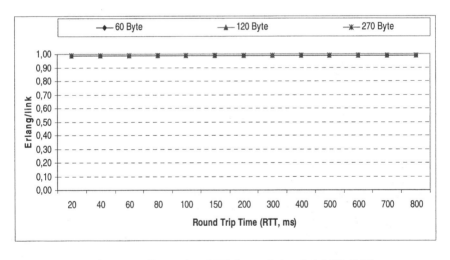

Fig. 8. SS7 Traffic Load vs. RTT (1 association, Rel. MB9-SAT)

3.2   Bandwidth Availability Effects

In order to evaluate satellite bandwidth availability effects, we observe system reactions increasing SS7 traffic, with PAMA Band set first to 2048 Kb/s and then to 1024

Kb/s; thank to Operative System change, there is no initial congestion, but two critical consequences appear (see Figure 9):

1)   when Ethernet Band of generated traffic exceeds PAMA Band even only by 5%, about the 50% of messages are lost (Used Band lower than Expected Band);

2)   SS7 traffic has to be reduced to 50% of PAMA Band to clear congestion.

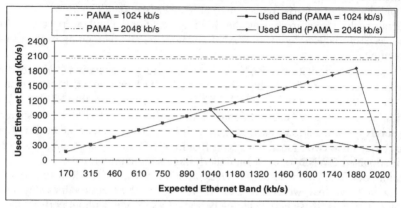

Fig. 9. Examples of Used Ethernet Band vs. Expected Ethernet Band

We can explain this behaviour by the following observations:

• the amount of acknowledge waiting data (so called OUTSTAND) grows with SS7 traffic band (B_{SS7}) and with the Acknowledge Time T_{ACK}, needed by SCTP to receive a transmitting data acknowledge and made up by Round Trip Time, possible DAMA Band Allocation Time (T_{ALL}) and possible Queuing Time on SS7 receiving interface (T_Q), according to:

$$OUTSTAND = B_{SS7} \cdot T_{ACK} \qquad T_{ACK} = RTT + T_{ALL} + T_Q{}^1 \qquad (1)$$

• OUTSTAND and CWND define respectively the traffic band injected in the network (named B_{IN}) and its maximum threshold (named $B_{IN,\,max}$), beyond which Congestion Avoidance (CA) Algorithm takes action, according to:

$$B_{IN} = OUTSTAND \ [Bytes] \cdot 8 \ [bit] / T_{ACK} \qquad (2)$$

$$B_{IN,\,max} = CWND \ [Bytes] \cdot 8 \ [bit] / T_{ACK} \qquad (3)$$

When B_{SS7} is constant and lower than PAMA Band, OUTSTAND is constant too, T_{ACK} is just equal to RTT and B_{IN} is equal to B_{SS7}; apparently, this situation leads to set CWND at the highest value, so that Congestion Time T_C, needed by OUTSTAND to reach CWND, is as long as possible (at least longer than T_{ACK}) and the Satellite Band B_S (PAMA+DAMA) can be fully employed, without congestion limit.

---

[1] T_Q will be omitted from now on, since it can be avoid by generating less than 1 Erlang/link on each of 30 Signalling Links per SG.

But when B_{SS7} grows up of ΔB, exceeding PAMA Band before $B_{IN, max}$, the Satellite Allocation/De-Allocation (SAD) Algorithm causes a T_{ALL} (1÷2 s), which makes T_{ACK} surely longer than T_C: because of this, not only OUTSTAND (and thus B_{IN}) grows faster to CWND ($B_{IN, max}$) causing congestion, but also the higher CWND has been set, the heavier congestion goes, with both CWND and OUTSTAND falling down and oscillating, triggering SAD and CA Algorithms in cycle. The system returns to a stable condition only by traffic reduction to 50% of PAMA Band.

Facing such effects, increasing the SCTP associations' number appears no longer useful, as easy to check by using WAN Emulator first and then going back to satellite connection:

- without band limitation (WAN Emulator), setting Associations' Number $N_A=2$ makes accepted traffic double, RTT and CWND being equal, because accepted traffic is proportional to N_A and CWND, inversely proportional to RTT;
- with band limitation (satellite connection), available band is however shared between $N_A=2$ associations, each of them going congested to half the traffic of previous case, since two associations with fixed CWND are equal to single association with doubled CWND, once again underlining its basic importance.

Therefore our final goal is to define the appropriate rules, which allow to correctly set CWND value, so that, when OUTSTAND reaches it, there both values stay still and any other traffic increase is rejected by periodic loss events, without performance collapse and simultaneously without wasting B_S.

3.3   Defining an Operative Reference Model

We can model the transmitting side of the system under test as shown in Figure 10, where the SS7 traffic band (B_{SS7}, generated by 30 Signalling Links, each at 0.xx Erlang rate) feeds OUTSTAND for the time T_{ACK}, being injected in the Fast Ethernet network as $B_{ETH} = (1+ \alpha_{OH}) \cdot B_{IN}$ (with α_{OH} to calculate OverHead).

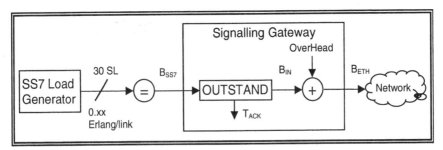

Fig. 10. System under Test transmitting scheme

Together with (1), (2), (3) and according to what expounded above, they let us formalize the following relations:

a)   when CWND is such that $(1+ \alpha_{OH}) \cdot B_{IN, max}$ is lower than PAMA Band and B_{SS7} increases of ΔB, OUTSTAND grows in function of ΔB as

$$OUTSTAND = B_{SS7} \cdot RTT + \Delta B \cdot RTT \qquad (4)$$

and, if CWND is reached, CA Algorithm is able to keep them both to maximum value, rejecting any other traffic increase by periodic loss events, without performance collapse;

b)   when CWND is such that $(1+ \alpha_{OH}) \cdot B_{IN, max}$ is greater than the whole B_s and B_{SS7} increases of ΔB over PAMA Band, OUTSTAND grows in function of ΔB and of T_{ALL} as

$$OUTSTAND = B_{SS7} \cdot RTT + \Delta B \cdot (RTT + T_{ALL}) \qquad (5)$$

where the second term implies a transient dynamic rise, making OUTSTAND suddenly exceed CWND, so that CA Algorithm triggers the cycled action of SAD Algorithm, which drives SCTP association to a continuous congestion, cleared only by traffic reduction to 50% of PAMA Band;

c)   when CWND is such that $(1+ \alpha_{OH}) \cdot B_{IN, max}$ is greater than PAMA Band, but lower than B_s, it's possible to overcome PAMA Band and to avoid congestion by keeping ΔB under the opportune threshold.

All these conditions are schematically summed up in the three working cases of (6), whose knowledge allows a right configuration of transport parameters:

Case A: when CWND is such that $(1+ \alpha_{OH}) \cdot B_{IN, max} > B_s$ (6)

$B_{ETH} < PAMA \implies B_{IN} = B_{SS7}$, Loss Rate = 0%

$B_{ETH} > PAMA \implies B_{IN}$ falls down, LR = 50% (congestion)

Case B: when CWND is such that $(1+ \alpha_{OH}) \cdot B_{IN, max} < PAMA$

$B_{ETH} < B_{IN, max} \implies B_{IN} = B_{SS7}$, LR = 0%

$B_{ETH} > B_{IN, max} \implies B_{IN} = B_{IN, max}$, LR $= (B_{SS7} - B_{IN, max}) / B_{SS7}$

Case C: when CWND is such that $PAMA < (1+ \alpha_{OH}) \cdot B_{IN, max} < B_s$

$\Delta B < \Delta B_{max} \implies$ case b.

$\Delta B > \Delta B_{max} \implies$ case a.

Finally, the study on N_A number of SCTP associations can be summed up in the following:

$$N_A \cdot CWND \cdot 8 / T_{ACK} = constant = N_A \cdot B_{IN, max} = B_{IN, MAX} \qquad (7)$$

where $B_{IN, MAX}$ is the total Maximum Injected Band, to be compared to B_s according to (6), that means $B_{IN, max}$ to be compared to B_s / N_A.

From this viewpoint, also statements in paragraph 3.1 about Transmit Delays (N_A = 8) find justification:

- 8 SCTP associations with CWND maximum value 64000 are equivalent to a single association with CWND maximum value 516000, enough to reach PAMA Band and fall in congestion with Loss Rate 50% (case A);
- initial congestion dues to CWND too slow rise from initial value.

Expressions (1), (2), (3), (4) and (5) build up an operative reference model about the system under test.

4   Test Methodology and Experimental Evidences

According to previous achievements, it follows that:

1) system congestion find the trigger event in band availability, when PAMA Band is over and DAMA Band gets allocated in T_{ALL};
2) two SCTP associations with fixed CWND are equivalent to one association with doubled CWND, on the basis of (5);
3) CWND is a significant parameter and shall be fixed on the basis of (6);
4) SS7 generated traffic increase shall take in consideration (6), as well.

To execute meaningful tests, system equipments are configured as follow:

- Satellite band: PAMA Band at both 2048 Kb/s and 1024 Kb/s with DAMA Band on demand till a total band of about 2150 Kb/s, configuration of SAD Algorithm in order to have the quickest allocation and the slowest de-allocation;
- Signalling Gateway: one SCTP association, with different CWND initial value.

From the whole tests we find that there isn't any dependence on SS7 routing (DPC or GTT) and different MSU length means essentially different OverHead fraction α_{OH} (inversely proportional to MSU length), SS7 generated traffic being equal.

4.1   Experimental Evidences

Starting with the suggested value for CWND (384000 Bytes), $B_{IN, max}$ is about 4600 Kb/s (considering T_{ACK} = RTT = 650 ms) and, whatever OverHead fraction we use, the system is in *Case A* for both PAMA Band choices. With 270 Bytes long MSUs, α_{OH} is about 0.16 and $\Delta B \approx 120$ Kb/s corresponds to steps of about 140 Kb/s in Ethernet Band. Tests for both PAMA values show that no messages are lost until PAMA Band is quite over; then, Ethernet Band falls down and start to oscillate, the system goes under congestion with Loss Rate of about 50% and turns stable only after B_{IN} is hardly reduced (as yet shown in Figure 9).

Changing CWND value to 154000 Bytes, when using 270 Bytes long MSUs, the system is in *Case B* with PAMA Band set to 2048 Kb/s and a null value for DAMA Band, because RTT rises from 650 ms to 750 ms while approaching PAMA, so that $B_{IN, max} \approx 1650$ Kb/s and $(1 + \alpha_{OH}) \cdot B_{IN, max} \approx 1910$ Kb/s.

Tests show that B_{IN} rises till $B_{IN, max}$ and then any traffic increase is periodically rejected, without compromising system performances (see Figure 11).

If DAMA Band is set to 250 Kb/s, RTT is about 650 ms also while approaching PAMA Band, so that $B_{IN, max} \approx 1850$ Kb/s and $(1+ \alpha_{OH}) \cdot B_{IN, max} \approx 2150$ Kb/s: the system is lightly in *Case C*.

A test with 270 Bytes long MSUs shows that, with $\Delta B \approx 130$ Kb/s (it corresponds to steps of about 150 Kb/s in Ethernet Band), congestion comes only when $B_{IN, max}$ exceeds PAMA Band, being kept at about 2100 Kb/s by periodic loss.

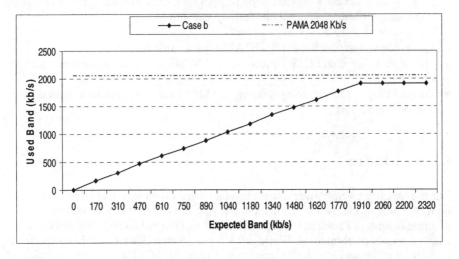

Fig. 11. Examples of tests results in case B

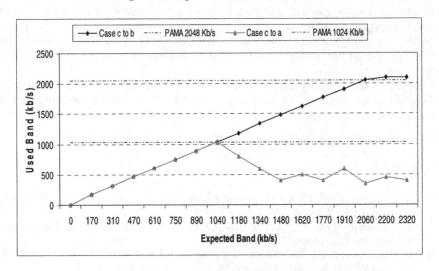

Fig. 12. Examples of tests results in case C

Results with 60 Bytes long MSUs are quite the same: RTT grows to 750 ms and $(1+ \alpha_{OH}) \cdot B_{IN, max} \approx 2300$ Kb/s, the same ΔB is accepted and $B_{IN, max}$ stay around 2100 Kb/s by periodic loss.

The situation is stressed by setting PAMA Band to 1024 Kb/s, where $\Delta B \approx 190$ Kb/s keeps the system in *Case B*, while $\Delta B \approx 250$ Kb/s drives it to *Case A* (see Figure 12).

4.2   Open Issues

Since the system behavior appears quite complicated, there are still some details to be clarified, that our future experimental activity will aim to.

The main aspects to be investigated are:

- T_{ALL} dynamic contribution to OUTSTAND quick growth;
- ΔB_{max} correlation with SCTP parameters, as CWND, and with the system's parameters, as T_{ACK}, T_{ALL}, etc.;
- Transit Delays of SS7 messages during DAMA Band allocation may exceed specifications' time-outs.

5   Conclusion

Our trial activity on SoIP over Satellite connection shows that it can be used in operations choosing in the right way the mentioned parameters. It has been underlined how its critical aspects (Transmit Delay and Bandwidth Availability) can influence the whole system's performances. While delay consequences (RTT 640-680 ms) seems to be overcome by configuring the maximum size of the SCTP Congestion Window at higher value (or equivalently by using more than one SCTP association), the fact that satellite bandwidth can be provided both as permanent (PAMA) and dynamic (DAMA) appears not to be solved at all by these actions, because the Satellite Allocation/De-allocation Algorithm can interact with SCTP Congestion Avoidance Algorithm in a dangerous way for system stability, if parameters aren't configured with special attention.

In order to guide configuration choices we propose an operative reference model, whose usefulness has been confirmed by testing validation, even if still more study is needed to have it completed.

References

[1]   R. Stewart et al. "SCTP: Stream Control Transmission Protocol", IETF RFC 2960, October 2000.
[2]   K. Morneault et al., "SS7 MTP2-User Adaptation Layer (M2UA) – draft-ietf-sigtran-m2ua-15 work in progress", February 2002.
[3]   G. Sidebottom et al., "SS7 MTP3-User Adaptation Layer (M3UA) – draft-ietf-sigtran-m3ua-12 work in progress", February 2002.
[4]   J. Loughney et al., "SS7 SCCP-User Adaptation Layer (SUA) – draft-ietf-sigtran-sua-12 work in progress", February 2002.
[5]   T. George et al., "SS7 MTP2-User Peer-to-Peer Adaptation Layer (M2PA) – draft-ietf-sigtran-m2pa-04 work in progress", February 2002.
[6]   G. Maggiore , F. Piovan et al., "VoIP and SoIP testing methodology, TIM experience", SCI2002 Orlando, July 2002

[7]   ITU-T Recommendation Q.543, Digital Exchange Performance Design Objectives, ITU-T, March 1993.
[8]   ITU-T Recommendation Q.706, Signalling System N.7 – Message Transfer Part Signalling Performance, ITU-T, March 1993
[9]   ITU-T Recommendation Q.716, Signalling System N.7 – Signalling Connection Control Part (SCCP) Performance, ITU-T, March 1993

Generation of Optimized Testsuites for UML Statecharts with Time

Tilo Mücke and Michaela Huhn[*]

Technical University of Braunschweig, 38106 Braunschweig , Germany,
{tmuecke,huhn}@ips.cs.tu-bs.de,
www.cs.tu-bs.de/ips

Abstract. We present an approach to automatically generate time-optimized coverage-based testsuites from a subclass of deterministic statecharts with real-time constraints. The algorithms are implemented as a plugin for a standard UML tool (Poseidon for UML). The statecharts are extended to accomplish common and new coverage criteria inspired by the experience of test experts and translated into timed automata. The model checker UPPAAL then searches a trace with the fastest diagnostic trace option which provides the basis for the testsuite.

1 Introduction

Model based software development is applied successfully in many application domains. In the embedded domain, the model based approach is well accepted since several years. Tool supported graphical modelling languages are a great help to master the complexity of modern embedded applications that results from safety requirements, the distribution of the components or real-time constraints. Statecharts introduced by Harel [1] are widely used in state based modelling and in particular the UML variant of statecharts is supported by various tools.

In practise, testing is the major technique for software validation and an important expense and time factor in the software development process. For embedded software, testing has become the predominant effort in the development since enhanced safety and reliability requirements have to be guaranteed if the software is employed in hundreds of technical everyday products or highly sensitive systems.

A straightforwared idea for automated test design is so-called model based testing, i.e. to generate tests from (semi-)formal state based design models. In the area of communication systems FSM based testing has been exercised since several decades [2,3,4] and was transferred to statecharts e.g. in [5]. Since the behaviour of a statechart is infinite in general, exhaustive testing is impossible. Thus it is common practise to create a testsuite, i.e. a finite set of tests that cover the system with respect to certain criteria. In software testing coverage criteria related to control flow like state or transition coverage and criteria related to the

---

[*] This research was supported in part by a grant of the DFG (Deutsche Forschungsgemeinschaft) - SFB562.

R. Groz and R.M. Hierons (Eds.): TestCom 2004, LNCS 2978, pp. 128–143, 2004.

data flow are well established [6,7]. Alternatively, functional queries generalizing the experience of test experts are used to create a small but expressive testsuite [8]. Recently, many authors [9,10,11,12,13] employ a model checker or other efficient search algorithms [14] to cope with the state explosion problem which is dominant in automated testcase generation. The procedure of this approach is depicted in Figure 1.

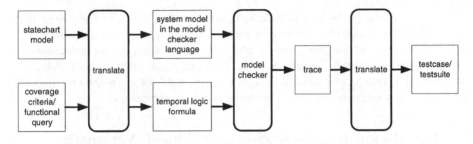

Fig. 1. Using a model checker for testcase generation

In this paper we use a model checker for testsuite generation from statecharts, too. Our approach concentrates on testcases to validate the real-time behaviour of statecharts because in the real-time domain the correct timing of operations is as important as pure functionality. We use the UPPAAL model checker [15] that is specialized for the verification of real-time systems.

As [10] we start with statecharts as a standard modelling notation which is automatically transformed into a formal model suitable as input to a model checker. Depending on the coverage criterion for which a testsuite shall be generated the model is prepared by introducing specific variables. The coverage criterion or functional query is translated into a temporal logic formula, e.g. for state coverage into a query for a path on which each state is visited which is indicated by the introduced variables. Here we follow the work of [10,16] and [12, 9] (for real-time systems) which we have extended by a new coverage criterion called *boundary coverage*. Then the model checker searches the state space of the model which results in a trace that is retranslated to be interpreted as a testcase.

For testcase generation tool support is mandatory ([17] gives an overview). [10,16,18] start with a formal system model ready for a model checker like Spin or SMV, [9,12] use timed automata as the system model. [3] (ObjectGeode), [5] (Rational Rose), and [8] (AutoFokus) have implemented tools as additional modules for various CASE tools. This corresponds to our approach. So the user can conveniently move from modelling to testcase generation and the formal methods behind are mainly hidden.

Even with the excellent algorithms implemented in model checkers, state explosion still is the major problem in testcase generation. [16] shows that the generation of the shortest testsuite is NP-complete and suggests the use of a greedy-algorithm to choose an adequate subset from the generated testcases.

Since version 3.3, UPPAAL contains the feature of emitting the fastest diagnostic trace. This feature provides the generation of the testsuite with the shortest test-execution-time as is shown in [9]. We use this feature to obtain a time-optimal testsuite. However, we show that the search for the fastest trace heavily suffers from the state explosion. Therefore we discuss several heuristics to palliate the storage consumption of the model checker for the price of a time-optimized but possibly non-optimal testsuite.

The rest of the paper is organized as follows: In Section 2 we briefly describe how to transform a family of deterministic statecharts into a system of UPPAAL timed automata. In Section 3 we explain how the statecharts are extended to accomplish the coverage criteria. Section 4 is concerned with our tool *TestGen* and Section 5 with an example. In Section 6 we evaluate the approach and discuss heuristic improvements. Section 7 presents concluding remarks.

2   Translation from Statecharts to Timed Automata

Our approach to generate testcases for statecharts is based on the transformation of UML statecharts to UPPAAL timed automata introduced in [19]. The transformation is restricted to a subclass of UML statecharts (condition 1-3). We put a fourth constraint on the set of suitable statecharts which is specific for testcase generation.

1. Concurrency is restricted to the top level (object level), i.e. within the statecharts AND-states must not be used. This is adequate in our system model, where statecharts model the behaviour of a family of objects without intra-object concurrency.
2. In guards and actions only expressions may be used that have a one-to-one correspondence in the UPPAAL language.
3. So far composite transitions, history connectors, entry-, exit-actions and do activities are not supported by the transformation tool, but these elements can be handled by an extension.
4. Statecharts have to be deterministic in the sense that in the semantics at most one transition is enabled at each moment. Therefore we require that for each two transitions with the same source state the enabling conditions (triggers, guards, timing constraints) are never satisfied both.

In addition to the UML standard syntax, an *after* construct with two parameters is supported to specify real-time constraints: The parameters give a time interval measured from the moment the state has been entered in which the source state may be left via this timing transition.

2.1   Syntax of the Statechart Model

Statecharts extend finite state machines by the concepts of hierarchy, concurrency and communication via events. A UML statechart model consists of states and transitions.

States can be basic or composite. A composite state has at least one substate, while the basic state has none. This hierarchy might be considered as a tree with composite states as internal nodes and basic states as leaves. The root of the tree is the top level composite state containing a complete statechart. Each composite state contains one initial state defining the default entry point. A composite state may contain at most one final state by which the composite state can be left via a so-called completion transition.

Transitions connect a source state with a target state. A transition is labelled by an expression $e[g]/a$, where:

1. e is an event triggering the transition. It can be a signal event, which has been sent from a concurrent statechart, a time event, triggering the transition in a given time interval after entering of the source state, or a completion event, if there is no explicit trigger.
2. g is a guard which has to be evaluated to true, to allow the transition to fire. For a straightforwarded translation to UPPAAL we allow only conjunctions of simple expressions[1].
3. a is a list of actions, which are executed when the transition fires. Actions can be assignments which conform to UPPAAL as above or send actions.

2.2   Statecharts Semantics

Our semantics for statecharts conforms to the UML standard with an extension to handle a family of concurrent statecharts on the object (top) level.

At the beginning, root and all recursively reachable initial substates are marked *active*. All variables are initialized.

A transition is *enabled* if its source is an active state and its trigger is the first in the event queue, in case of a signal or completion event, or if the correct time is reached, in case of a time event, and if its guard evaluates to true.

If several transitions are enabled at the same time, the one with its source state lower in the state hierarchy, has a higher priority. Since the statecharts are deterministic as explained above, with the priority scheme exactly one transition is left.

If a transition fires, the source state and all recursively reachable active substates are left and the target state and all recursively reachable initial substates are marked *active*. The actions are performed in the order of their occurrence. If the action is an assignment, the variable on the left hand is assigned its new value according to the evaluation of the right hand side. If the action is a send action, the send event is enqueued in the event queue of the receiver object.

Signal and completion events are stored in event queues, but completion events are always inserted at the beginning of the queue. If an event causes a transition to fire or is not able to trigger any transition, it is dequeued.

All variables are global.

---

[1] We only allow real-time clocks and integer variables. Timing contraints are restricted to expressions $c_1 \approx x \approx c_2$ and $c_3 \approx x - y \approx c_4$ where c_i is a non-negative constant or ∞, x, y are real-time clocks, and $\approx \in \{=, \leq, \geq\}$, see [15] for details.

For a basic state, a completion event is generated, whenever the state is entered. For a composite state, a completion event is generated, if its final state is entered.

A family of statecharts is executed in parallel and communicates via events which are addressed to a specified receiver object. Time elapses only, if all event queues are empty. If more than one statechart has a non-empty event queue, the next one to become active is selected non-deterministically. It consumes and processes an event without time delay. This will be repeated without time consumption until all queues are empty. When the system is stable, time elapses and the next time event starts a new sequence of steps.

2.3 Transformation into Timed Automata

A family of UML statecharts is transformed into UPPAAL timed automata in three steps: First, each statechart is flattened, meaning the hierarchical structure is removed because timed automata lack hierarchy. Next, the family of flat statecharts is transformed to a family of timed automata. In a last step, control automata are added to enforce the UPPAAL model to behave consistently to the statechart semantics. The transformation is described formally and in detail in [19].

After flattening the statecharts, the states are translated into locations and transitions into switches. Since we restricted the transition labels accordingly, the translation of transitions triggered by signal or completion events is straight-forward.

Next, the after events $after(min, max)$ are translated. For each state s with a leaving transition triggered by an after event, a clock c_s is introduced. Whenever s is entered, the clock c_s is reset. The after event is replaced by two guards on one transition $c_s > min, c_s < max$. To prevent the timed automaton from staying in the state s forever, an invariant $c_s < \text{MAX}$, with MAX being the maximum of all after transitions leaving s, is added to s.

In UPPAAL timed automata, two transitions may synchronize, but there is no way of asynchronous communication. Thus, event queues are modelled explicitly in the timed automata model.

In statecharts events that may not trigger any transition are removed from the head of the queue, thus in the timed automata model, message consuming self loops are added to all states where for some variable configuration and signal or completion event there is no corresponding transition leaving the state.

In UPPAAL timed automata, enabled transitions need not proceed, hence a control automaton, which enforces a timed automaton with a non-empty event queue to fire, is added.

3 Test Generation

To generate test cases we follow a coverage criteria based approach. Control flow can be covered by state, transition, condition, and boundary coverage. Data flow coverage is possible, too.

For some coverage criteria it is sufficient to generate queries to obtain test cases. To find a trace covering a state s, the query $E <> s$ (there exists a path reaching the state s) might be used. But for other coverage criteria, even a CTL^*-formula would not be sufficient [16].

Thus we decided to add Boolean coverage variables c_i to the model. These variables are set to true, whenever a certain coverage is achieved, e.g. a certain state is entered in case of state coverage. To find a trace providing the desired coverage a query $E <> \bigwedge_i c_i$ is used. The augmentation of coverage variables enlarges the statespace as mentioned in Section 6.

State Coverage requires a set of testcases (traces), so that every state is visited at least once. This is done by adding a new Boolean variable for each basic state and adding an assignment to every transition setting the new variable appropriately to the target basic state of the transition to *true*. The initial set of states is visited before any transition fires, therefore the coverage of these states does not need to be verified.

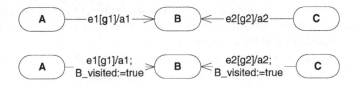

Fig. 2. A first statechart fragment and its state coverage extension

The results of this transformation can be observed in Figure 2.

It is reasonable for all coverage criteria that a coverage must only be achieved if possible. That means, if a state is unreachable, it does not have to be reached to accomplish state coverage.

The name spaces for the variables of the genuine statechart and the added coverage variables have to be disjoint. If necessary, variables have to be renamed before transformation.

Transition Coverage demands a testsuite in which every transition fires at least once. To do this, a Boolean coverage variable for each transition has to be added to the model. Next the actions for each transition are extended, so that the appropriate variable is set to *true*.

The statechart fragment from Figure 2 is therefore transformed to Figure 3. As can be seen, transition coverage is stronger than state coverage.

Condition Coverage can be achieved, evaluating the guard of every transition of the statechart at least once to *true* and once to *false*. To achieve multiple condition coverage [6], the expressions within every guard of each transition of

Fig. 3. Transition coverage extension for the first statechart fragment

the statechart will have to be evaluated at least once to *true* and at least once to *false*. Multiple condition coverage is stronger than condition coverage.

Because in our model the atomic guards are combined using the and-operation, it is only possible to prevent (block) the transition from firing by evaluating one atomic guard to *false*. This is why we use an alternative of condition coverage which is in combination with transition coverage stronger than normal condition coverage, but weaker than multiple condition coverage.

For every state, all outgoing transitions are considered and loop-transitions are added for each combination of one blocking atomic guard from every transition. For this coverage a new Boolean variable for every atomic guard is added.

Condition coverage should be used on the flattened statechart. This is no problem, because the statechart is flattened in the first step of the transformation to timed automata. Using our alternative of condition coverage on the statechart before flattening could increase the execution time of test generation and test execution without providing a better coverage.

As an example, the transformation of a statechart fragment with two transitions each with two atomic guards is shown in Figure 4.

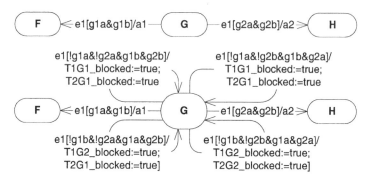

Fig. 4. Condition coverage extension for the second statechart fragment

Boundary Coverage requires that every guard with a relational operator enables its transition to fire at least once with the closest operands possible. Boundary coverage is used to test the limits of guards explicitly, because these are common failure sources.

Boundary coverage is a new development and is achieved by splitting each transition with the relation $<$, $<=$, $>$ or $>=$ in its guard in two transitions:

- $a < b$ is splitted in $a = b - 1$ and $a < b - 1$ (only for $a, b \in \mathbb{Z}$)
- $a <= b$ is splitted in $a = b$ and $a < b$

- $a > b$ is splitted in $a = b+1$ and $a > b+1$ (only for $a, b \in \mathbb{Z}$)
- $a >= b$ is splitted in $a = b$ and $a > b$

The remaining guards, the triggering event, and the actions are copied to both transitions. The first transition gets an extra action, setting the corresponding Boolean boundary coverage variable to true.

The effect of this transformation can be seen in Figure 5.

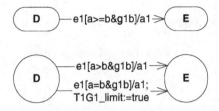

Fig. 5. Boundary coverage extension for the third statechart fragment

Data Flow Coverage demands that every path from an assignment of a variable to the usage of this variable without reassignment is used at least once.

To achieve this kind of coverage, for every variable another variable memorizes where this variable has been set previously. Whenever a variable gets used, a field of a matrix over the definitions and the usages of one variable is set to *true*. The usages are partitioned in predicate uses (p-use) and uses in all other expressions (c-use).

This transformation can be understood more easily looking at the statechart fragment and its transformation in Figure 6.

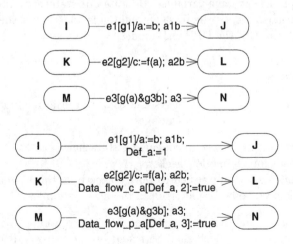

Fig. 6. Data flow coverage extension for the fourth statechart fragment

3.1   Reset Automaton and Satisfiability

Sometimes it is not possible to find a path for some coverage variable because e.g. a state cannot be reached or a transition can never fire. Coverage variables belonging to unreachable features are found, using a query $A[]c == false$ for $c \in C$, and are eliminated. A warning for the designer of the statechart is generated, too.

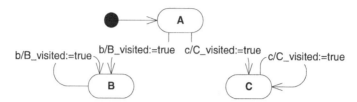

Fig. 7. An example statechart transformed for state coverage

Even if all of the coverage variables can be set to true, in general it is not the case, that a combination of all coverage variables will produce a trace, too. Figure 7 shows a statechart, where the states B and C can both be reached, but not in one trace.

To overcome this situation, a possibility to reset the whole system has to be added to the system. Because a reset of the system takes time in reality, it should take time in the model, too.

Therefore we introduce a synchronous *reset* event triggering transitions leading from every state of a statechart to its new *reset* state. After a given *reset-time* another transition, whose target is the *root* state, fires. This transitions resets all variables except the coverage variables. Because our statechart model does not support synchronous events, the reset-automaton is added after the transformation of the statechart to the UPPAAL-model.

3.2   Test Driver

Every statechart that is part of the system, can be transformed into UPPAAL-automata, but there are two disadvantages:

- A system consisting of several concurrent statecharts causes an explosion in the statespace for the model checker.
- The components are only tested to work correctly in this system but reused components need to be tested again in the new system.

Therefore, the user shall divide the components in two groups. The first group contains the components which shall be tested by the generated testsuite. The second group contains the components for which only test drivers have to be generated.

The test drivers must guarantee the following properties:

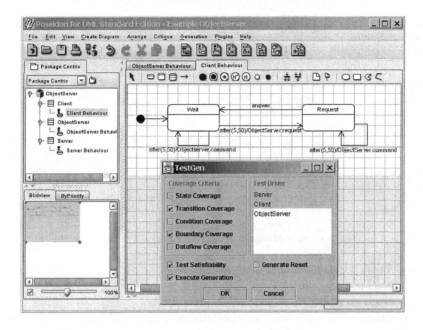

Fig. 8. Screenshot of TestGen

- Replacing a component by its test driver does not inhibit any behaviour of the remainder of the system.
- The test driver needs less state space than the original component.

To accomplish these properties, the test driver should to be able to:

- send any event, the component has been able to send before,
- change every shared variable to any possible value, if the component has been able to modify this variable before,
- receive every event,
- and wait any amount of time.

This can be done with a simple UPPAAL-automaton with only one state and several self loops, changing the shared variables and sending events.

4   The *TestGen*-Plugin

Our tool "TestGen" (see the screenshot in Figure 8), implementing the algorithms described in Section 2 and 3 in JAVA, has been realized as a plugin for the UML tool *Poseidon for UML*. A testsuite for a family of suitable statecharts modelled in *Poseidon for UML* can be generated as follows:

- Activate the testsuite generation by the plugin button (rightmost button in the menu).

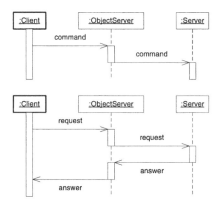

Fig. 9. The two modi of communication provided by the object server

- In a Pop-up menu the user may select:
  - which coverage criteria shall be used
  - which components shall build the test drivers
  - if the satisfiability for each coverage variable shall be tested
  - if a reset automaton shall be included
  - if the generation of the testsuite shall be started after the model transformation
- Then pressing the "Ok"-button starts the testsuite generation

In the moment, the output is a sequence of testcases in a textual representation. We are working on a graphical display of testcases in terms of sequence diagrams.

5   Example: Object Server

As a case study we consider a lightweight real-time middleware called *object server* which was developed within the Sonderforschungsbereich (SFB) 562[2]. The object server [20] serves as a middleware for highly dynamic processes of robot controls and builds a gateway from the external sensors communicating via a high speed industrial communication protocol (IAP) based on the IEEE 1394 standard (firewire) to the main processes of the robot control.

The object server supports two modi of data exchange (see Figure 9):

- command mode: The client sends an asynchronous command to the server which starts executing it.
- request mode: The client sends a request to the server which calculates an answer and sends it back to the client.

Figure 10 shows a simplified version of the object server. The model contains only one server and client and does not include the data possibly associated with

---

[2] The SFB 562 is promoted by the DFG (Deutsche Forschungsgemeinschaft).

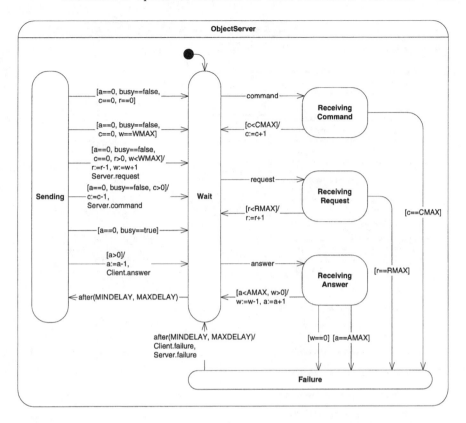

Fig. 10. Statechart of the object server

the messages, but it can store incoming messages in several queues and delivers them, when the server is not busy with incoming messages. An error occurs in case of queue overflows and in case of a mismatch between requests and answers. Then the server and the client are informed.

If a command, a request, or an answer is received, it is stored in the corresponding queue. The fill status of the queues is memorized in the variables c, r and a. If the appropriate queue is already full or an answer is received which is not expected, the object server sends a failure message to both, the server and the client. If no message arrives for a given period of time (MINDELAY, MAXDELAY), the object server starts to deliver messages from the queues. Answers have the highest priority of delivery. Commands may only be delivered if the queue for the answers is empty and the server is not busy. Requests may only be delivered if the other queues are empty and the server is not busy.

Generating a testsuite for this statechart using transition and boundary coverage results in the testcase which is depicted in Figure 11. Modifying the model requires only a single run of the testcase generator to automatically generate a new testsuite.

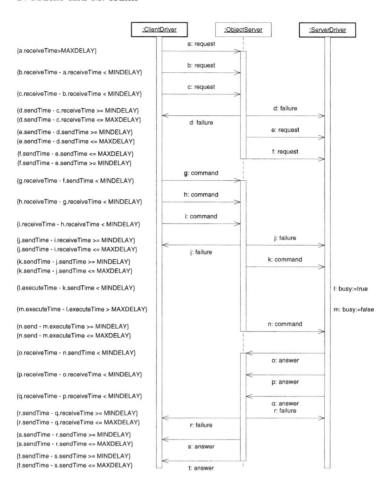

Fig. 11. Testsuite for the object server

6 Problems of the Method

The main problem using our approach is an exponential coherence between the length of a trace and the amount of memory used by UPPAAL for testcase generation, as depicted in Figure 12. This problem has two main causes:

– The state space is enlarged by the boolean coverage variables.
– A long trace is searched, because the whole testsuite is calculated by one single run of the model checker.

Both problems can be overcome with a simple variation of the algorithm.

1. In the first step, for some coverage variable not reached so far a path is calculated.

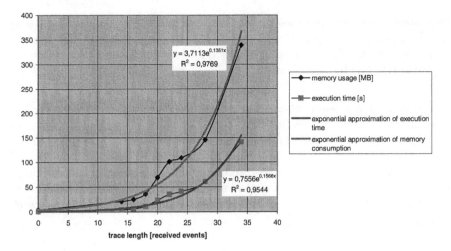

Fig. 12. Complexity trace-length dependency

2. Next, for the calculated path the coverage variables are determined which are reached additionally to the searched one.
3. If there are still reachable coverage variables which are not reached so far then we proceed to step 1 with the end configuration of the calculated path as a new start configuration.

Doing so, only one coverage variable is needed. The trace length of each run of the model checker is shortened, for the price of starting the model checker several times. The improvement of the algorithm results in lower memory consumption but higher execution time for the model checker.

This kind of search can be improved by a branch and bound algorithm like A^* [21], but has one disadvantage: It is not assured any more that the shortest testcase is generated if the implementation reacts as fast as possible. However, it is obvious that the concept provides shorter testsuites than the greedy algorithm. Heuristics like testcase ranking, to cut off some search paths, can be incorporated in the search algorithm, to improve the execution time of the testcase generation.

7   Conclusion and Future Work

We have presented a method for the automated generation of time-optimized testsuites for UML statecharts. The method is based on a transformation of statecharts to timed automata. For testcase generation the tool adds coverage variables and a reset automaton to the UPPAAL model. The testsuite is derived from a trace generated by UPPAAL in a model checking run with the "fastest trace"-option. Components can be tested stand-alone using test drivers for their environment, so that they can be reused without further testing. In difference to other approaches to testcase generation for statecharts using model checkers like Spin and SMV [18,10] our work aims for the testing of the timing behaviour.

In addition to [9] we offer tool support as a plugin for *Poseidon for UML* and an additional coverage criterion. To reach our goal to develop an environment for automatic conformance testing of a model and its implementation, there are several extensions to be explored:

Variations of the generation algorithm. Next we will implement the improvements mentioned in Section 6 to overcome the problems resulting from the enormous memory consumption. For us it seems to be more promising to optimize the testcase generation procedure for the price of good but non-optimal testsuites than to keep to the time-optimal testsuite, because the memory problem is the major restriction for practical applications. The algorithm would benefit further from the use of an optimized model checker and a modifiable search strategy as recommended in [14].

Syntax checks on statecharts. For the convenience and understanding of the user, we plan to implement a syntax check on statecharts that points out model elements that cannot be processed by TestGen.

Test execution via middleware will allow to run the test suite without adaption of the implementation. The components in the environment of the CUT (component under test) will be replaced by the corresponding test drivers, each of which sends the events noticed in each testcase to the CUT and checks its reactions for compliance with the testcase.

References

1. Harel, D.: Statecharts: A visual formalism for complex systems. Science of Computer Programming **8** (1987) 231–274
2. Bochmann, G., Petrenko, A.: Protocol testing: Review of methods and relevance for software testing. In: Proc. International Symposium on Software Testing and Analysis. (1994) 109–124
3. Kerbra, A., Jéron, T., Groz, R.: Automated test generation from SDL specifications. In: SDL Forum. (1999) 135–152
4. Rapps, S., Weyuker, E.: Selecting software test data using data flow information. In: IEEE TSE. Volume 11. (1985) 367–375
5. Offutt, J., Abdurazik, A.: Generating tests from UML specifications. In: UML'99. (1999) 416–429
6. Peled, D.: 9. Software Testing. In: Software Reliability Methods. Springer-Verlag (2001)
7. Friedman, G., Hartman, A., Nagin, K., Shiran, T.: Projected state machine coverage for software testing. In: ACM SIGSOFT European Software Engineering Conference and International Symposium on Foundations of Software Engineering. (2002) 134–143
8. Pretschner, A., Lötzebeyer, H.: Model based testing with constraint logic programming. In: Workshop on Automated Program Analysis, Testing and Verification (WAPATV). (2001) 1–9

9. Hessel, A., Larsen, K., Nielsen, B., Pettersson, P., Skou, A.: Time-optimal real-time test case generation using UPPAAL. In: Workshop on Formal Approaches to Testing of Software (FATES). (2003)
10. Hong, H., Lee, I., Sokolsky, O., Cha, S.: Automatic test generation from statecharts using model checking. In: Workshop on Formal Approaches to Testing of Software (FATES). (2001) 15–30
11. Rayadurgan, S., Heimdahl, M.: Coverage based test-case generation using model checkers. In: Intl. Conf. and Workshop on the Engineering of Computer Based Systems. (2001) 83–93
12. Nielsen, B., Skou, A.: Automated test generation from timed automata. In: Tools and Algorithms for the Construction and Analysis of Systems. (2001) 343–357
13. Jéron, T., Morel, P.: Test generation derived from model-checking. In: International Conference on Computer Aided Verification. Volume 1633. (1999)
14. Pretschner, A.: Classical search strategies for test case generation with constraint logic programming. In: Workshop on Formal Approaches to Testing of Software (FATES). (2001) 47–60
15. Larsen, K.G., Pettersson, P., Yi, W.: UPPAAL in a nutshell. International Journal on Software Tools for Technology Transfer **1** (1997) 134–152
16. Hong, H., Lee, I., Sokolsky, O., Ural, H.: A temporal logic based theory of test coverage and generation. In: Tools and Algorithms for the Construction and Analysis of Systems. (2002)
17. Goga, N.: Comparing TorX, autolink, TGV and UIO test algorithms. Lecture Notes in Computer Science (2001)
18. Gragantini, A., Heitmeyer, C.: Using model checking to generate tests from requirements specification. In: ACM SIGSOFT European Software Engineering Conference and International Symposium on Foundations of Software Engineering. (1999) 146–162
19. Diethers, K., Goltz, U., Huhn, M.: Model checking UML statecharts with time. In: UML 2002, Workshop on Critical Systems Development with UML. (2002)
20. Diethers, K., Kohn, N., Finkemeyer, B.: Middleware zur Realisierung offener Steuerungssoftware für hochdynamische Prozesse. it - Information Technology (2003)
21. Nilsson, N.: Principles of Artificial Intelligence. Springer Verlag (1982)

Communication Patterns for Expressing Real-Time Requirements Using MSC and Their Application to Testing

Helmut Neukirchen[1], Zhen Ru Dai[2], and Jens Grabowski[1]

[1] Institute for Informatics, University of Göttingen
Lotzestr. 16-18, D-37083 Göttingen, Germany
{neukirchen,grabowski}@informatik.uni-goettingen.de
[2] Fraunhofer FOKUS, Competence Center TIP
Kaiserin-Augusta-Allee 31, D-10589 Berlin, Germany
dai@fokus.fraunhofer.de

Abstract. This paper introduces real-time communication patterns (RTC-patterns) for capturing real-time requirements of communication systems. RTC-patterns for some of the most common real-time requirements are presented. They are formalized by using Message Sequence Charts (MSCs). The application of RTC-patterns to testing is explained by an example. The example shows how real-time requirements which are expressed using RTC-patterns can be related to *TIMED*TTCN-3 evaluation functions.

1 Introduction

The motivation for the work presented in this paper comes from our research on test specification and test generation for testing real-time requirements of communication systems. Especially, we investigate graphical specification methods that can be used in all phases of an integrated system development methodology and that allow an automated generation and implementation of test cases.

We use the *Testing and Test Control Notation* (TTCN-3) [5] as test implementation language and developed *TIMED*TTCN-3 [3] as an associated real-time extension to support the test of real-time requirements. For graphical test specification, we apply the *Message Sequence Chart* (MSC[1]) language [13]. The MSC-based specification of real-time test cases and generation of *TIMED*TTCN-3 code from MSC test specifications is explained in [4].

Even though it is possible to generate *TIMED*TTCN-3 code automatically for each MSC test description, we would like to facilitate and harmonize the use of *TIMED*TTCN-3 by providing a common set of test evaluation functions. This would make test results more comparable and avoid misinterpretations due to the use of different or erroneous evaluation functions. The key issue of this

---

[1] The term *MSC* is used both for a diagram written in the MSC language and for the language itself.

R. Groz and R.M. Hierons (Eds.): TestCom 2004, LNCS 2978, pp. 144–159, 2004.

approach is the identification of commonly applicable evaluation functions for *Timed*TTCN-3 test cases. Such functions are used to evaluate relations among time stamps of events, which are observed during a test run. An evaluation function is related to the number of interfaces of the system under test, the number of time stamps to be considered and the number of relations among these time stamps. It would be necessary to provide an infinite set of evaluation functions to cover all cases. This is not possible and, therefore, we look for a mechanism to identify evaluation functions for the most common cases.

Our idea is to use *real-time communication patterns* (RTC-patterns) for expressing real-time requirements and to provide evaluation functions for these patterns only. By using RTC-patterns during test design or by scanning test specifications for RTC-patterns, it is possible to use predefined evaluation functions in *Timed*TTCN-3 test descriptions.

The idea of patterns is not new. *Software patterns* as described in [6,2] focus on structural aspects of software design. Conventional software patterns are independent of an implementation language and described in a rather informal manner. Different from software patterns, *SDL patterns* [7] are tailored to the development of SDL [12] systems. They benefit from the formal SDL semantics, which offers the possibility of precisely specifying how to apply a specific pattern, under which assumptions this will be allowed, and what properties result for the embedding context.

RTC-patterns are used to describe real-time requirements in form of time relations among communication operations at the interfaces of a communication system. We use MSC for the pattern description. The formality of MSC allows formalizing at least some parts of the pattern instantiation. Even though the application domain of testing communication systems motivates our work on RTC-patterns, we believe that such patterns are of general interest for system development. Therefore, we present RTC-patterns independent of the testing domain (Section 2) and explain afterwards their application to testing (Section 3).

2   MSC and Patterns

This section gives a short introduction into the subset of the MSC language, which is used in this paper, and presents MSC patterns for capturing real-time requirements.

2.1   MSC

Basically, an MSC describes the flow of *messages* between the *instances* of a communication system. For example, the MSC Referenced (Fig. 1c) includes three instances, i.e., PCO, System$_1$ and System$_2$, and specifies that message m3 is sent from System$_1$ to System$_2$.

The MSC language supports abstraction from and refinement of behavior by *decomposed instances* and *references*. The decomposition mechanism allows to refine the behavior of an instance. This is shown in Fig. 1a and 1b. The keywords

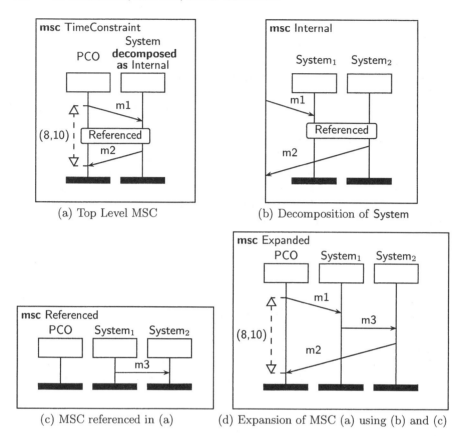

(a) Top Level MSC   (b) Decomposition of System

(c) MSC referenced in (a)   (d) Expansion of MSC (a) using (b) and (c)

Fig. 1. Used MSC Constructs

decomposed as followed by the name Internal in the header of instance System
(Fig. 1a) indicates that System is an abstraction of the behavior specified by MSC
Internal (Fig. 1b). The MSCs in Fig. 1a and 1b also contain reference symbols,
which both refer to the MSC Referenced. The semantics of a reference symbol is
given by the referenced MSC, i.e., the behavior of the referenced MSC replaces
the reference. By applying the rules for decomposed instances and references,
the MSC TimeConstraint can be expanded to the MSC shown in Fig. 1d.

For the specification of complex communication behavior in a compact manner within one diagram, MSC provides *inline expressions*. In this paper, we only
use **loop** inline expressions to specify the repeated occurrence of events. Fig. 4
presents an example, the behavior of the reference symbols loopedPreamble, ResponseTimePattern and loopedPostamble is repeated n times.

MSC allows to attach time annotations to events like sending or receiving a
message. In this paper we make use of relative *time constraints* which limit the
duration between two events. A time constraint is shown in Fig. 1a: the time
difference between sending m1 and receiving m2 at instance PCO is restricted to
be between 8 and 10 seconds. The value of a time constraint is specified using

intervals. The interval boundaries may be open, by using parenthesis, or closed, by using square bracket. An omitted lower bound is treated as *zero*, an omitted upper bound as *infinite*.

Time constraints can also be attached to the beginning and end of an inline expression (Figures 4 and 5). In this case, the constraint refers to the first or last event respectively which occurs inside the inline expression.

In addition to such relative time constraints, Fig. 7 contains a time constraint for a cyclic event (sending message m1) every $\bar{t}$ seconds) inside a loop inline expression. The definition of such periodic events is not supported in the MSC standard. Therefore, we use an extension proposed in [14].

2.2   RTC-Patterns and MSC

In the following, MSCs are used to present RTC-patterns for the most common hard real-time requirements [1,9,10].[2] Since real-time requirements are always related to some functional behavior on which they are imposed, it is not possible to provide patterns for pure real-time requirements. Therefore, the RTC-patterns contain communication events on which the real-time requirements are imposed.

In order to ease specification and testing of real-time communication systems, it was our intention to provide patterns for testable real-time requirements only. In general, testable requirements can be obtained if the involved events of the system can be observed and stimulated. Thus, we assume that the system for which the requirements are specified has appropriate interfaces called *points of control and observation (PCOs)*.

In our RTC-patterns, we represent each PCO as one MSC instance. The system is described by a single decomposed instance with the name System. We abstract from the internal structure of the system by omitting in the System instance header the actual reference to an MSC that refines the system behavior. Hence, we obtain a black-box view of the system.

The most common real-time requirements are related to *delay, throughput, periodic events* and *jitter* respectively. Basically, those requirements describe time relations between one sending and one receiving event, or the repeated occurrence of one sending and one receiving event. Depending on the number of PCOs of a system, the RTC-pattern for a certain requirement may look different, i.e., several pattern variants may exist for describing the same real-time requirement in different system configurations. In this paper, we provide RTC-patterns for systems with one or two PCOs only.

Delays: Latency/Response Time. The term *delay* is often used as an umbrella term for both *latency* and *response time* [9], since both only differ in the number of PCOs which are involved in the requirement. Hence, patterns for both types of real-time requirements are given.

---

[2] Note, that MSC is not well suited for expressing requirements involving statistical properties like soft real-time requirements or loss distributions.

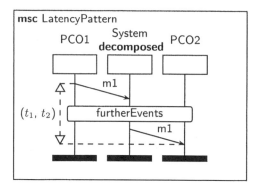

Fig. 2. Latency pattern

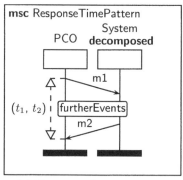

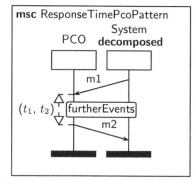

(a) Response time pattern   (b) Response time for the PCO pattern

Fig. 3. Response Time Patterns

Latency describes the delay which is introduced during the transmission of a signal by a component (the system), which is responsible for forwarding this signal [10]. The RTC-pattern for the latency requirement is given by the MSC LatencyPattern in Fig. 2. The allowed latency between sending message m1 via PCO1 and receiving it at PCO2 should be between t_1 and t_2 time units. The delay may be introduced by some further events that may include communication with the system environment (indicated by the MSC reference furtherEvents), the transmission times for message m1[3], and additional computations inside the system (indicated by the **decomposed** keyword in the heading of the System instance).

Response time is a delay requirement where the same PCO is used for sending a message and receiving the corresponding answer. The *response time* pattern is shown in Fig. 3a. In contrast to the latency pattern, the messages in the response time pattern usually differ significantly, e.g., request (message m1) and response

---

[3] Even though in this pattern the same message name is used for both transmissions, the actual contents of the forwarded message may differ due to changes introduced by the system, e.g., updated hop counters or processing of the actual payload.

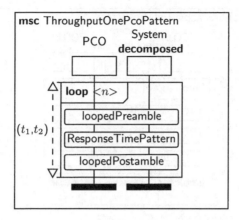

Fig. 4. Throughput pattern with one PCO

(message m2) in a client-server system. The given MSC shows a pattern for a response-time of t_1 and t_2 time units between sending message m1 and receiving message m2.

The response time requirement can also be turned into an requirement or assumption for the system environment or tester. This is necessary, if a timely behavior of the environment is needed by the system to fulfill some other requirements. This requirement can be specified using the *response time PCO* pattern given in Fig. 3b.

Throughput. While delay-based real-time requirements focus on a systems performance for a single set of events, *throughput* requirements consider a systems performance over a longer duration. This means, the number of messages per time that a system has to deliver or to process repeatedly is constrained [9]. In MSC, this can be expressed using loop inline expressions with time constraints.

The *throughput one PCO* pattern shown in Fig. 4 captures a throughput requirement for communication which is observed at one PCO.

The loop inline expression includes the references loopedPreamble, ResponseTimePattern and loopedPostamble. ResponseTimePattern refers to RTC-patterns *response time* (Fig. 3a) or *response time PCO* (Fig. 3b). The response time patterns define the functional behavior, which is part of the throughput requirement. Additional behavior, which precedes or follows the response pattern, may be contained in the MSC references loopedPreamble and loopedPostamble.

Even if a throughput requirement is fulfilled, this does not necessarily imply that all response time requirements are fulfilled for each of the loop's iteration (e.g., due to bursty behavior and buffers inside the system). Thus, when inserting a response time pattern into the throughput pattern, it has to be considered whether only the functional behavior of a response time pattern is desired or also an additional real-time constraint. In the first case, the delay pattern has to be instantiated with the time interval $[0, \infty)$ which is equivalent to removing

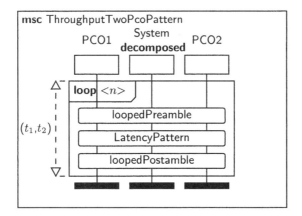

Fig. 5. Throughput pattern with two PCOs

the real-time constraint from the response time pattern. The latter case leads to requirements for periodic events and their jitter (see next section).

The given throughput pattern constrains a throughput TP to be $\frac{n}{t_2} < TP < \frac{n}{t_1}$ events per time unit. Note, that those "events" typically consist of a set of events, in particular such according to one of the delay patterns presented before.

For specifying a throughput requirement, which is observed at two PCOs, the *throughput two PCO* pattern shown in Fig. 5 is appropriate. This RTC-pattern re-uses the latency pattern (Fig. 2) for describing the functional behavior, which is part of the throughput requirement.

Periodic Events and Jitter. In contrast to throughput requirements, requirements for periodic events have to hold for each single execution of a periodic event. Like for the throughput requirement, iteration of events can be obtained using MSC loop inline expressions — but for periodic requirements, the time constraint is contained inside the loop. Depending on the numbers of involved PCOs, several patterns are possible. In this paper, we can only present some selected cases.

The first class of periodic requirements can be obtained, if delay patterns are put inside the loop. As an example, Fig. 6 shows a *cyclic response time* pattern, where the response time pattern from Fig. 3a has been chosen as delay pattern. Thus, the expressed real-time requirement is that the response time needs to hold every iteration of the loop.

Such MSCs can also be interpreted as *delay jitter* specifications. Delay jitter describes the variation of the delay during repetition. Note, that several interpretations of "jitter" exist [11]. Here, we use the following definition: $J_i = D_i - \overline{D}$, where $\overline{D}$ is the ideal (target) delay, D_i the actual delay of the ith pair of events and thus J_i the jitter in the ith repetition. Hence, a delay jitter requirement for the overall sequence of delays is expressed by the following inequation: $\forall i : J^- < J_i < J^+$, where J^- is the maximal allowed deviation below and J^+ the maximal allowed deviation above the target delay $\overline{D}$.

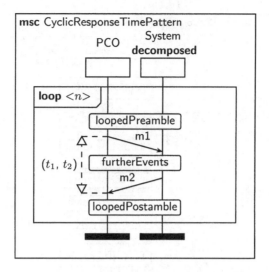

Fig. 6. Expansion of a looped response time pattern

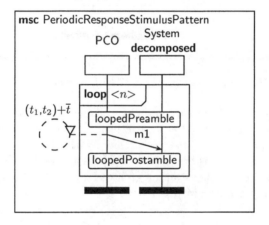

Fig. 7. Periodic response stimulus pattern

The RTC-pattern in Fig. 6 expresses a target delay $\overline{D}$ for which $t_1 < \overline{D} < t_2$ holds and a delay jitter requirement with $J^- = t_1 - \overline{D}$ and $J^+ = t_2 - \overline{D}$. I.e., the interval (t_1, t_2) could alternatively be written as $(\overline{D} + J^-, \overline{D} + J^+)$.

While time constraints for delays can be easily expressed using MSC, it is not possible to express the periodicity of cyclic events, i.e., a frequency. The reason is, that standard MSC does not allow to attach time constraints to a pair of events which spans over adjacent repetitions of a loop. Thus, MSC extensions for either high-level MSC [15] or plain MSC [14] have been suggested. The notation for the extension of plain MSC is shown in Fig. 7. The semantics of this extension can be obtained by unrolling that loop as shown in Fig. 8.

The *periodic response stimulus* pattern in Fig. 7 specifies a periodic sending of message m1 to the system. The requested periodicity $\bar{t}$ is specified as an

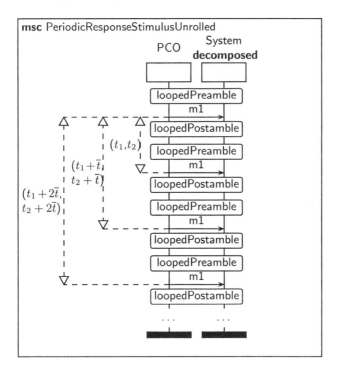

Fig. 8. Pattern of Fig. 7 with unrolled loop

additional parameter of the time interval. Likewise to delay jitter, a *jitter for the periodicity* or *frequency jitter* respectively is also specified by this pattern via $t1$ and $t2$, i.e. periodicity jitter requirement with $J^- = t_1 - \bar{t}$ and $J^+ = t_2 - \bar{t}$.

Further patterns can be obtained if two PCOs are used or the periodicity constraint is attached to another event, e.g., if the frequency of a message reception at a PCO should be constrained.

3   Application to Testing

In the previous section, it was shown how MSC RTC-patterns can be applied for specifying real-time requirements. In this section, we demonstrate how the RTC-patterns can be used for test development with *TIMED*TTCN-3. First, we describe how to associate RTC-pattern to *TIMED*TTCN-3. Then, we provide an application of this approach using an example.

3.1   Applying RTC-Patterns to *TIMED*TTCN-3

*TIMED*TTCN-3 [3] is a real-time extension for TTCN-3 [5]. It introduces the concept of absolute time, extends the TTCN-3 logging mechanism, supports online and offline evaluation of tests and adds the new test verdict **conf** to the existing TTCN-3 test verdicts.

```
      ...
(1)   var float timeA, timeB;
      ...
(2)   timeA := self.now;
(3)   PCO1.send(m1);
(4)   furtherEvents();
(5)   PCO2.receive(m1);
(6)   timeB := self.now;
(7)   setverdict(evalLatencyOnline(timeA, timeB, t1, t2));
      ...
```

Fig. 9. *TIMED*TTCN-3 Code for online latency evaluation

This section does not introduce the *TIMED*TTCN-3 language in detail. However, the presented *TIMED*TTCN-3 code should be understandable for readers with some basic knowledge of common programing languages like, e.g., C++. Further details about TTCN-3 and *TIMED*TTCN-3 can be found in [3] and [5].

*TIMED*TTCN-3 distinguishes between two different evaluation mechanisms for real-time requirements. On the one hand, *online evaluation* refers to the evaluation of a real-time requirement during the test run. On the other hand, *offline evaluation* means to evaluate a real-time requirement after the test run. We explain both by presenting the online evaluation of a latency requirement and by describing the offline evaluation of a throughput requirement.

Fig. 9 shows the *TIMED*TTCN-3 code fragment, which is related to the *latency* RTC-pattern. The relevant events for measuring the latency of two events are the sending of message m1 and receiving of message m1 (cf. Fig. 2). Thus, before m1 is sent to the SUT and after m1 is received, the points in time are measured and stored in the variables timeA and timeB (lines 2 and 6 of Fig. 9). The online evaluation function for latency is called in Line 7 with the parameters of the measured time values, i.e., timeA and timeB, and the allowed timebounds which are supposed to be stored in t1 and t2.

The definition of the function evalLatencyOnline can be found in the lines 6–15 of Fig. 11. Fig. 11 is an excerpt of the library module EvaluationFunctionModule, which embodies all functions for real-time evaluations.

In Fig. 9, function evalLatencyOnline is called in Line 7 within a **setverdict** operation. Depending on the time measurement, the function returns a **pass** verdict, if the real-time requirement is met, or a **conf** verdict (=non-functional fail) if the requirement is not met. The **setverdict** operation sets the verdict of the test case to the result of evalLatencyOnline.

Lines 1–10 in Fig. 10 depict a code fragment for a test case developed with the *throughput two PCO* pattern (cf. Fig. 5) that uses the offline evaluation mechanism for the throughput requirement. The events relevant for throughput are executed in a loop. Since for throughput only the overall duration is of interest, only the time points immediately before and after the execution of the

```
(1)   testcase ThroughputOffline(integer n) {
(2)     var integer i;
        . . .
(3)     log(myTimestampType:{"loopBegin", self.now});
(4)     for (i:=0; i < n; i:=i+1) {
(5)       loopedPreamble();
(6)       LatencyPattern();
(7)       loopedPostamble();
(8)     }
(9)     log(myTimestampType:{"loopEnd", self.now});
        . . .
(10) }
(11) control {
(12)   var testrun myTestrun;
(13)   var logfile myLog;
(13)   var verdicttype myVerdict;
(14)   myTestrun := execute(ThroughputOffline(n));
(15)   myVerdict := myTestrun.getverdict;
(16)   if (myVerdict == pass) {
(17)     myLog := myTestrun.getlog;
(18)     myVerdict := evalThroughputOffline("loopBegin", "loopEnd",
                         n/upperbound, n/lowerbound, n, myLog);
(19)     myTestrun.setverdict(myVerdict);
(20)   }
(21) }
```

Fig. 10. *TIMED*TTCN-3 Code for offline throughput evaluation

loop construct are measured and stored in a logfile (lines 3 and 9 of Fig. 10). Each entry of the logfile contains the name of the event and the associated time value, which is gained by the self.now statement.

In order to perform the offline evaluation, first test case ThroughputOffline is invoked in the control part of the *TIMED*TTCN-3 module (Line 14 of Fig. 10) and afterwards, the verdict of the functional behavior is checked (lines 15 and 16). If the functional verdict is a **pass** verdict, the real-time requirement will be evaluated. For that, the logfile is retrieved (Line 17) and the evaluation function evalThroughputOffline is called (Line 18). The parameters of the function are the identifiers of the logfile entries, the upper and lower throughput bounds[4], the number of iterations and the logfile generated by the test case.

The definition of function evalThroughputOffline can also be found in the library module EvaluationFunctionModule (lines 16–40 of Fig. 11). The function has six parameters: the labels of the entry and exit time stamps of the loop (loopEntry, loopExit), the lower and upper throughput bounds (lowerThroughput, upperThroughput), the number of iterations (n) and the logfile to evaluate (timelog). Lines 19–32 navigate to the relevant time stamps in the logfile and retrieve the entries: The operation **first** (Line 19) sorts the logfile entries and moves a cursor to the first

---

[4] The throughput bounds are calculated from the number of iterations and the interval bounds.

```
(1)  module EvaluationFunctionModule() {
(2)   type record ThroughputTimestampType {
(3)     float logTime,
(4)     charstring id
(5)   };
(6)   function evalLatencyOnline(float sendSigTime, float receiveSigTime,
           float lowerbound, float upperbound) return verdicttype {
(7)     var float timeDiff;
(8)     timeDiff := receiveSigTime - sendSigTime;
(9)     if ((lowerbound <= timeDiff) and (timeDiff <= upperbound)) {
(10)      return pass;      // non-functional pass
(11)    }
(12)    else {
(13)      return conf; // non-functional fail
(14)    }
(15)  }
(16)  function evalThroughputOffline(charstring loopEntry, charstring loopExit,
           float lowerThroughput, float upperThroughput, integer n, logfile timelog)
           return verdicttype {
(17)    var TimestampType stampA, stampB;
(18)    var float timeDiff;
(19)    if (timelog.first(TimestampType:{?,-}, TimestampType:{?, loopEntry}) == true) {
(20)      stampA := timelog.retrieve;
(21)      // Get current timestamp entry
(22)      if (timelog.next(TimestampType:{?, loopExit}) == true) {
(23)        stampB := timelog.retrieve;
(24)        // Get current timestamp entry
(25)      }
(26)      else {
(27)        return fail; // Error while retrieving log
(28)      }
(29)    }
(30)    else {
(31)      return fail; // Error while retrieving log
(32)    }
(33)    timeDiff := stampB.logTime - stampA.logTime;
(34)    if ((lowerThroughput < n/timeDiff) and (n/timeDiff < upperThroughput)) {
(35)      return pass;      // non-functional pass
(36)    }
(37)    else {
(38)      return conf;      // non-functional fail
(39)    }
(40)  }
(41) }
```

Fig. 11. Module with evaluation functions

matching entry in the logfile. A "?" indicates the field that is used as a sorting key. The second parameter of the **first** operation is used to move the cursor to the entry which relates to the loopEntry. The logfile entry which matches, is extracted by the **retrieve** operation (Line 20). The operation **next** (Line 22) advances the

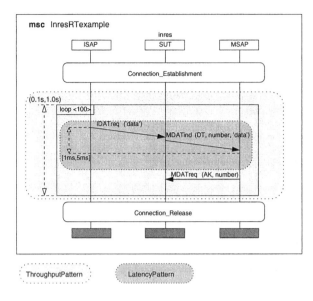

Fig. 12. Test purpose for the Inres example

cursor to the subsequent time stamp with a label identified by loopExit. The calculation of the actual throughput value is performed in lines 33–39 based on the
arithmetic expression for throughput presented in Section 2.2. Depending on the
evaluation, the function returns a **pass** verdict, if the real-time requirement is
met, or a **conf** verdict if the requirement is violated.

In Fig. 10, the offline evaluation function is called in Line 18. The result of
the function call is then used to set the final verdict of the test case (Line 19).

3.2 The Inres Example

Fig. 12 shows an MSC test purpose for testing an Initiator implementation of the
Inres protocol [8] with real-time requirements. The Inres system can be accessed
via the PCOs ISAP and MSAP. The functional requirement of the test purpose
is to test 100 data transfers. For doing this, a connection needs to be established.
After the test, the connection has to be released. The real-time requirements of
the test purpose are to test:

1. a latency constraint between the signals IDATreq and MDATind, and
2. a throughput constraint on the loop construct.

When scanning through the given MSC diagram, the RTC-pattern for *latency*
and *throughput with two PCOs* (Section 2.2) can be recognized. The shaded areas
in Fig. 12 show where both patterns are located in the diagram.

In this example, the latency between IDISreq and MDATind shall be evaluated
during the test execution (i.e., online) and the throughput of the loop construct
after the test execution (i.e., offline). The MSC diagram does not define which

```
(1)  module InresRTexampleModule() {
(2)    import all from EvaluationFunctionModule;
(3)    testcase InresRTexample() runs on inres {
(4)      var integer i;
(5)      var float timeBegin, timeEnd;
(6)      var verdicttype myVerdict;
(7)      Connection_Establishment();
(8)      // throughput pattern scheme begin
(9)      log(ThroughputTimestampType:{self.now, "loopBegin"});
(10)     for (i:=0; i<100; i:=i+1) {
(11)       // latency pattern scheme begin
(12)       timeBegin := self.now;
(13)       ISAP.send(IDATreq:{"data"});
(14)       MSAP.receive(MDATind:{DT, number, "data"});
(15)       timeEnd := self.now;
(16)       myVerdict := evalLatencyOnline(timeBegin, timeEnd, 0.001, 0.005);
(17)       setverdict(myVerdict);
(18)       // online evaluation of latency.
(19)       // latency pattern scheme end;
(20)       MSAP.send(MDATreq:{AK, number});
(21)     }
(22)     log(ThroughputTimestampType:{self.now, "loopEnd"});
(23)     // offline evaluation of throughput in control part;
(24)     // throughput pattern scheme end.
(25)     Connection_Release();
(26)     setverdict(pass);
(27)     stop;
(28)   }
(29)   control {
(30)     var testrun myTestrun;
(31)     var logfile myLog;
(32)     var integer i;
(33)     var verdicttype myVerdict;
(34)     myTestrun := execute(InresRTExample);
(35)     myVerdict := myTestrun.getverdict;
(36)     if (myVerdict == pass) {
(37)       myLog := myTestrun.getlog;
(38)       myVerdict := evalThroughputOffline("loopBegin", "loopEnd",
                                 100/1.0, 100/0.1, 100, myLog);
(39)                       // offline evaluation function of throughput
(40)       myTestrun.setverdict(myVerdict);
(41)     }
(42)   }
(43) }
```

Fig. 13. Test case generated from Fig. 12

evaluation mechanism is desired since the MSC language does not provide the possibility to express those kind of requirements. We consider such information as directives for a code generation algorithm.

In the previous section, we have introduced the *TIMED*TTCN-3 code fragments and evaluation functions for online latency and offline throughput requirements (Figures 9, 10 and 11). Now, we shall utilize them in our example.

Fig. 13 shows the *TIMED*TTCN-3 code for the Inres example, which can be generated automatically from the MSC diagram in Fig. 12. The module Inres-RTexampleModule (Fig. 13) imports all evaluation functions and types from the library EvaluationFunctionModule (Line 2). It contains only one test case called InresRTexample (lines 3–28) and the module control part (lines 29–42).

Test case InresRTexample starts with a connection establishment (Line 7). After connection establishment, points in time for the throughput measurement are logged. Analogous to the throughput code fragment, the time value and the event names are stored in the logfile just before the for loop contruct starts and just after it terminates (lines 9 and 22 in Fig. 13). These logged informations are accessed after the test run for the offline evaluation of the throughput requirement.

The online evaluation of latency between the signals IDATind and MDATreq is executed within the test case in lines 12–16. According to the code fragment presented in Section 3.1, the time before and after the time-critical events IDATreq and MDATreq are stored in the variables timeBegin and timeEnd. The evaluation is performed during the test run (Line 16) and the verdict of the test case is set in Line 17.

In the control part (lines 29–42), the throughput evaluation function is invoked. After the test case InresRTExample has been successfully executed regarding its functional behavior (lines 34–36), the logfile is fetched (Line 37) and the offline evaluation function evalThroughputOffline is called (Line 38). The final verdict is set with respect to the outcome of the evaluation function (Line 40).

4   Summary and Outlook

In this paper, MSC-based RTC-patterns for the specification of delay, throughput and periodic real-time requirements of communication systems have been presented. We demonstrated, how test development is eased, since pre-defined *TIMED*TTCN-3 evaluation functions can be associated to each RTC-pattern.

RTC-patterns may also improve the requirements definition and the specification phase of an integrated development methodology for real-time communication systems. For this, the formalisation of instantiation and composition of MSC-based RTC-patterns has to be studied. A formalization is possible due to the formality of MSC. Further investigations on the required MSC extensions, tool support and the usability of such an approach is necessary. Such investigations will be the focus of our future work.

Furthermore, we will implement support for RTC-patterns in our tool, which translates MSC test descriptions into *TIMED*TTCN-3 test cases. This includes also the provision of a library of generic evaluation functions for the RTC-patterns.

References

1. ATM Forum Performance Testing Specification (AF-TEST-TM-0131.000). The ATM Forum Technical Committee, 1999.
2. F. Buschmann, R. Meunier, H. Rohnert, P. Sommerlad, and M. Stal. *Pattern-Oriented Software Architecture – A System of Patterns*. Wiley, 1996.
3. Z.R. Dai, J. Grabowski, and H. Neukirchen. *TIMED*TTCN-3 – A Real-Time Extension for TTCN-3. In I. Schieferdecker, H. König, and A. Wolisz, editors, *Testing of Communicating Systems*, volume 14, Berlin, March 2002. Kluwer.
4. Z.R. Dai, J. Grabowski, and H. Neukirchen. *TIMED*TTCN-3 Based Graphical Real-Time Test Specification. In D. Hogrefe and A. Wiles, editors, *Testing of Communicating Systems*, volume 2644 of *Lecture Notes in Computer Science (LNCS)*. Springer, May 2003.
5. ETSI European Standard (ES) 201 873-1 (2002). The Testing and Test Control Notation version 3; Part 1: TTCN-3 Core Language. European Telecommunications Standards Institute (ETSI), Sophia-Antipolis (France), also published as ITU-T Rec. Z.140.
6. E. Gamma, R. Helm, R. Johnson, and J. Vlissides. *Design Patterns – Elements of Reusable Object-Oriented Software*. Addison Wesley, 1995.
7. B. Geppert. *The SDL Pattern Approach – A Reuse-Driven SDL Methodology for Designing Communication Software Systems*. PhD thesis, University of Kaiserslautern (Germany), July 2001.
8. D. Hogrefe. Report on the Validation of the Inres System. Technical Report IAM-95-007, Universität Bern, November 1995.
9. Request for Comments 1193: Client requirements for real-time communication services. Internet Engineering Task Force (IETF), 1990.
10. Request for Comments 1242: Benchmarking Terminology for Network Interconnection Devices. Internet Engineering Task Force (IETF), July 1991.
11. Request for Comments 3393: IP Packet Delay Varation Metric for IP Performance Metrics (IPPM). Internet Engineering Task Force (IETF), November 2002.
12. ITU-T Rec. Z.100 (1999). Specification and Description Language (SDL). International Telecommunication Union (ITU-T), Geneve.
13. ITU-T Rec. Z.120 (1999). Message Sequence Chart (MSC). International Telecommunication Union (ITU-T), Geneve.
14. H. Neukirchen. Corrections and extensions to Z.120, November 2000. Delayed Contribution No. 9 to ITU-T Study Group 10, Question 9.
15. T. Zheng and F. Khendek. An extension to MSC-2000 and its application. In *Proceedings of the 3rd SAM (SDL and MSC) Workshop*, 2002.

From Safety Verification to Safety Testing

Vlad Rusu, Hervé Marchand, Valéry Tschaen, Thierry Jéron, and
Bertrand Jeannet

IRISA/INRIA Rennes, France
First.Last@irisa.fr

Abstract. A methodology that combines verification and conformance
testing for validating safety requirements of reactive systems is presented.
The requirements are first automatically verified on the system's specification. Then, test cases are automatically derived from the specification
and the requirements, and executed on a black-box implementation of
the system. The test cases attempt to push the implementation into violating a requirement. We show that an implementation conforms to its
specification if and only if it passes all the test cases generated in this
way.

Keywords: verification, conformance testing, safety properties.

1 Introduction

Formal verification and conformance testing are two well-established methods
for validating software systems. In *verification* [14], a formal *specification* of the
system is proved correct with respect to some higher-level *requirements*. In *conformance testing* [10] the external, observable traces of a black-box *implementation* of the system are compared to those of its formal specification, according
to a *conformance relation*. For validating reactive systems (such as communication protocols) the two methods play complementary roles: the former ensures
that the operational specification S meets its requirements R, while the latter
checks that the implementation I of the system conforms to its specification S.
Thus, through verification and testing, a connection between a system's final
implementation and its initial requirements can be established:

1. first, satisfaction of the requirements by the specification is automatically
   verified, e.g., by model checking;
2. then, the user (or a test coverage tool, e.g., the TestComposer module of
   ObjectGeode [16]) produces *test purposes*, which are abstract scenarios to
   be tested on the implementation I;
3. next, a test generation tool, e.g., Autolink [18], TorX [1] or TGV [11] uses
   the test purposes to generate test cases from the specification;
4. finally, the test cases are executed on the implementation I, and verdicts are
   issued regarding its conformance with the specification.

R. Groz and R.M. Hierons (Eds.): TestCom 2004, LNCS 2978, pp. 160–176, 2004.
© IFIP 2004

This validation process corresponds to the current state-of-the-art use of formal methods in the telecom world [2]. The main problem with this process is that it does not guarantee that what is being tested on the implementation of the system (at Step 4) are the same requirements that have been verified to hold on the specification (at Step 1).

This is because the test generation step (Step 3) uses *test purposes*, which are a pragmatic means (actually, an essential one) to achieve test generation; but test purposes are typically written (at Step 2) independently of the requirements, that is, there is no *formal* connection between the test purposes and the requirements. If some crucial safety requirement is missed by all the test purposes, the final implementation may violate that requirement, and this violation remains undetected.

In this paper we propose a methodology to integrate verification and conformance testing into a seamless, sound validation process between *safety* requirements, specification, and implementation. The above validation process is then reformulated as follows: Step 1 is standard verification; Step 2 may be skipped (there is no need here to write test purposes by hand, but, of course, this is not forbidden either); Step 3 is a test generation algorithm that takes the specification and a safety requirement, and produces a test case for checking the requirement on the implementation; and Step 4 is standard conformance test execution.

Framework. The specification is given by IOLTS (Input-Output Labeled Transition Systems, i.e., finite, labeled transition systems with inputs, outputs, and internal actions). The requirements express safety properties on observable behaviors of the specification and are described by means of a particular class of IOLTS: *observers*, which enter a dedicated "*Violate*" location when the property is violated. Finally, the conformance relation between a black-box implementation and a specification is **ioco**, a standard relation used in conformance testing [19], which requires that after each visible trace of the specification, the observed outputs and blockings of the implementation are among those allowed by the specification.

Results. The meaning of requirement *relevant* for a specification is formally defined in the paper. We prove that an implementation conforms to a specification if and only if it satisfies all the relevant safety requirements that are also satisfied by the specification. This result is interesting because it establishes a formal connection between conformance and property satisfaction. However, it does not say how to actually check the safety requirements on the implementation. Moreover, the result is restricted to *relevant* requirements.

Hence, we propose a test generation algorithm, which takes a specification and a safety requirement (relevant or not), and produces a test case that, when executed on an implementation, attempts to push the implementation into violating the requirement. It is shown that an implementation conforms to a specification if and only if it passes all the test cases generated by the proposed algorithm.

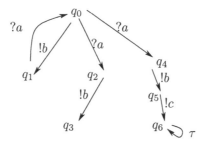

Fig. 1. Example of IOLTS $\mathcal{S}$

The rest of the paper is organized as follows. In Section 2, the main concepts from verification and conformance testing are recalled. In Section 3, the notion of a safety property *relevant* to a specification is defined, and a result that connects conformance testing and satisfaction of relevant safety properties is proved. In Section 4, the previous result is extended to take into account arbitrary safety properties. This directly induces a sound and complete test generation algorithm for checking safety properties on the implementation. We conclude in Section 5.

2   Verification and Conformance Testing

Definition 1 (IOLTS). *An IOLTS is a tuple $M = (Q, A, \rightarrow, q_0)$ where Q is a finite, non-empty set of states; $q_0 \in Q$ is the initial state; $\rightarrow \subseteq Q \times A \times Q$ is the transition relation; and A is a finite alphabet of actions, partitioned into three sets $A = A_? \cup A_! \cup I$, where $A_?$ is the set of input actions, $A_!$ is the set of output actions, and I is the set of internal actions.*

The actions in $A_? \cup A_!$ are also called *visible actions*. In the examples, a question mark placed before the name of an action (as in "$?a$") denotes the fact that a is an input $a \in A_?$. An exclamation mark (as in "$!b$") denotes an output $b \in A_!$. Internal actions are generically denoted by τ.

Example 1. The IOLTS depicted in Figure 1 describes a simple nondeterministic system. In the initial state q_0, the system can either spontaneously emit $!b$ and block itself waiting in state q_1 for an $?a$; or directly wait for an $?a$ in q_0 and then, nondeterministically go to either q_2 or q_4. In q_2, the system may only emit $!b$ and deadlock in q_3, while in q_4, $!b$ then $!c$ are emitted, followed by a loop of internal actions (a livelock).

2.1   Notations and Basic Definitions

Let $M = (Q, A, \rightarrow, q_0)$ be an IOLTS. The notation $q \xrightarrow{a} q'$ stands for $(q, a, q') \in \rightarrow$ and $q \xrightarrow{a}$ for $\exists q' : q \xrightarrow{a} q'$. An IOLTS is sometimes identified with its initial state, i.e., we write $M \rightarrow$ for $q_0 \rightarrow$. Let $\mu_i \in A$ denote some actions, $a_i \in A \setminus I$ some visible actions, $\tau_i \in I$ some internal actions, $\sigma \in (A \setminus I)^*$ a sequence of visible actions, $q, q' \in Q$ some states.

- We write $q \xrightarrow{\mu_1 \cdots \mu_n} q'$ for $\exists q_0, \ldots, q_n : q = q_0 \xrightarrow{\mu_1} q_1 \xrightarrow{\mu_2} \cdots \xrightarrow{\mu_n} q_n = q'$.
- The notation $\Gamma(q)$ stands for $\{\mu \in A \mid q \xrightarrow{\mu}\}$, i.e., the set of fireable actions in q. Similarly $\Gamma^{-1}(q)$ denotes the set $\{\mu \in A \mid \exists q'.q' \xrightarrow{\mu} q\}$.
- Visible behaviors are described by the $\Rightarrow$ relation, defined by $q \xRightarrow{\varepsilon} q' \triangleq q = q'$ or $q \xrightarrow{\tau_1 \cdot \tau_2 \cdots \tau_n} q'$ and $q \xRightarrow{a} q' \triangleq \exists q_1, q_2 : q \xRightarrow{\varepsilon} q_1 \xrightarrow{a} q_2 \xRightarrow{\varepsilon} q'$. We also write $q \xRightarrow{a_1 \cdots a_n} q'$ for $\exists q_0, \ldots, q_n : q = q_0 \xRightarrow{a_1} q_1 \cdots \xRightarrow{a_n} q_n = q'$
- $Traces(q) \triangleq \{\sigma \in (A \setminus I)^* \mid q \xRightarrow{\sigma}\}$ (resp. $Traces(M) \triangleq Traces(q_0)$) denotes the sequences of visible actions that are fireable from a state q (resp. from the initial state of the IOLTS M).
- For $q \in Q$ and a trace $\sigma \in Traces(q)$, we denote by q after $\sigma \triangleq \{q' \in Q \mid q \xRightarrow{\sigma} q'\}$ (resp. P after $\sigma \triangleq \bigcup_{q \in P} q$ after σ) the set of states that are reachable from the state q (resp. from the set of states P) by sequences of actions whose projection onto visible actions is σ.
- For $q \in Q$, $Out(q) \triangleq \Gamma(q) \cap A_!$ is the set of fireable outputs in q. This notion is naturally extended to sets of states: for $P \subseteq Q$, $Out(P) \triangleq \bigcup_{q \in P} Out(q)$. Likewise, $In(q)$ (resp. $In(P)$) denote the set of fireable inputs in $q \in Q$ (resp. in $P \subseteq Q$).
- Finally, an IOLTS M is *input-complete* whenever $\forall q \in Q$, $In(q$ after $\epsilon) = A_?$, that is, in each state, all inputs are accepted, possibly after a sequence of internal actions (here, ϵ denotes the empty trace).

Based on the previous notations we introduce some common definitions.

Definition 2 (Deterministic IOLTS). *An IOLTS M is* deterministic *if $I^M = \emptyset$, and for all $q, q', q'' \in Q^M$ and $a \in A^M$, $q \xrightarrow{a} q'$ and $q \xrightarrow{a} q''$ imply $q' = q''$.*

Given an arbitrary IOLTS M, one can construct a deterministic IOLTS $det(M)$ with the same visible behavior, i.e., $Traces(M) = Traces(det(M))$.

Definition 3 (Determinization). *The* deterministic IOLTS *of an IOLTS $M = (Q, A, \rightarrow, q_0)$ is $det(M) = (2^Q, A \setminus I, \rightarrow_d, q_0$ after $\varepsilon)$, whose transition relation $\rightarrow_d$ is the smallest relation defined by: $P \xrightarrow{a}_d P'$ if $P' = P$ after a.*

The *synchronous composition* of two IOLTS performs synchronization on their common visible actions and lets them evolve independently by internal actions:

Definition 4 (Synchronous composition). *Let $M_i = (Q_i, A^i, \rightarrow_i, q^i_o)$, $i = 1, 2$ be two IOLTS, with I_i the internal actions of M_i. The synchronous composition $M_1 \parallel M_2$ of M_1 and M_2 is an IOLTS $(Q, A, \rightarrow, q_o)$ such that:*

- $Q = Q^1 \times Q^2$, $q_o = (q^1_o, q^2_o)$, $A = A^1 \cap A^2 \cup (I^1 \cup I^2)$
- $\rightarrow$ *is the smallest relation in $Q \times A \times Q$ satisfying*

$$(q_1, q_2) \xrightarrow{a} \begin{cases} (q'_1, q'_2) \text{ if } a \in A \setminus (I^1 \cup I^2) \ \wedge \ q_1 \xrightarrow{a}_1 q'_1 \ \wedge \ q_2 \xrightarrow{a}_2 q'_2 \\ (q'_1, q_2) \text{ if } a \in I^1 \ \wedge \ q_1 \xrightarrow{a}_1 q'_1 \\ (q_1, q'_2) \text{ if } a \in I^2 \ \wedge \ q_2 \xrightarrow{a}_2 q'_2 \end{cases}$$

It is not hard to show that $Traces(M_1 \parallel M_2) = Traces(M_1) \cap Traces(M_2)$.

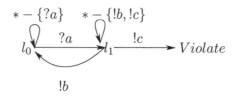

Fig. 2. Sample observer. For $A \subseteq A^\omega$, the notation $* - A$ is a shortcut for $A^\omega \setminus A$.

2.2 Verification of Safety Properties

The verification problem considered here is : given a reactive system M and a property ψ, does M satisfy ψ ($M \models \psi$)? We model properties using observers, which are a particular class of IOLTS.

Definition 5 (Observer). *An observer for an IOLTS M is a deterministic IOLTS $\omega = (Q^\omega, A^\omega, \rightarrow_\omega, q_0^\omega)$ such that $A^\omega = A^M \setminus I^M$, and there exists a unique state $Violate_\omega \in Q^\omega \setminus \{q_0^\omega\}$ such that $\Gamma^{-1}(Violate_\omega) \subseteq A_!^M$ and $\Gamma(Violate_\omega) = \emptyset$. Its language is $\mathcal{L}(\omega) = \{\sigma \in (A^\omega)^* \mid q_0^\omega \xrightarrow{\sigma}_\omega Violate_\omega\}$.*

An observer expresses the negation of a safety property on the visible behavior of a system. The *Violate* state is entered when the system emits an undesired output. We note that Definition 5 matches the class of Büchi automata obtained from negations of LTL safety formulas [13], except for the self-loop on the *Violate* accepting state, and for the propositions labelling transitions (rather than states).

Example 2. Consider the property: between each $?a$ and $!c$, there must be at least one $!b$. The negation of this property is expressed by the observer depicted in Figure 2. Here, an action $?a$ followed by a $!c$ goes to the Violate location, meaning that the property was violated as there has been no $!b$ between $?a$ and $!c$. However, if $!b$ occurs after $?a$, the property cannot be violated unless another $?a$ occurs, hence, the observer goes back to its initial location to wait for another $?a$.

Let $\Omega(M)$ denote the (infinite) set of observers for an IOLTS M. The following definition formalizes the *satisfaction* of $\omega \in \Omega(M)$ by M:

Definition 6 (Satisfaction relation). *An IOLTS M satisfies an observer $\omega \in \Omega(M)$, denoted $\mathcal{S} \models \omega$, if and only if $Traces(M) \cap \mathcal{L}(\omega) = \emptyset$.*

$M \models \omega$ holds whenever no state $(q, Violate_\omega)$ with $q \in Q^M$ is reachable in $M \parallel \omega$.

Example 3. The IOLTS $\mathcal{S}$ depicted in Figure 1 satisfies the observer ω depicted in Figure 2. Indeed, there is no way that in $\mathcal{S}$ an $?a$ can be directly followed by $!c$ without $!b$ occurring in between. As these are the only traces that may lead to Violate in ω, we conclude that $\mathcal{S} \models \omega$.

2.3   Conformance Testing

The goal of conformance testing is to establish whether a black-box implementation $\mathcal{I}$ conforms to its formal specification $\mathcal{S}$. In our framework, the specification is given by an IOLTS $\mathcal{S} = (Q^s, A^s, \rightarrow_s, q_0^s)$. The implementation $\mathcal{I}$ is not a formal object (it is a physical system) but, in order to reason about conformance, it is necessary to assume that the behavior of $\mathcal{I}$ can be modeled by a formal object in the same class as the specification and having a *compatible interface* with it, i.e., having the same set of visible actions. Moreover, the implementation can never refuse an input from the environment (it is *input-complete*).

These assumptions are called *test hypothesis* in conformance testing [19]. Thus, the implementation is modeled by an input-complete IOLTS $\mathcal{I} = (Q^{\mathcal{I}}, A^{\mathcal{I}}, \rightarrow_{\mathcal{I}}, q_0^{\mathcal{I}})$ with $A^{\mathcal{I}} = A_?^{\mathcal{I}} \cup A_!^{\mathcal{I}} \cup I^{\mathcal{I}}$, $A_?^s = A_?^{\mathcal{I}}$, and $A_!^s = A_!^{\mathcal{I}}$.

Quiescence: The tester observes not only responses of the implementation, but also *absence of response* (i.e., in a given state, the implementation does not emit any output for the tester to observe). This is called *quiescence* in conformance testing. There are three possible reasons for quiescence:

- A *deadlock* state is a state where the system cannot evolve: $\Gamma(q) = \emptyset$.
- An *output quiescent* state is a state where the system is waiting only for an input from the environment, i.e. $\Gamma(q) \subseteq A_?$.
- A *livelock* state is a state from which the system diverges by an infinite sequence of internal actions. In the case of finite state systems that we consider, a livelock is a loop of internal actions, i.e., $\exists \tau_1, \ldots \tau_n, q \overset{\tau_1 \cdots \tau_n}{\rightarrow} q$.

In practice, quiescence is observed using timers : a timer is reset whenever the tester sends a stimulus to the implementation; when the timer expires, the tester observes quiescence. It is assumed that the timer is set to a value large enough such it only expires only when no response will ever occur.

At the model level, however, quiescence is materialized by adding a special output action δ that manifests itself in quiescent states [19].

Definition 7 (Suspension IOLTS). *The* suspension IOLTS *of an IOLTS $\mathcal{S} = (Q, A, \rightarrow, q_0)$ is an IOLTS $\mathcal{S}^\delta = (Q^\delta, A^\delta, \rightarrow_\delta, q_0^\delta)$ with $Q^\delta = Q$, $q_0^\delta = q_0$, $A^\delta = A \cup \{\delta\}$ and $\delta \in A_!^\delta$ (δ is an output of $\mathcal{S}^\delta$). The transition relation of $\mathcal{S}^\delta$ is $\rightarrow_\delta = \rightarrow \cup \{q \overset{\delta}{\rightarrow} q | q$ is quiescent$\}$. The traces of $\mathcal{S}^\delta$ are the* suspension traces *of $\mathcal{S}$.*

Example 4. For $\mathcal{S}$ depicted in Fig. 1, q_3 is a deadlock, q_1 is an output-lock, and q_6 is a livelock. $\mathcal{S}^\delta$ (cf. Fig. 3) is obtained by adding a δ-labeled self-loop to them.

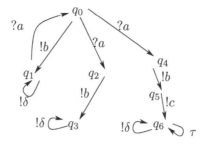

Fig. 3. The suspension IOLTS $\mathcal{S}^\delta$ for the IOLTS $\mathcal{S}$ depicted in Figure 1

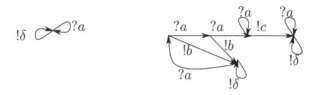

Fig. 4. Suspension IOLTS of Implementations $\mathcal{I}_1$ and $\mathcal{I}_2$ from Example 5.

Conformance relation. A *conformance relation* formalizes the set of implementations that behave consistently with a specification. Here, we use the classical **ioco** relation defined by Tretmans [19]. Intuitively, an implementation $\mathcal{I}$ **ioco**-conforms to its specification $\mathcal{S}$, if, after each suspension trace of $\mathcal{S}$, the implementation only exhibits outputs and quiescences that are possible in $\mathcal{S}$. Formally:

Definition 8 (Conformance). *For IOLTS $\mathcal{S}, \mathcal{I}$ such that $\mathcal{I}$ is interface compatible with $\mathcal{S}$, $\mathcal{I}$ **ioco** $\mathcal{S} \triangleq \forall \sigma \in Traces(\mathcal{S}^\delta), Out(\mathcal{I}^\delta \, after \, \sigma) \subseteq Out(\mathcal{S}^\delta \, after \, \sigma)$.*

Remember that the black-box implementation $\mathcal{I}$ is assumed to be input-complete, but the specification $\mathcal{S}$ is not necessarily so. Hence, in this framework, the specification is *partial* with respect to inputs, i.e., after an input that is not described by the specification, the implementation may have any behavior, without violating conformance to the specification. This corresponds to the intuition that a specification models a minimal set of services that must be provided by a system. A particular implementation of the system may include more services than what is specified, but these services should not influence conformance to the specification.

Example 5. First, consider the implementation $\mathcal{I}_1$ whose suspension IOLTS is depicted in Figure 4 (left), which only accepts inputs $?a$ and emits no outputs but quiescence. For $\mathcal{S}$ depicted in Figure 1, $\mathcal{I}_1$ **ioco** $\mathcal{S}$ does not hold, because quiescence is not allowed initially in the suspension IOLTS $\mathcal{S}^\delta$ (Figure 3). On the other hand, the implementation $\mathcal{I}_2$ whose suspension IOLTS is depicted in

Figure 4 (right) does conform to $\mathcal{S}$: the first divergence between $\mathcal{I}_2^\delta$ and $\mathcal{S}^\delta$ is on the second input ?a in line, which does not violate conformance.

The mechanism for testing the conformance of an implementation with its specification consists in generating *test cases* from the specification, and running them in parallel with the implementation to detect non-conformances between the two representations of the system. Test cases are essentially deterministic, input-complete IOLTS. In Section 4 we show how to generate test cases from the specification using observers for safety properties, in order to test both the satisfaction of the properties by the implementation and its conformance to the specification.

Example 6. To see why it is important to extract test cases from the specification, consider a tester that initially stimulates the implementation $\mathcal{I}_1$ from Example 5 using two consecutive ?a actions. This behavior does not belong to the specification $\mathcal{S}$, which only allows one ?a initially (cf. Fig 1). Although $\mathcal{I}_1$ ioco $\mathcal{S}$ does not hold, this particular tester cannot observe it, because it has forced the implementation to diverge from the specification by the second ?a. When this happens, the implementation is free to do anything without violating the conformance.

3   Connecting Conformance and Property Satisfaction

In this section we establish a relation between conformance ($\mathcal{I}$ **ioco** $\mathcal{S}$) and the satisfaction of safety properties by the specification and the implementation ($\mathcal{S} \models \omega, \mathcal{I} \models \omega$). Properties are expressed using observers $\omega \in \Omega(\mathcal{S})$. Remember that a specification $\mathcal{S}$ is a *partial* specification in the sense defined in Section 2.3: the specification does not say what happens after an unspecified input. Hence, an observer is *relevant* for a specification $\mathcal{S}$ if it may only diverge from $\mathcal{S}$ by outputs:

Definition 9 (Relevant observer). *An observer $\omega \in \Omega(M)$ is relevant for M if $\mathcal{L}(\omega) \subseteq Traces(M) \cdot A_!^M$. The set of relevant observers for M is denoted $\varrho(M)$.*

Example 7. The observer ω depicted in Figure 2 is not relevant for the specification $\mathcal{S}$ depicted in Figure 1. This is because ω accepts arbitrarily many ?a's initially, while $\mathcal{S}$ accepts only one. Intuitively, ω is not relevant because it says something about behaviors that diverge from $\mathcal{S}$ through an unspecified input.

Relevant observers play an essential role in Theorem 1 below, which establishes a relation between conformance testing and property satisfaction.

To prove Theorem 1 the following technical lemma will be employed.

Lemma 1. *For A, B, C arbitrary sets, $\forall x \in A.(x \notin B \Rightarrow x \notin C)$ implies $(A \cap B = \emptyset \Rightarrow A \cap C = \emptyset)$.*

Theorem 1. *For all IOLTS $\mathcal{I}, \mathcal{S}$: $\mathcal{I}$ ioco $\mathcal{S} \Leftrightarrow \forall w \in \varrho(\mathcal{S}^\delta). \ \mathcal{S}^\delta \models w \Rightarrow \mathcal{I}^\delta \models w.$*

Proof : ($\Rightarrow$): $\mathcal{I}$ ioco $\mathcal{S}$ is $\forall \sigma \in Traces(\mathcal{S}^\delta).Out(\mathcal{I}^\delta \, after \, \sigma) \subseteq Out(\mathcal{S}^\delta \, after \, \sigma)$
(Definition 8). By definition of $Out(\mathcal{S}^\delta \, after \, \sigma)$, $Out(\mathcal{I}^\delta \, after \, \sigma)$ (cf. Section 2.1):

$$\forall \sigma \in Traces(\mathcal{S}^\delta), \forall a \in A_!^{\mathcal{S}^\delta}. \ \sigma \cdot a \in Traces(\mathcal{I}^\delta) \Longrightarrow \sigma \cdot a \in Traces(\mathcal{S}^\delta)$$

which is clearly equivalent to

$$\forall \sigma \in Traces(\mathcal{S}^\delta), \forall a \in A_!^{\mathcal{S}^\delta}. \ \sigma \cdot a \notin Traces(\mathcal{S}^\delta) \Longrightarrow \sigma \cdot a \notin Traces(\mathcal{I}^\delta) \quad (1)$$

Now, consider an arbitrary relevant observer $w \in \varrho(\mathcal{S}^\delta)$. By Definition 9, all the sequences $\sigma' \in \mathcal{L}(w)$ are of the form $\sigma' = \sigma \cdot a$, where $\sigma \in Traces(\mathcal{S}^\delta)$ and $a \in A_!^{\mathcal{S}^\delta}$. Hence, the implication (1) can be rewritten equivalently as

$$\forall w \in \varrho(\mathcal{S}^\delta). \forall \sigma' \in \mathcal{L}(w). \ \sigma' \notin Traces(\mathcal{S}^\delta) \Longrightarrow \sigma' \notin Traces(\mathcal{I}^\delta) \quad (2)$$

Using Lemma 1 with $A = \mathcal{L}(w)$, $B = Traces(\mathcal{S}^\delta)$, $C = Traces(\mathcal{I}^\delta)$, we obtain

$$\forall w \in \varrho(\mathcal{S}^\delta). \mathcal{L}(w) \cap Traces(\mathcal{S}^\delta) = \emptyset \Longrightarrow \mathcal{L}(w) \cap Traces(\mathcal{I}^\delta) = \emptyset \quad (3)$$

which, by Definition 6 is $\forall w \in \varrho(\mathcal{S}^\delta). \ \mathcal{S}^\delta \models w \Rightarrow \mathcal{I}^\delta \models w$: this direction is done.
($\Leftarrow$) Assume $\neg(\mathcal{I}ioco \, \mathcal{S})$. We prove that there exists a relevant observer $w \in \varrho(\mathcal{S}^\delta)$ such that $\mathcal{S}^\delta \models w$ but $\mathcal{I}^\delta \not\models w$. This leads to a contradiction and completes the proof. To build w, from $\neg(\mathcal{I}$ ioco $\mathcal{S})$ we obtain that there exists a sequence of the form $\sigma \cdot a$ with $a \in A_!^{\mathcal{S}^\delta}$ such that $\sigma \in Traces(\mathcal{S}^\delta)$, $a \in Out(\mathcal{I}^\delta \, after \, \sigma)$ but $a \notin Out(\mathcal{S}^\delta \, after \, \sigma)$. Let w be an observer such that $\mathcal{L}(w) = \{\sigma \cdot a\}$.
    Then, clearly, w is relevant for $\mathcal{S}^\delta$ as $\mathcal{L}(w) \subseteq Traces(\mathcal{S}^\delta) \cdot A_!^{\mathcal{S}^\delta}$. Also, $\mathcal{S}^\delta \models w$ as $a \notin Out(\mathcal{S}^\delta \, after \, \sigma)$, therefore, $\sigma \cdot a \notin Traces(\mathcal{S}^\delta)$, i.e., $\mathcal{L}(w) \cap Traces(\mathcal{S}^\delta) = \emptyset$; and $\mathcal{I}^\delta \not\models w$ as $a \in Out(\mathcal{I}^\delta \, after \, \sigma)$ and therefore $\sigma \cdot a \in Traces(\mathcal{I}^\delta) \cap \mathcal{L}(w) \neq \emptyset$. Hence, the observer w is relevant for $\mathcal{S}^\delta$, $\mathcal{S}^\delta \models w$, and $\mathcal{I}^\delta \not\models w$: the proof is done.$\square$

Interpretation. Theorem 1 can be interpreted as follows: an implementation $\mathcal{I}$ **ioco**-conforms to its specification $\mathcal{S}$ if, whenever $\mathcal{S}^\delta$ satisfies a relevant safety property, $\mathcal{I}^\delta$ satisfies it as well. Hence, in order to establish conformance, it is enough to prove that all relevant safety properties satisfied by the specification are also satisfied by the implementation. This is a completeness result, which is impossible to achieve in practice because there may be infinitely many relevant properties that hold on a specification.
    On the other hand, Theorem 1 also says that, to detect conformance violation, it is enough to exhibit one relevant property that is satisfied by the specification, but violated by the implementation. This a soundness result and is achievable in practice. However, it does not say how to actually check the violation of the property by the implementation (the observer is not a test case, for example, it is not necessarily input-complete) and, more importantly, it is limited to properties expressed by observers that are relevant to the specification.

These limitations are raised in Section 4. We conclude this section by an example showing that the *relevance* hypothesis is essential for Theorem 1 to hold.

Example 8. *Consider the observer ω, which was shown in Example 7 to be irrelevant for $\mathcal{S}$ (Fig. 1). For the same reason, ω is irrelevant for $\mathcal{S}^\delta$ (Fig.3). Consider now implementation $\mathcal{I}_2$ whose suspension IOLTS is depicted in Figure 4. We have shown in Example 5 that $\mathcal{I}_2$* **ioco** *$\mathcal{S}$, and in Example 1 that $\mathcal{S}^\delta \models \omega$, but clearly, $\mathcal{I}_2^\delta \not\models \omega$ because $\mathcal{I}_2^\delta$ admits a !c directly after an ?a. That is, except for its irrelevance, the observer ω falsifies Theorem 1.*

4   Test Generation from Safety Requirements

This section shows how to generate test cases from a specification using a safety requirement as a guide. Intuitively, such a test case guides the implementation, and attempts to "push" it into violating the requirement.

It should be clear from the previous examples that writing a relevant requirement for a given specification (in the sense of Definition 9) is not always easy. For example, the requirement expressed by the observer ω from Examples 2 to 8 is a natural (and true) property of $\mathcal{S}$, but it is nevertheless irrelevant for $\mathcal{S}$.

However, when an observer as a whole is irrelevant for a given specification, a subset the observer of it may still be relevant. For example, the sequence $?a\cdot!c \in \mathcal{L}(\omega)$ is in $Traces(\mathcal{S}^\delta) \cdot A_!^{\mathcal{S}^\delta}$, i.e., it is relevant for $\mathcal{S}^\delta$ in the sense of Definition 9.

Hence, we need a test generation algorithm that takes a specification $\mathcal{S}$ and an *arbitrary* requirement $\omega \in \Omega(\mathcal{S})$, and automatically sorts out from ω what is relevant for $\mathcal{S}$ and what is not. This is done by the following operation.

Definition 10 (Forcing). Let $M = (Q^M, A^M, \rightarrow_M, q_0^M)$ be a deterministic IOLTS and $\omega = (Q^\omega, A^\omega, \rightarrow_\omega, q_0^\omega)$ an observer for M. The forcing of M by ω, denoted $M \triangleright \omega$, is an IOLTS $(Q^\triangleright, A^\triangleright, \rightarrow_\triangleright, q_o^\triangleright)$ such that

- the set of states $Q^\triangleright$ is $(Q^M \times Q^\omega) \cup \{Violate, Fail\}$, where $Violate, Fail \notin Q^M \times Q^\omega$
- the initial state $q^\triangleright{}_o$ is (q_0^M, q_0^ω)
- the alphabet $A^\triangleright$ is A^M (same partitioning between inputs and outputs)
- the transition relation $\rightarrow_\triangleright$ of $Q^\triangleright$ is the smallest relation defined as follows. For all states $(p, q) \in Q^\triangleright$ and action $a \in A^\triangleright$:

  - if $p \xrightarrow{a}_M p'$, $q \xrightarrow{a}_\omega q'$ then $(p, q) \xrightarrow{a}_\triangleright (p', q')$ [α]
  - if $a \in A_!$, $p \not\xrightarrow{a}_M$, $q \xrightarrow{a}_\omega Violate_\omega$ then $(p, q) \xrightarrow{a}_\triangleright Violate$ [β]
  - if $a \in A_!$, $p \not\xrightarrow{a}_M$, $\neg(q \xrightarrow{a}_\omega Violate_\omega)$, then $(p, q) \xrightarrow{a}_\triangleright Fail$.   [$\gamma$]

Example 9. *For the IOLTS $\mathcal{S}^\delta$ depicted in Figure 1 and ω depicted in Fig. 4, the IOLTS $det(\mathcal{S}^\delta) \triangleright \omega$ is depicted in Figure 4 (note that $\omega \in \Omega(det(\mathcal{S}^\delta))$). For better readability, the Violate and Fail locations have been duplicated.*

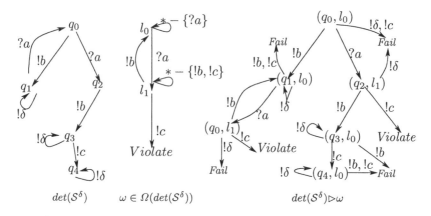

$$det(\mathcal{S}^\delta) \qquad \omega \in \Omega(det(\mathcal{S}^\delta)) \qquad det(\mathcal{S}^\delta) \triangleright \omega$$

Fig. 5. The $\triangleright$ operation between $det(\mathcal{S}^\delta)$ and ω

Definition 10 deserves some comments. The forcing operation performs synchronization on visible actions whenever it is possible (line $[\alpha]$). However, for each *output a* that is not allowed by the specification M, $M \triangleright \omega$ performs this output anyway. Intuitively, this is because the forcing operation is the first step towards test case generation, and the test cases are executed in parallel with an implementation $\mathcal{I}$ of the system to detect property violation and/or non-conformance:

– If the output a is not allowed by the specification M and leads the observer ω into its *Violate$_\omega$* state, then $M \triangleright \omega$ goes into its *Violate* state as well - cf. line $[\beta]$. If this happens when running $M \triangleright \omega$ in parallel with an implementation $\mathcal{I}$, this means that $\mathcal{I}$ violates both the conformance to M and the property defined by ω. This is formalized by Theorem 2 below.
– if the output a is not allowed by M but does not lead the observer into its *Violate$_\omega$* state (line $[\gamma]$), then $M \triangleright \omega$ goes into its *Fail* state. If this happens when running $M \triangleright \omega$ in parallel with an implementation $\mathcal{I}$, then $\mathcal{I}$ violates the conformance to M (but does not necessarily violate the property defined by ω). This is formalized by Theorem 3.

Note that if M is a deterministic IOLTS and $\omega \in \Omega(M)$, then $M \triangleright \omega$ is an observer for M as well, i.e., $M \triangleright \omega$ satisfies all the conditions of Definition 5. In particular, its language $\mathcal{L}(M \triangleright \omega)$ is defined. The following lemma characterizes this language.

Lemma 2. *For IOLTS M and $\omega \in \Omega(M)$, $\mathcal{L}(M \triangleright \omega) = \mathcal{L}(\omega) \cap [Traces(M) \cdot A_!^M]$.*

Proof : We prove for an arbitrary sequence $\sigma \in (A^M)^*$ that $\sigma \in \mathcal{L}(M \triangleright \omega)$ iff $\sigma \in \mathcal{L}(\omega) \cap [Traces(M) \cdot A_!^M]$.

First, by Definition 5, a sequence σ that belongs to either of these sets cannot be empty, because *Violate* cannot be the initial state of an observer.

Then, $\sigma = \sigma' \cdot a \in \mathcal{L}(M \triangleright \omega)$ iff a is an output that has been forced to go to *Violate* in $M \triangleright \omega$ by rule $[\beta]$ of Definition 10. But, by the same rule, this happens if and only if $\sigma \in \mathcal{L}(\omega)$ and $\sigma' \in Traces(M)$, i.e., $\sigma \in \mathcal{L}(\omega) \cap [Traces(M) \cdot A_!^M]$.   □

Lemma 2 says that $M \triangleright \omega$ is a relevant observer for M (it actually says that $M \triangleright \omega$ defines the strongest safety requirement weaker than ω and relevant for M).

Theorem 2 below is a refinement of Theorem 1, obtained by dropping the *relevance* hypothesis for the observer. Its proof invokes Theorem 1 and Lemma 2.

Theorem 2. *Let $\mathcal{I}$ and $\mathcal{S}$ be two IOLTS, then*
$$\mathcal{I} \text{ ioco } \mathcal{S} \iff \forall \omega \in \Omega(\mathcal{S}^\delta).\mathcal{S}^\delta \models \omega \Rightarrow \mathcal{I}^\delta \models (det(\mathcal{S}^\delta) \triangleright \omega).$$

Proof : ($\Rightarrow$) Assume $\mathcal{I}$ **ioco** $\mathcal{S}$ and let ω be an arbitrary observer in $\Omega(\mathcal{S})$ such that $\mathcal{S}^\delta \models \omega$. Thus, $Traces(\mathcal{S}^\delta) \cap \mathcal{L}(\omega) = \emptyset$, which implies $Traces(\mathcal{S}^\delta) \cap \mathcal{L}(\omega) \cap [Traces(\mathcal{S}^\delta) \cdot A_!^{\mathcal{S}^\delta}] = \emptyset$, which, by Lemma 2 is just $\mathcal{S}^\delta \models (det(\mathcal{S}^\delta) \triangleright \omega)$.

Still by Lemma 2 we know that $det(\mathcal{S}^\delta) \triangleright \omega$ is a relevant observer for $\mathcal{S}^\delta$. Then, using Theorem 1 we obtain: $\mathcal{S}^\delta \models (det(\mathcal{S}^\delta) \triangleright \omega) \Rightarrow \mathcal{I}^\delta \models (det(\mathcal{S}^\delta) \triangleright \omega)$.

By transitivity of $\Rightarrow$, we have $\mathcal{I}^\delta \models (det(\mathcal{S}^\delta) \triangleright \omega)$, and this direction is done.

($\Leftarrow$): Assume $\forall \omega \in \Omega(\mathcal{S}^\delta).\mathcal{S}^\delta \models \omega \Rightarrow \mathcal{I}^\delta \models (det(\mathcal{S}^\delta) \triangleright \omega)$. Then, in particular, we have that this implication is true for all *relevant* observers $\omega \in \varrho(\mathcal{S}^\delta)$, that is, $\forall \omega \in \varrho(\mathcal{S}^\delta).\mathcal{S}^\delta \models \omega \Rightarrow \mathcal{I}^\delta \models (det(\mathcal{S}^\delta) \triangleright \omega)$. However, by Lemma 2, $\mathcal{I}^\delta \models (det(\mathcal{S}^\delta) \triangleright \omega)$ implies $Traces(\mathcal{I}^\delta) \cap \mathcal{L}(\omega) \cap [Traces(\mathcal{S}^\delta) \cdot A_!^{\mathcal{S}^\delta}] = \emptyset$, and, by Definition 9, $\mathcal{L}(\omega) \subseteq [Traces(\mathcal{S}^\delta) \cdot A_!^{\mathcal{S}^\delta}]$. Hence, we have $Traces(\mathcal{I}^\delta) \cap \mathcal{L}(\omega) = \emptyset$, which implies $\mathcal{I}^\delta \models \omega$.

We have obtained that, for all *relevant* observers $\omega \in \varrho(\mathcal{S}^\delta)$, $\mathcal{S}^\delta \models \omega \Rightarrow \mathcal{I}^\delta \models \omega$ holds. By Theorem 1, we obtain $\mathcal{I}$ **ioco** $\mathcal{S}$, and the proof is done.   □

Interpretation. For observers ω that represent *true* safety properties of a specification $\mathcal{S}$, whenever $det(\mathcal{S}^\delta) \triangleright \omega$ enters its *Violate* state when executed in parallel with an implementation $\mathcal{I}$, then $\mathcal{I}$ violates both the safety property defined by ω (cf. Lemma 2) and the conformance to the specification (cf. Theorem 2).

Hence, $det(\mathcal{S}^\delta) \triangleright \omega$ is the basis for a potentially interesting test case. When it enters its *Violate* state, the implementation will be assigned the **Violate** verdict:

> **Violate:** The implementation violates both the property and the conformance

We now consider the situation when $det(\mathcal{S}^\delta) \triangleright \omega$ enters its *Fail* state.

Theorem 3. *For IOLTS $\mathcal{I}$, $\mathcal{S}$ and $\omega \in \Omega(\mathcal{S}^\delta)$, if there exists $\sigma \in Traces(\mathcal{I}^\delta) \cap Traces(det(\mathcal{S}^\delta) \triangleright \omega)$ such that Fail $\in (det(\mathcal{S}^\delta) \triangleright \omega)$ after σ, then $\neg(\mathcal{I}$ ioco $\mathcal{S})$.*

Proof : By Definition 10 line $[\gamma]$, *Fail* $\in (det(\mathcal{S}^\delta) \triangleright \omega)$ *after* σ means that $\sigma = \sigma'a$, where a is an output ($a \in A_!$) which is not fireable in $det(\mathcal{S}^\delta)$ after the sequence σ', i.e., $a \notin Out(\mathcal{S}^\delta \text{ after } \sigma')$. However, by $\sigma \in Traces(\mathcal{I}^\delta)$ we have that $a \in Out(\mathcal{I}^\delta \text{ after } \sigma')$. Then, by Definition 8, $\neg(\mathcal{I}$ **ioco** $\mathcal{S})$.   □

Interpretation. Theorem 3 says that when $det(S^\delta)\rhd\omega$ enters *Fail* when run on an implementation, the latter violates conformance to the specification (but not necessarily the property ω). In this case, the **Fail** verdict is given:

> **Fail**: The implementation violates the conformance but not necessarily the property

What remains to do is to build from $det(S^\delta)\rhd\omega$ an actual test case.

Mirror. The next step consists in transforming all inputs of $det(S^\delta)\rhd\omega$ into outputs and reciprocally. This is called the mirror operation. It is necessary because, in the test execution process, the actions of the implementation and those of the test case must complement each other.

Pruning. This operation consists in suppressing from $det(S^\delta)\rhd\omega$ the subgraphs that cannot lead to *Violate*. Here, the main goal of testing is to check the violation of the requirement after a trace of the specification, and, if an implementation leads a tester (extracted from the specification) into a subgraph that cannot lead to *Violate*, the current test experiment will never be able to achieve this goal.

There are two situations, depending on whether the subgraph (from which *Violate* is unreachable) was entered through an input or an output:

- the subgraph has been entered by an *output* of the tester. In this case, the transition labeled by that output (together with the whole subgraph), are removed. Intuitively, the tester has control over its outputs, thus, it may decide not to stimulate the implementation with an output if it knows that this will never lead to a **Violate** verdict.
- the subgraph has been entered by an *input* of the tester (that does not directly lead to *Fail*). In this case, only the transition labeled by that input is kept (the rest of the graph is removed). The destination of the transition is set to a new state called *Inconc*, which means that no *Violate* verdict can be given any more (but the conformance was not violated). Hence, for completeness, in this situation the verdict will be **Inconc** (inconclusive).

> **Inconc**: neither **Fail** nor **Violate** have occurred and **Violate** cannot occur any more

Let $test(S,\omega) = prune(mirror(det(S^\delta)\rhd\omega))$ denote the IOLTS obtained after these operations. $test(S,\omega)$ is the test case generated from specification S and observer ω. It is not hard to see that by replacing $det(S^\delta)\rhd\omega$ by $test(S,\omega)$ in the statements of Theorems 2, 3 the proofs still hold. This is because $test(S,\omega)$ satisfies Lemma 2 as well, i.e., $\mathcal{L}(test(S,\omega)) = \mathcal{L}(det(S^\delta)\rhd\omega) = \mathcal{L}(\omega) \cap [Traces(S^\delta) \cdot A_!^{S^\delta}]$, as only subgraphs that *cannot lead to Violate* have been suppressed by pruning.

The above property of the language of $test(S,\omega)$ is enough to establish Theorem 2.

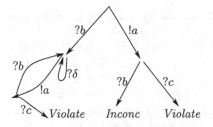

Fig. 6. Test case generated from $\mathcal{S}$ and ω (except the *Fail* location).

On the other hand, Theorem 3 is concerned with traces of $det(\mathcal{S}^\delta)\rhd\omega$ that lead to *Fail*, and a trace that leads to *Fail* in $test(\mathcal{S}, \omega)$ also leads to *Fail* in $det(\mathcal{S}^\delta)\rhd\omega$.

This establishes that Theorem 3 still holds when $det(\mathcal{S}^\delta)\rhd\omega$ is replaced by $test(\mathcal{S}, \omega)$.

Example 10. The test case depicted in Figure 6 checks the property: "between each ?a and !c, there is at least one !b" (cf. Example 2). The Fail location has not been represented; there is an implicit transition to Fail from each state, labeled by all the input actions that do not go anywhere else. Implementation $\mathcal{I}_2$ from Example 5, which initially receives an ?a and then emits !b (cf. right of Figure 4) violates neither the property nor conformance to $\mathcal{S}$ on this trace, and our test case will never be able to detect violation of the requirement in the future, hence, the **Inconc** *verdict is assigned. An implementation that receives an ?a initially and then directly emits !c violates both the property and the conformance, hence, the verdict is* **Violate**. *Finally, an implementation that emits !δ initially, violates the conformance to the specification (but not the property): the verdict is* **Fail**.

5   Conclusion, Related Work, and Future Work

We now recall the framework proposed in the paper and the main results obtained. A system is viewed at three different levels of abstraction: high-level *requirements* $\mathcal{R}$, operational *specification* $\mathcal{S}$, and final, black-box *implementation* $\mathcal{I}$. In the proposed framework, all three views are modeled using Input-Output Labeled transition systems, which are labeled transition systems whose actions are partitioned into inputs, outputs, and internal actions.

The conformance relation **ioco** [19] links $\mathcal{I}$ and $\mathcal{S}$, and the satisfaction relation $\models$ links $\mathcal{S}$ (or $\mathcal{I}$) and requirements $\mathcal{R}$. A notion of requirement that is *relevant* for a specification is defined, which essentially means that the requirement does not refer to features that are not incorporated into the specification.

Our first result says intuitively that $\mathcal{I}$ **ioco**-conforms to $\mathcal{S}$ if and only if $\mathcal{I}$ satisfies all relevant requirements that are satisfied by $\mathcal{S}$. While it is interesting from a theoretical point of view, because it gives an alternative definition of **ioco**-conformance, this result is not practical as it is restricted to *relevant* requirements (which are not always easy to come up with) and it does not say how to actually check a requirement on a black-box implementation.

This can be done by testing, and therefore we propose a test generation algorithm that takes an IOLTS specification S, and an arbitrary requirement ω (relevant or not) expressed using specific IOLTS called *observers*, and produces an IOLTS test case, denoted $test(S, \omega)$. The tester emits verdicts: **Violate**, **Fail**, and **Inconc**, which express relations between $\mathcal{I}$, S, and $\mathcal{R}$.

Our second result says intuitively that $\mathcal{I}$ **ioco** S holds if and only if, for all observers ω that express *true* properties of the specification S, by executing $test(S, \omega)$ in parallel with the implementation $\mathcal{I}$, the **Violate** verdict is not obtained.

The "only if" part of this result is a theoretical completeness result: in order to establish conformance, an infinite number of test cases should be executed, and each execution is a potentially infinite process as well.

More interesting in practice is the "if" part of the result, which is a soundness property. Going back to the validation approach proposed in Section 1, it implies that every requirement that holds on the specification allows to automatically generate a test case to check the requirement on the implementation as well.

A similar soundness result holds for the **Fail** verdict, which says that, if the **Fail** verdict is obtained by executing $test(S, \omega)$ in parallel with the implementation $\mathcal{I}$, then $\mathcal{I}$ **ioco** S does not hold. The **Fail** verdict plays the role of a warning in the proposed validation process: when it is issued, the implementation has violated conformance to the specification, and the trace that led to this violation can be examined to check whether this corresponds to a serious problem or not.

Finally, an **Inconc** (inconclusive) verdict means that the current test experiment will never be able to detect the violation of a requirement in the future, therefore, the user may stop the current test experiment and start another one.

Related Work. There exists a lot of interest in formal verification from researchers and, recently, formal verification has started to penetrate the industry. More recently, conformance testing (and other forms of testing) have become a topic of interest to the verification community. This has resulted in new algorithms and tools for testing based on verification technology (mainly model checking) [1,4,11,18].

In [6] the authors describe an approach to generate tests from observers describing linear-time temporal logic requirements and to execute the tests directly on the implementation. This is similar to what we do, except for the logic and one more important point: [6] does not require verification of the property on the specification prior to conformance testing, and the test cases do not check conformance, but only that the implementation does not violate the requirements.

The authors of [15] have ideas similar to ours. Given a specification S, and an invariant P assumed to be satisfied by S, mutants S' of S are built using standard mutation operators. Then, a combined machine is generated, which extends sequences of S with sequences of S'. Next, the SMV model-checker is used to generate sequences that violate P, i.e., sequences that prove that S' is a mutant of S violating P. Finally, the sequences are interpreted as test cases. The construction of the combined machine is quite similar to our forcing operation (with S' interpreted as ω). Several other papers, like [7,5], start from a specification S and a property P in a temporal logic (CTL or LTL) satisfied by S, and use the counter-example facility of a model checker (SMV, SPIN) to generate counter-examples of $\neg P$, thus, witnesses of P in S. Some papers like [8] extend the idea to describe coverage criteria in temporal logic and generate test cases using model-checking.

However, all these papers suffer from the same drawbacks. They do not take nondeterminism into account, do not differentiate between inputs and outputs, and do not formally define conformance testing. Moreover, except [15], they do not relate satisfaction of properties to conformance testing.

In [17] another approach to combine test selection and verification is presented. The idea is to use symbolic test selection techniques to extract test cases from a specification, which, under some sufficient conditions, can be used to perform a compositional verification of the requirements. However, the test selection mechanism is not related to the requirements in a formal way, as it is in this paper.

Future work. In the near future we are planning to implement the test generation method for safety properties presented here in the TGV tool [11]. TGV uses *test purposes* as test selection mechanisms, which express *reachability* properties of the specification; a test case is generated for every witness (trace) showing that the specification satisfies a given reachability property [11]. Thus, to perform test generation from safety properties, it is *not* enough to take the negation of a safety property, and use TGV with the resulting reachability property as a test purpose: if the specification satisfies the safety property (as assumed everywhere in this paper), its negation has no witnesses, thus, TGV produces an empty test case.

Our symbolic test generation tool STG [4], based on abstract interpretation rather than enumeration, is another target for the new test generation algorithm.

We are also planning to extend this framework to LTL safety formulas [13] by a translation of LTL formulas on observable events into observers, and connect this work with that of [9,3]. The problem addressed by these papers is to check whether temporal logic formulas expressing safety requirements have a sufficient coverage of the specification. Here, coverage is defined by the ability of a formula to distinguish mutants. Thus, if a set of requirements has a good coverage of the specification, the test cases obtained by our method may have a good coverage on implementations, thus, a good chance of finding bugs during test execution.

Finally, in this paper the situation where the specification does *not* satisfy the requirements has not been considered. We are currently investigating an approach based on previous work [12] for automatically computing the largest specification contained in the original specification, which satisfies the requirements and does not change the set of implementations that conform to the original specification.

References

1. A. Belinfante, J. Feenstra, R. de Vries, J. Tretmans, N. Goga, L. Feijs, and S. Mauw. Formal test automation: a simple experiment. In *International Workshop on the Testing of Communicating Systems (IWTCS'99)*, pages 179-196, 1996

2. M. Bozga, J.-C. Fernandez, L. Ghirvu, C. Jard, T. Jéron, A. Kerbrat, P. Morel, and L. Mounier. Verification and test generation for the SSCOP protocol. *Science of Computer Programming*, 36(1):27–52, 2000.

3. H. Chockler, O. Kupferman, R.P. Kurshan, and M.Y. Vardi. A Practical Approach to Coverage in Model Checking. In *Computer-Aided Verification (CAV'01)*, number 2102 in LNCS, pages 66–78, 2001.

4. D. Clarke, T. Jéron, V. Rusu, and E. Zinovieva. STG: a Symbolic Test Generation tool. In *Tools and Algorithms for the Construction and Analysis of Systems (TACAS'02)*, number 2280 in LNCS, pages 470–475, 2002.

5. A. Engels, L.M.G. Feijs, and S. Mauw. Test Generation for Intelligent Networks Using Model Checking. In *Tools and Algorithms for the Construction and Analysis of Systems (TACAS'97)*, number 1217 in LNCS, pages 384–398, 1997.

6. J.C. Fernandez, L. Mounier, and C. Pachon. Property-oriented test generation. In *Formal Aspects of Software Testing Workshop (FATES'03)*, 2003.

7. A. Gargantini and C.L. Heitmeyer. Using Model Checking to Generate Tests from Requirements Specifications. In *ESEC / SIGSOFT FSE*, pages 146–162, 1999.

8. H. Hong, I. Lee, O. Sokolsky, and H. Ural. A temporal logic based theory of test coverage and generation. In *Tools and Algorithms for Construction and Analysis of Systems (TACAS'02)*, number 2280 in LNCS, pages 327–341, 2002.

9. Y.V. Hoskote, T. Kam, P.-H. Ho, and X. Zhao. Coverage Estimation for Symbolic Model Checking. In *Design Automation Conference*, pages 300–305, 1999.

10. ISO/IEC. International Standard 9646, OSI-Open Systems Interconnection, Information Technology – Conformance Testing Methodology and Framework, 1992.

11. T. Jéron and P. Morel. Test generation derived from model-checking. In *Computer-Aided Verification (CAV'99)*, number 1633 in LNCS, pages 108–122, 1999.

12. T. Jéron, H. Marchand, V. Rusu, and V. Tschaen. Synthèse de contrôleurs pour une relation de conformité. In *Modélisation des systèmes réactifs (MSR'03)*, 2003.

13. O. Kupferman and M.Y. Vardi. Model Checking of Safety Properties. *Formal Methods in System Design*, 19(3):291–314, 2001.

14. Z. Manna and A. Pnueli. *Temporal verification of reactive systems. Vol. 1: Specification, Vol. 2: Safety*. Springer-Verlag, 1991 and 1995.

15. P. Ammann, W. Ding and D. Xu. Using a Model Checker to Test Safety Properties. In *International Conference on Engineering of Complex Computer Systems (ICECCS'01)*. IEEE Computer Society, 2001.

16. Telelogic SDL products. http://www.telelogic.com/products/sdl.

17. V. Rusu. Combining Formal Verification and Conformance Testing for Validating Reactive Systems. *Software Testing, Verification, and Reliability*, 13(3):157–180, 2003.

18. M. Schmitt, A. Ek, J. Grabowski, D. Hogrefe, and B. Koch. Autolink – putting SDL-based test generation into practice. In *International Workshop on the Testing of Communicating Systems (IWTCS'97)*, pages 227–244, 1997.

19. J. Tretmans. Testing concurrent systems: A formal approach. In *Concurrency Theory (CONCUR'99)*, number 1664 in LNCS, pages 46–65, 1999.

Derivation of Abstract Protocol Type Definitions for the Conformance Testing of Text-Based Protocols

Stephan Schulz

Nokia Research Center
P.O. Box 407
FIN-00045 NOKIA GROUP
Stephan.Schulz@nokia.com

Abstract. In today's specification and implementation of conformance test systems the derivation of a proper abstract protocol type definition for text-based protocols remains an open issue. Contrary to conventional telecommunication protocol standards, text-based protocol standards do not specify such an abstract protocol syntax but instead its transfer syntax, i.e., information about message content in conjunction with its encoding. We present in this paper an approach, which allows to extract an abstract protocol type definition from a text-based protocol transfer syntax specified using the Augmented Backus Naur Form (ABNF). In addition, we briefly discuss how a protocol independent codec system can be implemented based for such protocol type definitions.

1 Introduction

The specification of conformance test suites, which verify that a protocol implementation adheres to the protocol syntax and semantics as specified in a specification or standard, has only recently started to be practiced for text-based protocols. Arguably one reason for this late recognition is that the ideas and methodology for conformance testing originate from the telecom community [1] whereas most text-based protocols have been standardized in the internet community, which has a separate standardization body as well as a different testing philosophy. The lack of established conformance testing has led to the common situation that correct protocol syntax and semantics for text-based protocols are commonly specified by an implementation (of an influential software vendor) rather than the protocol standard.

When looking at text-based protocol syntax definitions and their standards from a telecommunication perspective we notice a number of differences: Firstly, protocol syntax is specified as a transfer syntax - most commonly using the Augmented Backus Naur Form (ABNF) [13] - instead of an abstract syntax, e.g., using the Abstract Syntax Notation One (ASN.1) [2], along with an encoding rule, e.g., Basic Encoding Rules (BER). A transfer syntax like ABNF mixes message content (i.e., its abstract syntax) with encoding information. Possibly this approach for protocol syntax definition originated from the fact that textual encoding, contrary to its binary counterpart, was initially readable for humans. Nevertheless some textual encoding can already today turn out to be barely human readable, e.g., large textually encoded Media Gateway Control (MEGACO ABNF) [3] messages. Secondly, multiple ways

R. Groz and R.M. Hierons (Eds.): TestCom 2004, LNCS 2978, pp. 177–192, 2004.

of encoding the same information are commonly acceptable, e.g., short and long forms for text tokens, or the appearance of multiple headers in encoded Session Initiation Protocol (SIP) [4] messages. Also, the concept of white space, which is a well defined sequence of characters contributing no information content to a message for a given protocol, is a previously unknown concept to the telecommunication protocol world.

Another possible reason for the late start of conformance testing of text-based protocols may be that classical conformance testing has not properly addressed the testing needs of such protocols. Only recently the best established testing language in conformance testing, the Testing and Test Control Notation (TTCN), was extended to better support the testing of text-based protocols in its third release, TTCN-3 [5], which includes for example numerous string manipulation functions as well as regular expressions for the matching of strings.

But even the best testing language alone is only a start to a good conformance test suite. In order to minimize the source of error from test case specification and to increase its coverage, it is highly desirable to provide an abstract protocol type definition to test engineers which relieves them from the task to assure correct encoding of message content. As text-based protocol standards do not provide an abstract syntax, protocol type definitions need to be derived from the transfer syntax. Tightly coupled to the abstract type definition is the implementation of a textual encoder and decoder in a test system which automates the transition from abstract syntax to transfer syntax and vice versa. This part is more commonly called the "codec" implementation. In our paper, we present the derivation of abstract type definitions from the ABNF definition of text-based protocols. We also outline the implementation of a protocol independent text codec based on our approach.

2 Related Research

The first TTCN-3 conformance test suite for text-based protocols was developed by the Telecommunication and Internet Protocol Harmonization Over Networks (TIPHON) workgroup at the European Telecommunication Standardization Institute (ETSI). This group wrote a SIP test suite for testing voice over IP call handling using SIP, which was released for the first time in the summer of 2002 [6]. A major TTCN-3 SIP test suite update was then released in the first quarter of 2003. In both test suites, the origin of the SIP TTCN-3 type definition is unclear. The best presentation of their efforts can be found in [15]. The paper leaves still a lot of questions open, e.g., the approach taken to derive the actual TTCN-3 SIP type specification. ETSI SIP test suite implementers have mentioned to the author that internal representation of SIP messages in existing open source SIP implementations probably had a significant impact on the design of the protocol type definition. Notice that this work only encompassed TTCN-3 code but not the implementation of the remaining parts of test system, e.g., a SIP codec, which is required to make this TTCN-3 test suite executable.

The first executable commercial TTCN-3 test system for SIP was released by the Berlin based company <testing_tech> [7]. Their latest release constituted in essence a commercial full TTCN-3 test system release for the second ETSI SIP test suite. Therefore their abstract protocol definition was the same as specified by ETSI. Their codec implementation is mostly based on an open source SIP parser implementation.

The approach taken in both above cases, that is, to base the abstract protocol definition and its encoding for a TTCN-3 conformance test system on an open source parser implementation has two major drawbacks: First of all, the granularity of such a TTCN-3 type specification is likely to be driven by this parser implementation and not by the test purposes and syntax definition as it should be. Secondly, if there is a complete reliance on the codec implementation data structures, problems also arise when aspects of a protocol are to be tested which are not yet supported by any public parser implementations, e.g., 3GPP specific SIP extensions. Similarly, this solution is only suitable for protocols which have open source implementations available.

In other research, also at ETSI, S. Müller [8] has investigated the conformance testing of the text-based Open Settlement Protocol (OSP) using TTCN-3. In his documentation, he was the first to clearly and explicitly separate textual encoding from actual message content in a TTCN-3 data type definitions by isolating encoding information in TTCN-3 encoding attributes. Arguably the scope of his research was a little different than in the previous SIP cases. Contrary to SIP, OSP has a far simpler transfer protocol syntax and it is based on XML instead of ABNF.

Finally we want to mention that there have also been different approaches to test SIP, e.g., using XML [9] instead of TTCN. We feel a XML based test specification approach is not appropriate for conformance testing. Although XML is a widely accepted specification format it has not been designed nor standardized for conformance testing purposes. In essence, such an approach requires from its users to specify testing infrastructure, e.g., a rich type system, sophisticated matching mechanism, dynamic test configurations, test verdict management, which are already native in TTCN-3.

3 The Augmented Backus Naur Form

The Augmented Backus Naur Form (ABNF) is probably the best established method to specify protocol transfer syntax for text-based protocols in standardization. In particular, ABNF is used to specify the transfer syntax of many important text-based protocols which are to be used in future third generation telecommunication networks including Session Initiation Protocol (SIP) [4], Session Description Protocol (SDP) [10], the textual form of the Media Gateway Control protocol (MEGACO ABNF) [3], Real Time Streaming Protocol (RTSP) [11], and Hypertext Transfer Protocol (HTTP) [12]. This form of specification has been defined by the Internet Engineering Task Force (IETF) in their Request For Comments (RFC) 2234 [13]. Notice however that ABNF could also be used to described the syntax of text-based protocols which use currently another basis of specification, e.g., XML. In this section we provide a brief introduction into this specification format followed by an discussion of its limitations.

3.1 The Main Concepts

A ABNF based transfer syntax specification for a given protocol is generally specified by a set of ABNF rules, which first gradually define the structure of textually encoded messages and eventually specify a textual encoding for all possible atomic values. Such atomic values, i.e., rule elements which can not be further decomposed, are referred to as terminals. Each ABNF rule can be composed of one or more elements which may be combined using the operators defined in [13]: concatenation, optionality, repetition, and alternation. Each element may either be fixed character string or single character, i.e., a terminal, or a reference to another rule. Finally, an ABNF specification may also include descriptive comments. We illustrate these main concepts with some small ABNF rule examples taken from the SIP standard [4].

The concatenation operator defines that the elements this rule definition must always follow each other in the specified order in a correctly encoded protocol message. The optional operator indicates that one or more elements may be but also may not be present at the location specified by the rule.

SIP-URI   = "sip:" [userinfo] hostport uri-parameters [headers]   (1)

Our first ABNF example rule (1) illustrates a combination of concatenation and optional operators. Here the rule <SIP-URI> defines that its correct encoding must have the terminal "sip:" followed by the result of resolving rules <hostport> and <uri-parameters>. The encoded strings which are the result of resolving rules <userinfo> and <headers>, however, may be omitted in a syntactically correct encoding of a message. If, however, one or both of them are present then they must occur in the specified positions, i.e., between the terminal "sip:" and the encoded element <hostport> and immediately following the encoded element <uri-parameters>, respectively.

Via   = ("Via" / "v") HCOLON via-parm *(COMMA via-parm)   (2)

Our second example rule (2) illustrates that ABNF rules may contain more than one and different ABNF operators. Firstly, the concatenation, which is shown as a sequence listing of rule elements, mandates that the result of encoding the first alternation operator must be followed by the result of resolving rules <HCOLON>, <via-parm>, and finally that of the repetition operator. The alternation operator, illustrated as a backslash, requires that either the terminal string either "Via" or "v" to be present in a valid encoded message. The repetition operator, which is shown with a star followed by element to be repeated within parenthesis, always indicates that zero or more (i.e., no upper limit) occurrences of the element may be repeated at this point of the encoded string. Numbers before and after the star can be used to specify lower and upper bounds on the allowed number of repetitions.

A common naming convention found in ABNF specifications is that capitalized rule identifiers identify rules which specify basic values, e.g., <HCOLON> used in example rule (2), which is in [4] defined as the string ":" which may be preceded and superceded by white space.

3.2   Limitations of ABNF-Based Specification of Textual Encoding

Generally we find that an ABNF based specification textual encoding is not very concrete. Very commonly we find the concept of using repetition in combination with an alternation which essentially allows for information to occur in any given order and any number of times (including not at all). The problem here is that in practice the full capability of this loose specification is only rarely made use of but still the worst case needs to expected. Our example rule (3) from [14] specifies the list of parameters for HTTP digest computation. Based on a literal interpretation of this ABNF rule multiple occurrences of every element are allowed. Multiple occurrences however only make sense in this case for the extension element <auth-param>. Notice that this example also uses two extensions to the ABNF notation which are not defined in [13]: the hash sign, a shorthand notation to specify that repeated encoded elements are to be separated by a comma, and the optional operator for an alternation element.

$$\text{digest-challenge} = 1\#(\text{ realm } / [\text{ domain }] / \text{ nonce } / [\text{ opaque }] / [\text{ stale }] | \qquad (3)$$
$$[\text{ algorithm }] / [\text{ qop-options }] / [\text{ auth-param }])$$

A considerable difference compared to conventional telecom encoding is that many text-based protocols allow multiple forms of encoding to represent the same information. One example for that is the compact form concept which is commonly used, e.g., in SIP [4] and MEGACO ABNF [5]. The compact form allows that encoded messages may either use an explicit or an abbreviated form of a string token to indicate the presence of some information. An example of a compact form specification is our rule (1) which allows "Via" or "v" to be used to indicate the presence of a "Via" header field. One problem with such multiple forms of encoding is that their equivalent information content is not apparent from the ABNF itself, but it is instead specified in the verbal sections of text-based protocol standards, e.g., Sections 7.3.3 in the SIP standard [4].

A second difference to binary encoding schemes is the concept of compressible white space. Such white space can be loosely defined as a set of possible characters - usually including extra space, tabulator, and line feed characters - which may appear in various combinations at well defined positions within an textually encoded message. It does not contribute any information about the content of the message or even its encoding. Although the concept of compressible white space is a general one, it is not consistently defined across different text protocol standards.

The biggest problem with ABNF based transfer syntax specifications, which may be a result of the weakness of the ABNF specification format itself, are in general significant restrictions specified upon message encoding in the *verbal* sections of text-based protocol standards or within ABNF comments. The SIP standard [4] in Section 20.10, for example, prohibits the appearance of URL parameters and headers in the plain addresses within "Contact", "To" and "From" header fields which are not reflected in the definition of their ABNF rules. Another example is Table 2 in the SIP standard which specifies optional and mandatory headers for different SIP request kinds, whereas the SIP ABNF only defines one single SIP request kind which if literally followed allows the appearance of any header (in any number). The comment for the <serviceChangeParm> rule in the MEGACO ABNF specification [3] - an alternation - requires two of its alternation elements to be always present and only one of two other elements to be present at any time, which severely restrict this ABNF rule.

4 Derivation of Abstract Syntax from ABNF Specifications

Now that we have an idea on how textual encoding can be defined using ABNF, we want to present an approach which can be used to extract an abstract syntax from ABNF based transfer syntax specifications. More concretely we want to isolate the information from its encoding as much as feasible. We discuss here first a one-to-one mapping of ABNF rules to type definitions. After that we will discuss how the results of this mapping can easily be improved further - especially in the context of the previously discussed limitations of ABNF based specifications.

We will use the TTCN-3 type system to illustrate our derived abstract syntax, i.e., our abstract protocol type definition. Notice that our derivation itself is also applicable to other Abstract Syntax Notation One (ASN.1) [2] like type systems. We still promote the use of TTCN-3 as in our opinion only this testing language currently offers the required language support, e.g., access, checking, and manipulation of character string values, to properly specify conformance test cases for text-based protocols.

4.1   Requirements for an Abstract Syntax Definition

First we would like to specify the requirements guide the derivation:

1. The abstract syntax shall follow the ABNF structure and naming as closely as possible. That means that based on the name of a data type the test engineer should be able to identify the location in the ABNF specification where its possible (encoded) values are defined.
2. The protocol type definition should consist of a minimum amount of data type definitions, i.e., its specification complexity should be minimized. It is in our opinion this is a critical requirement to derive protocol type definitions comprehensible to a test engineer.
3. When a textual encoding is much more intuitive than their more structured counterpart for an information element, e.g., IPv4 address specification, then the less structured representation should be chosen in the protocol type definition as long as our previous, second requirement is met.
4. The level of structuring imposed by the abstract protocol type definition must at least allow direct access to all information within a protocol message which are to be validated by a given test purposes or needed in order to communicate sensibly with the implementation under test, i.e., the test engineer shall not need to parse for information within an information element.
5. A protocol type definition must only be based on one single encoding of each information element. That format should be the more readable to the test engineer, e.g., long format instead of the compact format.
6. The derived data types shall enable a test engineer at least to send all possible valid message content. This requirement does not imply that all valid encodings are to be supported for sending purposes. Similarly, it does not exclude the possibility to accept protocol messages that arrive with different encoding than the selected one or with invalid content.

4.2   Handling of White Space and Multiple Encoding Representations

Since white space does not represent any information of value for conformance testing it does not get any representation in our abstract protocol definition. This in essence allows us to edit a given ABNF based protocol transfer syntax specification and substitute all occurrences white space in ABNF rules with its minimal representation, i.e., no or a single space terminal. That also means that test engineers have no means to specify or test for valid extra white space occurrence in a message which is specified based on this abstract protocol type definition.

Another result of the requirements listed in the previous section is that only one of multiple encoding schemes has to be selected in prior to the derivation of the abstract data types. In this case, we advise to choose the long and more meaningful form over the compact form. Therefore, like in the case of white space handling, this could be interpreted as a replacement of all occurrences of compact form related alternation rules in the ABNF specification with the long form terminal only.

4.3   Delimiters

Before we start our discussion of our derivation we still have to introduce the concept of delimiters. Delimiters encode structural information in text-based protocol messages. In the context of ABNF, a delimiter is usually one but possibly multiple concatenated terminal strings in a ABNF rule definition which identify an encoded ABNF rule element, i.e., another ABNF rule definition or basic encoded value. Examples for multiple terminal strings constituting a single delimiter are <"Via" HCOLON> in our example rule (2) and <ErrorToken EQUAL> in our rule (4). Notice that both elements in these rules define only a single terminal or character string since short form as well as white space definitions have been removed in our ABNF specification as discussed in the previous section.

$$\text{errorDescriptor} = \text{ErrorToken EQUAL ErrorCode} \tag{4}$$
$$\text{LBRKT [quotedString] RBRKT}$$

In delimiter kinds, we can firstly distinguish between element *pre-* and *post-* delimiters which may be specified for any element in a given ABNF rule. Element pre-delimiters have to precede in the encoded message the result of encoding a rule element, whereas post-delimiters must succeed the encoded form of an element. An example of a pre-delimiter for a rule element is the <COMMA> used in the ABNF rule definition in example rule (2).

In ABNF rules, which are defined using the concatenation operator, e.g., our rule (2), only optional elements allow a unique classification of a delimiter to be a pre or post-delimiter of that element and its preceding and following element. When two mandatory elements follow each other, however, a delimiter may be interpreted either as a post-delimiter of the first rule element or a pre-delimiter of the second element. Although from theoretical perspective the actual choice is irrelevant, from a practical perspective, i.e., the underlying codec implementation, choosing pre- over post-delimiter may be preferable to speed up the parsing process during decoding.

For ABNF rules, which are defined as a concatenation, there exists a similar concept of *rule* delimiters in addition to *element* delimiters. Rule pre- and post-delimiters follow the same principle as their element delimiter counterparts, only that they identify encoding information for the entire encoded rule instead of merely one element within that rule. Example rule (4) from [3] illustrates a rule post-delimiter <RBRKT>. The <RBRKT> rule can not be classified as a element post-delimiter of <quotedString> since its presence in an encoded message is only optional. Similarly like in the case of the element delimiters, a first element pre-delimiter may frequently be interpreted either as rule or element pre-delimiters, e.g., <ErrorToken EQUAL> in example rule (4), and last element post-delimiters may be interpreted either as rule or element post-delimiters. Again the best classification of the rule versus element delimiter may depend on the underlying codec implementation.

Although delimiters are a key concept in transfer syntax specification for text-based protocols, they do not have to be specified in every rule for every element. Frequently many ABNF rules do not have any delimiters specified [3]. This only occurs for rules based exclusively consisting of rule reference elements which structure the element further. Here, the referenced rule usually provides a pre-delimiter for its first element. And example for this is the <uri-parameters> field in our example rule (1) which appears to have no delimiters with its preceding <hostport> field. The rule <uri-parameters>, however, is defined as a repetition with the element pre-delimiter <COMMA>.

4.4   Mapping ABNF Rules to Abstract and Basic Data Types

In this section, we define a direct mapping of ABNF rules to different abstract data type definitions. This mapping assumes that each ABNF rule is specified using only one concatenation, alternation or repetition operator. As shown in example rules (2) and (3), these operators frequently occur in combination. In these cases the ABNF rule must be split into one rule per operator which reference each other.

4.4.1   Rules Defining Basic Encoded Values

The first step of our mapping is an analysis of the ABNF specification which identifies all ABNF rules specifying a textual encoding of basic values other than a character string, i.e., real numbers, whole numbers, and hexadecimal values.

The encoding for whole numbers is generally specified in a repetition of the <DIGIT> rule, e.g., in the <CSeq> rule of the SIP ABNF. It may also be specified as an alternation of terminal strings which encode specific number. Such rules should mapped to, e.g., the TTCN-3 integer type. Range restrictions or value lists should be used in the particular integer type definition to reflect, e.g., the limits in the digit repetition.

The encoding for real numbers is generally specified as a concatenation of a whole number followed by a "." and another whole number, e.g., in the <MIME-Version> rule of the SIP ABNF. This rule can be mapped to an TTCN-3 float type.

The encoding hexadecimal values is generally specified in a repetition of the <HEXDIG> rule, e.g., in the <SecurityParmIndex> rule of the MEGACO ABNF. Such rules should mapped to, e.g., the TTCN-3 hexstring type but also to the TTCN-3 octetstring type if applicable. Again range restrictions should be applied to reflect the ABNF repetition restrictions. Notice that encoding information, e.g., a pre-delimiter "0x", has to be contained in the abstract type definition either by creating hexstring alias type for this value or specified as field encoding information in its parent structured type(s) (see Section 4.4.3).

4.4.2 Rules Defining Alternations of Terminal Strings and Tokens

ABNF rules, which specify an alternation of terminal strings are mapped to a character string type, e.g., the TTCN-3 charstring or universal charstring. In this case, terminals are considered to not specify encoding information but a character string value. More specifically, the correct mapping of such an alternation is a character string type which is subtyped with a value list corresponding to the terminals used in the alternation.

The second use of character string type is to represent the commonly used <token> rule or its equivalent. This rule commonly acts as a placeholder in ABNF specifications for "any valid string value" or future protocol syntax extensions. Here, the use of subtyping is desirable but usually not practical.

```
errorDescriptor = ErrorToken EQUAL ErrorCode LBRKT [quotedString] RBRKT

type record ErrorDescriptor {
    ErrorCode errorCode,
    QuotedString quotedString optional
} with {
    encode "Error=_}"; // rule pre- and post-delimiter
    encode (errorcode) "_{"; // element post-delimiter
}
```

```
Contact = ( "*" / (contact-param *(COMMA contact-param)))

type union Contact {
    charstring wildCard("*"),
    Contact_param_list contact_params
} with {
    encode (wildCard)""; // no delimiter
    encode (contact_params) ""; // no delimiter
}

type set of Contact_param Contact_param_list
with { encode ","; } // element list-delimiter
```

Fig. 1. Example mappings of ABNF rule (4) and <Contact> [4] to structured types

When fields in structured types (see following section) are of character string type without any subtyping restrictions, the underlying codec implementation should check for ABNF specified syntax for that particular part in the encoded message. In cases, where the specified transfer syntax is not checked by the codec, test engineers must check compliance of character string values to be sent or received in charstring type fields within a test case, e.g., by using regular expressions in the corresponding TTCN-3 receive templates. Similarly as for hexadecimal values, encoding information of character string values, i.e., pre- and post-delimiters, has to be either captured by defining a charstring type alias or within its parent structured type(s).

4.4.3 Other Rules

Rules which do not only specify a basic value are mapped to structured types: rules which are defined as concatenations to an ordered sequence type, e.g., a TTCN-3 record type, alternations to a choice type, e.g., a TTCN-3 union type, and repetitions to an unordered list type, e.g., a TTCN-3 set of type. Optional elements within a concatenation get mapped to an optional field in the ordered sequence. Some mapping examples are shown in Figure 1. Notice that the concatenation in the second example <contact-param *(COMMA contact-param)> has been mapped to an unordered list based on our second simplification which we present later in Section 4.5.In the mapping, the name of the rule becomes the name of the structured type and the name of rule elements become field and field type names in the structured type definition. Notice again that information about delimiters used in these rules is not included in their structured type definition directly but may be reflected as encoding information. Our use of TTCN-3 encoding attributes will be discussed in more detail in Section 4.4.5.

```
digest-challenge  = 1#( realm / [domain] / nonce / [opaque] / [stale] / [algorithm] /
                   [qop-options] / [auth-param] )

type set Digest_challenge
{
    Realm            realm,
    Domain           domain optional,
    Nonce            nonce,
    Opaque           opaque optional,
    Stale            stale optional,
    charstring       algorithm optional,
    charstring       qop_options optional,
    Other_auth_param_list other_auth_params optional
} with {
    encode (algorithm) "algorithm=_"; // pre-delimiter
    encode (qop_options) "qop=_"; // pre-delimiter
    encode "," // list-delimiter
}

type set of Other_auth_param Other_auth_param_list
with { encode ","} // element list delimiter
```

Fig. 2. Example Mapping of ABNF rule (3) to a TTCN-3 set type

4.4.4 Repeated Alternations

Repeated alternations, e.g., our rule (2), we treat as a special cases in our mapping. Instead of mapping them individually to an unordered list and a choice type, we map them to an unordered list type, e.g., the TTCN-3 set type, where in our first mapping each field is optional and of an unordered list type.

The reason for mapping to an unordered sequence of unordered lists is that the latter has more expressive power than the alternative approach. In a unordered sequence of unordered lists, fields can be specified as optional or mandatory whereas an unordered list of choice does not allow such restriction. Also it allows more easily to place further restrictions on the number occurrences of individual alternation elements as we see in Figure 2. The problem which however remains is that the ABNF specifications itself do not necessarily contain the required information to make these restrictions, e.g., is a given alternation element mandatory. Such information is however frequently specified in the verbal section of text protocol standards. Therefore, in a second step we may then define the required presence of a particular unordered list field to mandatory.

Another simplification in this mapping is that commonly multiple occurrences of some alternation element(s) can not occur. In these cases, the type of the particular unordered list field should be changed from its unordered list type to directly refer to type definition for the alternation element. If the alternation element however is an extension placeholder, its field must always be defined as an unordered list type as illustrated in Figure 2. Only the <auth-param> field is specified here as an unordered list since only it may occur multiple times within a HTTP digest challenge.

A strong benefit of this special handling is that the abstract type specification is tightened but also that the access of values for rule elements becomes significantly easier within test cases. The alternative - a mapping to an unordered list of choice – would require a search through the list of elements whereas the unordered sequence allows a direct access of a desired element via its field name.

A drawback of this mapping is that the order used in the order of field value encoding can no longer be influenced to the same extend in sending, e.g., digest challenge values, within a test case as it would be if an unordered list of choice type definition was used. In the latter case it would be possible to send of multiple values from different fields in an interleaved manner. We argue that it is acceptable to loose this capability since it does not change the *information content* of a message - merely its *encoding*. Notice that in the decoding of unordered sequence values in the underlying codec implementation must of course be able to handle such scenarios.

4.4.5 Retaining Encoding Information

As we discussed in the previous sections, delimiters, i.e., encoding information, are eliminated in our mapping to basic and structured data types. In principle, there are two ways to retain this information.

One approach is to use structured type names or type aliases for basic types to enable to an underlying codec implementation to perform a lookup of encoding information via the type name. This solution as the drawback that protocol specific information is split across two information sources, one being the type definition and the other being an external table which maps type names to encoding information.

Arguably a more elegant solution is to use encoding attributes in the abstract type definition, as proposed in [8], to capture such encoding information. Firstly, it allows test engineers to relate each abstract type better to an ABNF rule in the text protocol standard, but more importantly it keeps all the information pertaining to a specific abstract protocol definition in one place.

In the latter approach, rule delimiters would be specified as TTCN-3 type encoding attributes and element delimiters would be specified as field encoding attributes. This has been illustrated in Figure 1 and 2. In the special case of the repeated alternation mapping the type encoding attribute of the unordered sequence would contain the delimiters specified for the repetition element and its field delimiters would contain the delimiters specified for each alternation element. Secondly, unordered list types used for unordered sequence fields would also use the repetition delimiters.

Notice that in the specific case of TTCN-3, encoding attributes have the limitation of allowing only a specification of a single string per field or type which conflicts with our need to specify pre- and post-delimiters. We show here one possible way of solving this problem is by encoding pre- and post-delimiter information for a given field, as shown in the previous Figure 1 and 2 (where a string if is present before an underscore character specifies a pre-delimiter and if present after specifies a post-delimiter).

4.4.6 Observations

In our mapping, string terminals may be either classified as encoding information or message content. This classification is not uniquely possible when an ABNF rule element models a signal, e.g., MEGACO ABNF <KeepActiveToken> rule [3]. In that case, the terminal should be interpreted as message content, i.e., a character string value.

Another possibility than representing an alternation of terminal strings by subtyping the character string type is to map this construct instead to an enumeration type. This approach has been taken in the ETSI SIP protocol type definition in [6]. It is also valid but has the drawback that the testing language limits the choice in enumeration value names which makes it hard to create an intuitive relation between enumeration name and value when the terminal string contains special characters. A drawback of the character string mapping in practice is that not all TTCN-3 tools may offer access to subtyping information for codec implementations.

One general problem which remains for our proposed mapping is the number of type definitions it generates, which can be significantly larger than the number of rules in the ABNF specification. The main reason for that is the necessity to have only one concatenation, alternation, and repetition per rule. Another issue is that the mapping only reflects aspects covered or expressible in the ABNF notation. There may however exist a number of restrictions in the informal part of a text protocol standard which could improve, i.e., tighten, the abstract protocol type definitions.

4.5   Further Improvements

As mentioned in our previous sections, text-based protocol standards frequently further restrict the valid textual encoding of protocol messages specified by ABNF in their informative sections. If these restrictions are not reflected in the protocol type definition, the protocol definition will allow the receipt of incorrect messages and leave the checking of their syntactical correctness to the test engineer. In most cases, these aspects can be compensated for within the test specification, e.g., checking that an omitted value is never received in a field which is declared optional by the mapping but mandatory in the informal section.

There is however one case where the abstract protocol type definition must be modified, which is when the arrival of list items is restricted to be ordered, e.g., via header field values in [4]. Here, the corresponding unordered list specifications must be changed an ordered list type, e.g., a TTCN-3 record of type, e.g., the derived "ViaParmList" set of type in Figure 1 must be modified into a record of type. Notice that there is no other alternative for a test engineer to reconstruct this particular information, i.e., the order of arrival.

All other improvements listed in this section are not mandatory but they help to solve the general problem of large number of type definitions or making abstract type definitions for text based protocols more readable:

1. Single field ordered sequences may be eliminated if that field is not optional. One reason to not remove such an ordered sequence may be that it carries some meaning, e.g., MEGACO ABNF [5] descriptors. In the case of a removal of the ordered sequence its delimiters or encoding information must be moved to its parent or child type definitions.

2. In ordered sequences where a field followed by a field list type of the same type, e.g., in the mapping of the <via-parm> and <via-parm> repetition in our example rule (2), can be simplified by removing that field from the sequence and placing lower length bound of 1 upon the list definition. This simplification also creates the need for a third element delimiter kind, the list-delimiter. A list delimiter must only appear between list elements but not before the first nor after the last element of a list value.
3. Structured type definitions, which have field types of the same type kind, may be combined into one definition, e.g., when a choice which defines the type of a field in another choice type they can be combined into a single choice. A condition for such a modification is that structured field type in question is only used in the definition of that structured type. In the specific case of choice types the parent choice also must not specify any element delimiters for the child choice type.
4. More aggressive subtyping restrictions may be defined for fields of basic type based on informal statements in the standard about the corresponding ABNF rule, e.g., MEGACO ABNF rule <UINT16> [3].
5. Finally, the character string type or aliases of it may be used is to abstract or replace unnecessarily complex type structures in appropriate places of a protocol type definition. This applies for example when a value is more intuitive to handle in its encoded form than its structured form, e.g., IP addresses or the SIP caller identification string. Secondly, this approach may be used if it is possible to ignore parts of protocol messages which are not of interest for a given test purpose, e.g., irrelevant SIP headers. As discussed in Section 4.4.2 and [15] this simplification in the protocol type definition may require test case engineers to check received values more closely for correctness.

5 A Generic Codec System Implementation

At Nokia the described derivation of protocol type definitions has been applied in a number of case studies in conformance testing for different text-based protocols, i.e., different SIP, SDP, and MEGACO ABNF test suites. These studies have shown that it is possible to implement one generic, protocol independent codec system based on the traversal of abstract TTCN-3 protocol type definitions, which can be used in real world text-protocol conformance testing. All protocol type definitions used in these studies have been derived from ABNF specifications as discussed in this paper. The implementation of the protocol type definition analysis by the codec implementation has been based on a TTCN-3 Control Interface (TCI) [16] like tool independent TTCN-3 type and value interface. In general the codec implementation can be split into three parts: an encoder, a pre-processor, and a decoder.

The purpose of the pre-processor is to examine and modify received encoded messages prior to passing them to the decoder, so that they conform to the encoding representation selected for the derivation of the TTCN-3 protocol type definition, e.g., to replace any occurrence of short with their corresponding long token forms or to combine multiple SIP header field occurrences into on header field value. Secondly, the pre-processor either removes or reduces white space in the places specified by the respective protocol standard.

The encoder traverses the TTCN-3 protocol type definition at run-time while building of the encoded message to be sent. From each structured type definition encoding information is read from TTCN-3 encoding attributes and added to the target encoded string. Basic values are converted into their corresponding string format and possibly also encoding information is added.

The decoder receives a normalized encoded message from the pre-processor and then gradually converts it into a structured value by traversing again the TTCN-3 protocol type definition at run-time. Given a specific structured type in the protocol type definition and the current position in the encoded message, the decoder attempts to find encoding information for the current structured type definition, e.g., its delimiters, at the proper places in the encoded message. If successful, a corresponding value is constructed, the current position in the message is advanced, and depending on the value found the next type definition is selected and checked for presence. Depending on the optionality of a type in its parent type(s) a failure to find encoding information for a given field of a structured type may be acceptable or not. If the information is optional, then the analysis attempts to check for the presence of the next field or other feasible type information in the encoded string. In case of a failure for mandatory presence, a decoding failure is reported. Basic types are treated similarly. Here, the decoder also attempt to find the encoded value and converts that information at the current position in the encoded string into basic value upon success. Given that an optimization can in most cases detect the presence of optional fields based on the presence of pre-delimiters, this decoder implementation follows the philosophy of a single parsing approach of the normalized encoded message.

6 Conclusions

We presented in this paper a structured approach which extracts an abstract protocol type definition for text-based protocols whose transfer syntax is specified using ABNF. A mapping of ABNF rules to structured and basic types represents the key contribution. It separates textual encoding information from the message content and structure of text-based protocol messages. It assumes that definitions of white space occurrence in the ABNF specification have been removed and that one encoding has been selected for multiple variants prior to this mapping.

We also presented some additional transformations which can reduce the possibly high specification complexity of the resulting protocol type definition. These transformations also help to address the major shortcoming of text-based protocol standards which is their restriction of valid textual encoding and message content outside of the ABNF specification.

Finally, we outlined the implementation of a text-based protocol codec system based on the traversal of this abstract protocol type definition, but independent of the protocol to be tested or the concrete type definition itself. Contrary to textual codec implementations used in current TTCN-3 conformance test systems, the primary design criteria is not based on an already existing parser implementation. Currently at Nokia such a text codec implementation is used in practice for the conformance testing of numerous text-based protocol implementations.

We believe that our research results could help to turn the current art of conformance testing of ABNF specified text-based protocols into a science. In addition, we hope that they could help to positively influence a future testing philosophy of the internet community (which is currently not much in favour of conformance testing) as well as the accuracy of the protocol syntax definitions in future text-based protocol standards. In addition, this derived abstract syntax could also be used to encode originally textually encoded information with a more efficient binary encoding instead.

Acknowledgements. The author would like to thank Martin Elger for his contributions to the implementation of text-based codec systems based on type information traversal. He has laid the foundation of our classification of different delimiters as well as their encoding in TTCN-3 encoding attributes. Also I would like to thank the members of the ETSI TIPHON work group for their helpful discussions and the reviewers of my paper for their helpful comments.

References

1. ISO/IEC 9646-1: "Information technology - Open Systems Interconnection – Conformance testing methodology and framework - Part 1: General Concepts". 2nd ed.. Geneva (December 1994).
2. ITU-T Recommendation X.680: "Information technology - Abstract Syntax Notation One (ASN.1): Specification of basic notation".
3. ITU-T Recommendation Series H: "Audiovisual and Multimedia Systems; H.323-System Recommendations Implementors' Guide". Version 11 (2000).
4. J. Rosenberg et al: "SIP: Session Initiation Protocol". IETF RFC 3261 (June 2002).
5. ETSI ES 201 837-1 (V2.1.0): "Methods for Testing and Specification (MTS); The Testing and Test Control Notation version 3; Part 1: TTCN-3 Core Language". Sophia Antipolis (February 2003).
6. ETSI DTS/TIPHON-06020-3 (V0.0.4): "Telecommunication and Internet Protocol Harmonization Over Networks (TIPHON); Conformance Testing for TIPHON Release 5; Session Initiation Protocol (SIP) Conformance Test Specifications; Part3: Abstract Test Suite (ATS) Specification". Sophia Antipolis (September 2001).
7. Testing Tech: TTsuite-SIP User Guide (2003). http://www.testingtech.de/products/TTsuite-SIP/index.html
8. ETSI DTS/TIPHON-6022-3 (V0.3.2): "Communication And Internet Protocol Harmonization Over Networks (TIPHON) Release 4; Technology Compliance Specifications; Open Settlement Protocol (OSP); Part 3: Abstract Test Suite (ATS) specification". Sophia Antipolis (January 2001).
9. M. Ranganathan, O. Deruelle, D. Montgomery: "Testing SIP Using XML Protocol Templates". Proceedings of Testcom Conference. Sophia Antipolis (May 2003).
10. M. Handley, V. Jacobson: "SDP: Session Description Protocol". IETF RFC 2327 (April 1998).
11. H. Schulzrinne, A. Rao, R. Lanphier: "Real Time Streaming Protocol (RTSP)", IETF RFC 2326 (April 1998)
12. R. Fielding et al.: "Hypertext Transfer Protocol – HTTP/1.1". IETF RFC 2616 (June 1999).
13. D. Crocker: "Augmented BNF for Syntax Specifications: ABNF". IETF RFC 2234 (November 1997).

14. J. Franks et al: "HTTP Authentication: Basic and Digest Access Authentication". IETF RFC 2617 (June 1999).
15. A. Wiles et al: Experiences of Using TTCN-3 for Testing SIP and OSP. Proceedings of first ACATS ATS Conference. Athens (February 2002).
16. ETSI ES 201 837-6 (Draft V1.0.0): "Methods for Testing and Specification (MTS); The Testing and Test Control Notation version 3; Part 6: TTCN-3 Control Interface". Sophia Antipolis (March 2003).

Mutation Testing Applied to Validate SDL Specifications

Tatiana Sugeta[1], José Carlos Maldonado[1], and W. Eric Wong[2]

[1] Universidade de São Paulo,
Instituto de Ciências Matemáticas e de Computacão,
São Carlos, São Paulo, Brazil,
P.O. Box 668, ZIP Code 13560-970,
{tatiana, jcmaldon}@icmc.usp.br
[2] University of Texas at Dallas,
Department of Computer Science,
Richardson, TX, USA,
ZIP Code 75083,
ewong@utdallas.edu

Abstract. Mutation Testing is an error-based criterion that provides mechanisms to evaluate the quality of a test set and/or to generate test sets. This criterion, originally proposed to program testing, has also been applied to specification testing. In this paper, we propose the application of Mutation Testing for testing SDL specifications. We define a mutant operator set for SDL that intends to model errors related to the behavioral aspect of the processes, the communication among processes, the structure of the specification and some intrinsic characteristics of SDL. A testing strategy to apply the mutant operators to test SDL specifications is proposed. We illustrate our approach using the Alternating-Bit protocol.

Keywords: Specification Testing, Mutation Testing, SDL.

1 Introduction

Testing is an important activity to guarantee the quality and the reliability of a product under development. The main objective of testing activity is to identify errors that were not yet discovered in software products. To obtain a reliable software, specification testing is as important as program testing since the earlier the errors are detected in the life cycle the less onerous is the process to remove them. The success of the testing activity depends on the quality of a test set. The quality of the testing activity is by itself an issue in the software development process. One way to evaluate the quality of a test case set T is to use coverage measures based on testing criteria.

Mutation Testing is a criterion initially proposed to program testing but some works have shown this criterion can also be applied to specification testing and conformance testing [6, 15, 16, 17, 18, 20, 25, 26, 29]. Mutation Testing consists

R. Groz and R.M. Hierons (Eds.): TestCom 2004, LNCS 2978, pp. 193–208, 2004.

of generating mutants of the program/specification, based on a mutant operator set that intents to model common, typical errors made during the development. The objective is to select test cases that are capable to distinguish the behavior of the mutants from the behavior of the original program/specification. Mutation Testing provides mechanisms to evaluate the quality of a test set and/or to generate test sets [11]. Mutation Testing has also been explored to support Integration Testing [10, 19]. Delamaro et al. [10] proposed Interface Mutation to explore interface errors related to the connections among program units, in a pairwise approach, and Ghosh and Mathur [19] proposed Interface Mutation to explore errors in the interface of components in a distributed application.

Formal techniques have been used to specify safety critical systems like bank control, air traffic control, metro control, patient hospital monitoring and communication protocols. Examples of these techniques are Statecharts, Petri Nets, Estelle and SDL. SDL (Specification and Description Language) is a language standardized and maintained by ITU-T (*International Telecommunications Union*) for the specification and description of telecommunications systems. Although this initial intention, SDL has been used to describe reactive systems such as real-time, event-driven and communicating systems. The behavior of a system modelled by SDL is described by processes, that behave like Communicating Extended Finite State Machines (CEFSMs).

Different techniques have been proposed to generate test cases from the SDL specifications [7, 20, 21, 32]. These techniques are applied to the conformance testing, that uses the test set generated to test the implementation of the system. In conformance testing it is supposed the specification is correct. An usual formal verification technique applied to guarantee the correctness of the specification is model checking. Model checking is based on state exploration and allows to verify some software properties. Although by using model checking some information of the structural coverage can be obtained, this technique do not stress to provide evidences about how much the specification was tested that could provide a quantitative measure about the testing being executed.

Motivated by previous researches that have investigated Mutation Testing to validate specifications based on formal techniques such as Finite State Machines [14, 16], Statecharts [18, 30], Petri Nets [17, 27, 28], Estelle [26, 29], in this paper we propose the Mutation Testing to test specifications written using SDL. We present a mutant operators set and a mutation-based testing strategy to guide the tester to apply the mutant operators and to explore the behavioral aspect, the communication among the processes and the structure of the SDL specification. To illustrate our definitions we use the well known Alternating-Bit protocol [31].

This paper is organized as follow: Section 2 contains an overview of some related works. In Section 3 we present an overview of basic concepts of SDL. The main concepts related to Mutation Testing are discussed in Section 4. The mutant operators set and a proposed Incremental Testing Strategy are presented in Section 5. In that section we also illustrate examples of application of some mutant operators. Our final comments are discussed in Section 6.

2   Related Work

Probert and Guo [26] proposed a technique to test Estelle specifications based on mutation, named E-MPT (Estelle-directed Mutation-based Protocol Testing). This technique validates the EFSMs defined in the specification. It generates the mutants from the specification and translates, using an Estelle compiler, the original specification and its mutants to C programs. The codes generated by the compiler are not completed and they need to be completed by the tester. The C programs generated are executed and the obtained results are compared.

Bousquet et al. [6] applied Mutation Testing in the conformance testing. In their experiment, the criterion is used to verify if the implementation of a conference protocol is according to its specification. The specification was written using Lotos. The test cases are generated based on the Lotos specification and the implementation is tested when using this test case set generated.

Ammann and Black use Mutation Testing and model checking to automatically produce tests from formal specifications [3] and measure test coverage [2]. The system is specified by Finite State Machines. To the former, each transition of the state machine is represented as a clause in temporal logic. To generate tests, the mutant operators are applied to all temporal logic clauses, resulting in a set of mutant clauses. The model checker compares the original state machine specification with the mutants. When an inconsistent clause is found, the model checker produces a counterexample if possible, and it is converted to a test case. To measure the coverage of a test set, each test is turned into a finite state machine that represents only the execution sequence of that test. Each state machine is compared by the model checker with the set of mutants produced previously. A mutation adequacy coverage metric is the number of mutants killed divided by the total number of mutants. Black et al. [5] refined the mutant operators set defined in Ammann et al. [3] and proposed new ones to be applied in the same approach that combines mutation testing and model checking.

Kov cs et al. [20] have used Mutation Testing to generate and select test cases to be applied at the conformance testing of communication protocols specified using SDL. The test cases generated at specification level are used to test the programs implemented based on the specification and its mutants. Two algorithms were proposed to select test cases. The first one has an SDL specification as input and the result is a test case set that is Mutation Testing-adequate. The second one has two inputs, an SDL specification and a finite test case set. This algorithm analyzes the initial test case set and only those ones that identify the mutants are selected. A tool was implemented using Java to automate the second algorithm.

Fabbri et al. [15, 16, 17, 18] have explored Mutation Testing at the specification level, analyzing the adequacy of this criterion on testing the behavioral aspects of reactive systems specified using Finite State Machines [16], Statecharts [18] and Petri Nets [17]. Fabbri et al. defined mutant operators for these three formal techniques. Mutants are generated by applying the mutant operators to the specification being tested. The mutant operators set models the more typical errors related to the specification technique in use. After the mutants generation, each mutant is simulated and the results are compared to the results of the original specification. These steps contribute to the analysis of the mutation testing adequacy.

Souza et al. [29] investigated the application of Mutation Testing to validate Estelle specifications, exploring with this criterion the behavioral aspect, the communication among the modules and the structure of the specification. Souza et. al present a more complete mutant operators set than the one proposed by Probert and Guo [26], considering aspects such as the interface among modules, the hierarchical structure and the parallelism of the specification.

Fabbri et al. [18] and Souza et al. [29] established Incremental Testing Strategies to aid the application of Mutation Testing to Statecharts and Estelle, respectively. By using these strategies it is possible to prioritize some specific aspects, according to the features the tester wants to explore in the testing activity.

3   SDL: Overview

SDL is a language standardized and maintained by ITU-T (*International Telecommunications Union*) for the specification and description of telecommunications systems. Its first version is from 1976 and since then the language has been modified and improved to be as complete as possible. The newest version is SDL 2000. Although SDL was initially proposed to telecommunications systems, it has been used to describe reactive systems such as real-time, event-driven and communicating systems.

An SDL specification consists of a system, blocks, processes and channels. An SDL system specification is compounded by blocks, which exchange messages or signals with each other and the environment through the channels. The blocks can be decomposed recursively into sub-blocks and in the last level of this decomposition are the processes. Communication between processes is asynchronous and is also through channels. Channels can be uni or bi-directional. All the signals received by a process are merged into the individual process First In First Out (FIFO) queue, in the order of their arrivals.

The behavior of an SDL system specification is described by processes, that behave like Communicating Extended Finite State Machines. A process consists of a set of states and transitions that connect the states. When in a state, a process initiates a transition by consuming an expected signal from its input queue. Non expected signals in a state are implicitly consumed, that means to discard them and remains in the same state. Sometimes, it can be interesting to keep a signal in the queue to be consumed later by the process. In this case, the *save* construction can be used and just change the order of signals consumption by a process. Consuming a signal can result in another signals and update in the variables values.

SDL process can access the global timer using *now* which returns the current time. A timer is set to expire after a certain time from the current time defined by *now*. When a timer expires it sends a signal with its name to the process and this signal arrives at the input queue of the process. After the timer signal is consumed the timer is reset.

4 Mutation Testing

Mutation Testing is used to increase the confidence that a software product P is correct by producing, through small syntactic changes, a set of mutant elements that are similar to P, and creating test cases that are capable of causing behavioral differences between P and each one of its mutants. These changes are based on an operators set called mutant operators. To each operator it is associated an error type or an error class that we want to reveal in P.

The definition of mutant operators is a crucial factor for the success of Mutation Testing. Very simple operators are usually defined based on the competent programmer hypothesis, which states that a program produced by a competent programmer is either correct or near correct. The tester must construct test cases that show that these transformations lead to incorrect programs. Another hypothesis considered by Mutation Testing is the coupling effect that, according to DeMillo et al. [12], can be described as "test data that distinguishes all programs differing from a correct one by only simple errors is so sensitive that it would also implicitly distinguish more complex errors".

Mutation Testing consists of four steps: mutant generation; execution of the program P based on a defined test case set T; mutant execution; and adequacy analysis. All the mutants are executed using a given input test case set. If a mutant M presents results different from P, it is said to be dead, otherwise, it is said to be alive. In this case, either there are no test cases in T that are capable to distinguish M from P or M and P are equivalent, that means they have the same behavior (or output) for any data of the input domain. The objective must be to find a test case set T to kill all non-equivalent mutants; in this case T is considered adequate to test P.

DeMillo [11] notes that Mutation Testing provides an objective measure for the confidence level of the test case set adequacy. The Mutation Score, obtained by the relation between the number of mutants killed and the total number of non-equivalent mutants generated, allows the evaluation of the adequacy of the test case set used and therefore of the program under testing. A test case set T is adequate to a program P with respect to mutation testing coverage if the mutation score is 1.

The computational cost can be an obstacle to the use of Mutation Testing due to the high number of mutants generated and to be analyzed so that the equivalent ones can be identified. Since, in general, the equivalence is an undecidable question the equivalent mutants are interactively obtained by the tester. Some alternatives were proposed to program testing [4, 23, 34]. Wong et al. [34] provide evidences that examining only a small percentage of the mutants may be an useful heuristic for evaluating the test sets. Offutt et al. [23] and Barbosa et al. [4] have proposed the use of an essential operator set, so that a high mutation score against this essential set would also determine a high mutation score against the full set of mutant operators. Another option is to automatically generate test cases and determine equivalent mutants [13, 24]. Sim o and Maldonado [27] proposed an algorithm to generate test cases based on Mutation Testing to validate Petri Nets. Although it is undecidable, in some cases equivalent mutants can be identified using this algorithm.

Although Mutation Testing, as mentioned before, was proposed for program testing, it can be of help for validating a specification even considering that there is no mutation that would "restore" the correct behavior of the specification. The mutations can lead the tester to an error-revealing mutant without leading to the correct behavior. If k-mutants (more than a single change in the mutant) are considered it can be argued that would exist a mutant that presents the correct behavior but always depending on the quality of the specification under test. By defining a set of mutant operators and considering just a single change in each mutant, in fact, the space of possible wrong specifications has been reduced, reducing the cost of the Mutation Testing and assuming that single errors would lead to discover multiple and more complex errors. This assumption has to be explored in further studies.

5   Mutation Testing Applied to SDL

Earlier researches on testing specifications using Mutation Testing indicate that this criterion may contribute to the improvement of these activities [16, 26, 29], since it can complement other testing methods. This fact motivates the analysis of the adequacy of Mutation Testing in the context of SDL specifications.

As commented before, the definition of mutant operators is a key factor for the success of this criterion. Like Fabbri et al. [15, 16, 17, 18] and Souza et al. [29], we propose a mutant operators set for SDL based on some previous works: the control structure sequencing error classes defined by Chow [8], the mutant operators for boolean expressions defined by Weyuker et al. [33] and the mutant operator set for C language defined by Agrawal [1], Delamaro and Maldonado [9], Delamaro et al. [10]. Added to them, we explore some intrinsics features of SDL like *save* and *task* commands.

To illustrate the application of Mutation Testing in an SDL specification we use the well known Alternating-Bit protocol, which is a simple form of the "sliding window protocol" with a window size of 1 [31]. This protocol provides a reliable communication over a non-reliable network service using a one-bit sequence number (which alternates between 0 and 1) in each message or acknowledgement to determine when messages must be retransmitted. This protocol is composed of a sender and a receiver processes that communicate through two channels (Medium1 and Medium2). Figure 1 illustrates the Alternating-Bit protocol at the system level, with three blocks: sender_block, medium and sender_block.

The mutant operators are divided into three different classes: Process Mutant Operators, Interface Mutant Operators and Structure Mutant Operators. Table 1 illustrates the set of mutant operators defined for SDL and the number of mutants generated by them for the Alternating-Bit protocol. All of the opera-

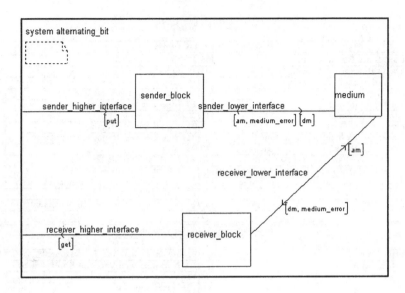

Fig. 1. System Level of the Alternating-Bit Protocol Specification in SDL

tors generated 261 mutants: 77, 51 and 133 by the Process Operators, Interface Operators and Structure Operators, respectively. Some operators do not generate any mutant since the syntactic structures that these operators act on do not occur in this protocol specification.

Given a specification S, a mutant set of S is generated, $\phi(S)$. A test set T is adequate for S with relation to $\phi(S)$ if for each specification Z of $\phi(S)$, either Z is equivalent to S, and in this case Z and S have the same behavior for T, or Z differs from S at least on a test point. To distinguish the mutant behavior from the original one, we analyze the final states of all processes reached after the execution with the test case set. Considering s a statement in a specification S and s_m the same statement but containing some mutation to generate the mutant Z. Three conditions must be satisfied by a test case T to distinguish Z from S [13]:

1. Reachability: s_m must be executed.
2. Necessity: The state of the mutant Z immediately after some execution of s_m must be different from the state of the original specification S after the execution of s.
3. Sufficiency: The difference in the states of S and Z immediately following the execution of s_m and s must be propagated until the end of execution of S or Z so that the final states reached by them when executed with T are different.

For SDL we consider that a typical test sequence is constituted by the sequence of signals exchanged during the execution of the specification. For example, a possible test sequence for the Alternating-Bit protocol is $ts = \mathit{¡put(m)},$

Table 1. Mutant Operators for SDL

Process Mutant Operators			
1. Origin State Replacement	03	15. Coverage of Code	15
2. State Definition Exchanged	01	16. Question of Decision Negation	04
3. Destination State Replacement	09	17. Answer of Decision Exchanged	04
4. State Missing	02	18. Answer of Decision Missing	08
5. Transition Missing	08	19. Stop Process Missing	0
6. Condition Missing	0	20. Save Missing	01
7. Negation of Condition	0	21. Signal Saved Missing	0
8. Boolean Assignment Replacement	0	22. Signal Saved Replacement	0
9. Variable by Variable Replacement	12	23. SET TIMER Missing	0
10. Variable by Constant Replacement	0	24. RESET TIMER Missing	0
11. Variables/Constants Increment/Decrement	0	25. CREATE Process Missing	0
12. Unary Operator Inclusion in Variables	0	26. Arithmetic Operator Replacement	0
13. Task Replacement	0	27. JOIN/LABEL Replacement	0
14. Task Missing	02	28. Relational Operator Replacement	08
		TOTAL	77
Interface Mutant Operators			
Group I: Calling Point		Group II: Called Process	
1. Output Missing	11	9. Interface Variables Replacement	08
2. Output Replacement	15	10. Non-Interface Variable Replacement	0
3. Output Destination Replacement	0	11. Variable Increment/Decrement	0
4. Signal Route of Output Replacement	06	12. Unary Operators Inclusion in Variable	0
5. Parameters Replacement	0	13. Boolean Assignment Replacement	0
6. Parameters Increment/Decrement	0	14. Input Missing	07
7. Order of the parameters Exchanged	0	15. Input Replacement	04
8. Unary Operators Inclusion in Parameters	0		
		TOTAL	51
Structure Mutant Operators			
1. Signal of Signal List Inclusion			44
2. Signal of Signal List Missing			12
3. Signal of Signal List Exchanged			35
4. Signal routes/Channels Missing			16
5. Connection between Channels and Signal routes Missing			08
6. Connected Channels/Signal routes Replacement			18
		TOTAL	133

$dm(m,0)$, $dm(m,0)$, $get(m) \wedge am(0)$, $am(0)$¿. This sequence corresponds to the following steps: Sender sends a message to Receiver ($put(m)$ signal). The message (m) is packed and it is sent to the Medium1 ($dm(m,0)$) with an identifier bit (0). Medium1 sends the message to Receiver ($dm(m,0)$). The message arrives to Receiver that verifies that it is the message it was expecting, stores the message ($get(m)$) and sends the acknowledgement to Sender ($am(0)$) through Medium2. Medium2 receives the acknowledgment and sends it to Sender ($am(0)$). The acknowledgment is received by the Sender and it is recognized as the expected acknowledgment.

For the test sequence ts, the final states activated are $sa = ¡$ ([(wait_- put)], [(wait_dm), (wait_am)], [(wait_dm)]) ¿, considering the following order of processes: ([Sender], [Medium1,Medium2], [Receiver]).

In the following we describe the three classes of mutant operators and present an informal definition of one mutant operator for each class. For each one of these mutant operators we illustrate one mutant generated and execute them with the test sequence ts.

5.1 Process Mutant Operators

The operators of this class model errors related to the behavior of processes that is similar to the Communicating Extended Finite State Machines (CEFSMs) behavior. To define this class of operators, we consider the particular features of SDL and two previous works: the set of mutant operators to Extended Finite State Machines (EFSMs) defined by Fabbri et al. [18] and the set of operators defined by Souza et al. [29] to explore mutation on modules of Estelle specifications that behave like EFSMs. Our mutant operators set models: transitions and states errors; expressions, mathematic operators, variables and constants errors, and; timers errors (set and reset).

– Example: Destination State Exchanged
  This operator models state errors by exchanging the destination of each transition. The state defined at the *nextstate* command is mutated by other states defined in the same process and by the – symbol.
  This operator is applied to the Sender process of the Alternating-Bit protocol. The transition fired by am(j) event when in the wait_am state has as destination state wait_put. To generate the mutants this state is replaced by the other state in the process, that is wait_am, and by the - symbol. Figure 2 illustrates the part of the original specification where one mutation is done and one of the mutants generated.
  When this mutant is executed with *ts* the final states activated are $sa = $ ¡ ([wait_am], [wait_dm, wait_am], [wait_dm]) ¿. The wait_am state in Sender process is different from the expected one which was the wait_put state. As a result, the mutant is distinguished from the original specification and so is considered dead. In other case, if the mutant is executed with ts_i = ¡put(m), dm(m,0), dm(m,0), get(m) ∧ am(0), medium_error¿, the final states activated are $sa = $ ¡ ([wait_am], [wait_dm, wait_am], [wait_dm]) ¿. The same final states are activated when the original specification is executed with ts_i. Thus, the test case ts_i is not able to distinguish this mutant from the original specification.

Original Specification	Mutant Specification
STATE wait_am;	STATE wait_am;
INPUT am (j);	INPUT am (j);
DECISION j = i;	DECISION j = i;
(TRUE):	(TRUE):
TASK i := inv(i);	TASK i := inv(i);
NEXTSTATE wait_put;	→ NEXTSTATE **WAIT_AM**;
ELSE:	ELSE:
. . .	. . .

Fig. 2. Process Mutant Operator Example: Destination State Exchanged

5.2   Interface Mutation

At program level, Delamaro et al. [10] defined Interface Mutation to test the interactions between the units compounding a software. Based on this concept, Souza et al. [29] defined interface mutant operators to Estelle applying the Interface Mutation to the specification level. In the same way, we propose an interface mutant operators set modelling communication errors among processes of an SDL specification, considering all the possible signals exchanges. Following these previous works, we divide the interface mutant operators in two groups: Group I, that explores the points where a process is called, i.e., at the *output* command; and Group II, that explores the process called, but the mutation is done in the *input* command and where computations are executed with the received signals.

– Example Group I: Output Missing
  This operator models output errors by excluding each output defined in the state transitions.
  One of the mutants generated when applying this operator to the Sender process of the Alternating-Bit protocol is presented in Figure 3. To generate this mutant, the operator is applied to the output of the transition of the `wait_put` state, excluding the "OUTPUT dm (m , i);" command.
  When this mutant is executed with ts the final states activated are $sa = ¡$ *([wait_am], [wait_dm, wait_am], [wait_dm]) ¿*. The `wait_am` state is different from the expected one, the `wait_put` state. As a result, the mutant is distinguished from the original specification and so is considered dead. In this case, the test sequence $ts_i = ¡put(m),\ dm(m,0),\ dm(m,0),\ get(m) \wedge am(0),\ medium\_error¿$ also distinguishes this mutant because the second signal `dm(m,0)` is not generated and the final states are $sa = ¡$ *([wait_am], [wait_dm, wait_am], [wait_dm]) ¿*.

Original Specification	Mutant Specification
STATE wait_put;	STATE wait_put;
INPUT put (m);	INPUT put (m);
OUTPUT dm (m , i);	$\rightarrow$
NEXTSTATE wait_am;	NEXTSTATE wait_am;
ENDSTATE;	ENDSTATE;

Fig. 3. Interface Mutant Operator Example: Output Missing

5.3   Structure Mutation

Structure Mutation explores errors in the architecture of the SDL specification that represents the hierarchical composition of the software components, their interaction and the data exchanged by them. The data flow is expressed by input and output signals and the local variables of the processes. It is worth to note that some interface aspects are presented by the software structure, then we can also consider interface errors in the structure mutation context.

The structure mutant operators set models errors in the definitions of signal routes and channels, in the connections between them and in the list of signals declared.

- Example: Signal routes/Channels Missing
  This operator models errors related to the signal routes or channels definitions. It excludes each signal route and channel that links processes and blocks of the SDL specification.
  Figure 4 illustrates the definition of one signal route and one of the mutants generated when applying this operator to it. This mutant does not have the signal route that links the environment to the Sender process.
  When executing this mutant with ts the final states activated are $sa = ¡$ ([wait_am], [wait_dm, wait_am], [wait_dm]) ¿. The wait_am state of the Sender process is different from the expected one which was the wait_put state. As a result, the mutant is distinguished from the original specification and so is considered dead. The test sequence $ts_i = ¡put(m), dm(m,0),$ $dm(m,0), get(m) \wedge am(0), medium\_error¿$ also distinguishes this mutant because the last signal medium_error is not received by the Sender process and the final states are $sa = ¡$ ([wait_am], [wait_dm, wait_am], [wait_-dm])¿.

Original Specification	Mutant Specification
SIGNALROUTE sender_lower_interface	SIGNALROUTE sender_lower_interface
FROM ENV TO sender_process	→
WITH am , medium_error;	
FROM sender_process TO ENV WITH dm;	FROM sender_process TO ENV WITH dm;

Fig. 4. Structure Mutant Operator Example: Signal Routes/Channels Missing

5.4   Incremental Testing Strategies and Automation Aspects

Incremental Testing Strategies can be established to orient the application of the mutant operators to the SDL specifications. We can consider the three classes of operators and prioritize some aspects such as: behavior of the processes, communication among processes and structure of the specification. We can also select a subset of operators in each step of the strategy. The steps of one possible testing strategy are:

1. to validate the behavior of processes of the SDL specification, for each process
   a) apply the Process Mutant Operators and determine an adequate test set;

2. to validate the communication among the processes, for each process

   a) apply the Interface Mutant Operators and determine an adequate test set;

3. to validate the structure of the SDL specification

   a) for each signal route and channel definition

      – apply the Structure Mutant Operator (operators 1 to 4) and determine an adequate test set

   b) for each connection between a channel and a signal route

      – apply the Structure Mutant Operators (operators 5 and 6) and determine an adequate test set

This testing strategy can be applied either top-down or bottom-up. In case an error is found during the application of this strategy, the specification should be corrected and the strategy applied again.

A testing tool to support the application of Mutation Testing is crucial since this activity can be error prone and unproductive if applied manually. Our work group has developed a family of tools to support Mutation Testing at the program and specification levels [22]. For testing C programs we have Proteum and Proteum/IM tools [9, 10]. For testing at the specification level, there are Proteum/FSM for the Finite State Machines based specifications [16]; Proteum/ST for Statecharts based specifications [18, 30]; and Proteum/PN for Petri Nets based specifications [28]. All these tools support the main functions related to the Mutation Testing: definition of a test case set, execution of the specification (or program), mutants generation, execution of the mutants, analysis of the mutants, computation of the mutation score and reports generation. When using these tools, the tester works in test sessions. In this way, the tester can start a test session, stop it at his/her convenience and resume the test session later from the point he/she has stopped. To allow this, the tools record the intermediate states of the test session. Information about mutants and test cases are maintained in a database. It is possible to select a subset of the mutant operators (constrained mutation) [23] or specify a percentage to be applied to generate the mutants. To analyze the mutants, the results obtained by their execution are compared to the result obtained by the original specification (or program) execution. Considering these features, we will develop a tool to support Mutation Testing to test SDL specifications. The preliminary results we present in this paper were obtained manually, but this was a very simple example and the development of a supporting tool is required. In fact we intend to add these functionalities into an existing tool named CAT_{SDL} [35], a coverage analysis tool that aids in testing specifications written in SDL. This tool supports control flow and data flow-based criteria.

Some problems existing in program testing also occur in specification testing, for example the oracle problem. The oracle problem remains in specification testing, either there is a formal mechanism to specify the expected behavior of the specification under test and then having an automated process to check the output or a human expertise is required. Other problem related to Mutation

Testing is the high computational cost caused by the large number of mutants that can be generated. To overcome this problem at the program level, Offutt et al. [23] and Barbosa et al. [4] proposed the determination of an essential operators set. In the same vein, we intend to investigate an essential operators set to SDL, based on our initial mutant operators set. At specification level, Sim o and Maldonado [27] proposed as an alternative to overcome the computational cost of Mutation Testing applied to Petri Nets, the automatic generation of test sequences that in some cases identify equivalent mutants. We also intend to investigate this approach in the context of SDL specification testing.

6   Final Remarks

In this paper we proposed the use of Mutation Testing to test specifications written in SDL. We use this criterion as a mechanism for assessing the SDL specifications testing adequacy. Kov cs et al. [20] use the test set generated by applying Mutation Testing to an SDL specification to test and validate the related implementation, i.e., it is applied in the conformance testing. Differently, we are interested in testing the specification itself. This is relevant so that the quality of the product can be guaranteed earlier in the development process. We were motivated by other works of our research group that have investigated Mutation Testing in the context of some formal techniques such as Finite State Machines, Statecharts, Petri Nets and Estelle. Although we are interested in specification testing, the test set generated based on the mutants can also be used to the conformance testing of implementations that claim to be conformed to the specification.

To propose a mutant operators set we took into account intrinsics features of SDL, the behavioral aspect of the processes, the communication among the processes and the structure of the SDL specification. These aspects were divided in three classes of mutant operators, that define a fault model to SDL: Process Mutation, Interface Mutation and Structure Mutation. Priority can be given to some aspects when the testing activity is conducted by a testing strategy. We also presented an incremental testing strategy for application of the Mutation Testing in this context.

The short term goals of our work on this subject is directed to three lines of research: improvement and refinement of the mutant operators (determining an essential operators set in the same line of Offutt et al. [23]), development of a tool to support Mutation Testing in the context of SDL and conduct empirical studies to compare Mutation Testing and Control and Data flow-based criteria.

Acknowledgements. The authors would like to thank the partial financial support from the brazilian funding agencies CNPq, CAPES and FAPESP, and from Telcordia Technologies (USA).

References

[1] Agrawal, H. (1989). Design of mutant operators for the C programming language. Technical Report SERC-TR-41-P, Software Engineering Research Center/Purdue University.

[2] Ammann, P. and Black, P. (1999). A specification-based coverage metric to evaluate test sets. In *Proceedings of Fourth IEEE International High-Assurance Systems Engineering Symposium (HASE 99)*, pages 239–248. IEEE Computer Society.

[3] Ammann, P., Black, P., and Majurski, W. (1998). Using model checking to generate tests from specifications. In *Proceedings of 2nd IEEE International Conference on Formal Engineering Methods*, pages 46–54, Brisbane, Australia. IEEE Computer Society.

[4] Barbosa, E. F., Maldonado, J. C., and Vincenzi, A. M. R. (2001). Toward the determination of sufficient mutant operators for C. *Software Testing, Verification and Reliability Journal*, 11(2):113–136.

[5] Black, P. E., Okun, V., and Yesha, Y. (2000). Mutation operators for specifications. In *Proceedings of 15th IEEE International Conference on Automated Software Engineering (ASE2000)*, pages 81–89.

[6] Bousquet, L. D., Ramangalahy, S., Simon, S., Viho, C., Belinfante, A., and Vries, R. G. (2000). Formal test automation: The conference protocol with TGV/TORX. In Ural, H., Probert, R. L., and v. Bochmann, G., editors, *IFIP 13th International Conference on Testing of Communicating Systems(TestCom 2000)*. Kluwer Academic Publishers.

[7] Bromstrup, L. and Hogrefe, D. (1989). TESDL: Experience with generating test cases from SDL specifications. In *Proceedings of Fourth SDL Forum*, pages 267–279.

[8] Chow, T. S. (1978). Testing software design modeled by Finite-State Machines. *IEEE Transactions on Software Engineering*, 4(3):178–187.

[9] Delamaro, M. E. and Maldonado, J. C. (1996). Proteum: A tool for the assessment of test adequacy for C programs. In *Conference on Performability in Computing Systems*, pages 79–95, Brunswick, NJ.

[10] Delamaro, M. E., Maldonado, J. C., and Mathur, A. P. (2001). Interface mutation: An approach for integration testing. *IEEE Transactions on Software Engineering*, 27(3):228–247.

[11] DeMillo, R. A. (1980). Mutation analysis as a tool for software quality assurance. In *Proceedings of COMPSAC80*, Chicago, IL.

[12] DeMillo, R. A., Lipton, R. J., and Sayward, F. G. (1978). Hints on test data selection: Help for the practicing programmer. *IEEE Computer*, 11(4):34–41.

[13] DeMillo, R. A. and Offutt, A. J. (1991). Constraint-based automatic test data generation. *IEEE Transactions on Software Engineering*, 17(9):900–910.

[14] Fabbri, S. C. P. F., Maldonado, J. C., Delamaro, M. E., and Masiero, P. C. (1999a). Proteum/FSM: A tool to support Finite State Machine validation based on mutation testing. In *Proceedings of XIX SCCC - International Conference of the Chilean Computer Science Society*, pages 96–104, Talca, Chile.

[15] Fabbri, S. C. P. F., Maldonado, J. C., and Masiero, P. C. (1997). Mutation analysis in the context of reactive system specification and validation. In *5th Annual International Conference on Software Quality Management*, pages 247–258, Bath, UK.

[16] Fabbri, S. C. P. F., Maldonado, J. C., Masiero, P. C., and Delamaro, M. E. (1994). Mutation analysis testing for Finite State Machines. In *Proceedings of ISSRE'94 - Fifth International Symposium on Software Reliability Engineering*, pages 220–229, Monterey, California, USA.

[17] Fabbri, S. C. P. F., Maldonado, J. C., Masiero, P. C., Delamaro, M. E., and Wong, E. (1995). Mutation testing applied to validate specifications based on Petri nets. In *Proceedings of FORTE'95 - 8th International IFIP Conference on Formal Description Techniques for Distributed Systems and Communications Protocol*, pages 329–337, Montreal, Canada.

[18] Fabbri, S. C. P. F., Maldonado, J. C., Sugeta, T., and Masiero, P. C. (1999b). Mutation testing applied to validate specifications based on Statecharts. In *ISSRE — International Symposium on Software Reliability Systems*, pages 210–219, Boca Raton, Flórida, EUA.

[19] Ghosh, S. and Mathur, A. P. (2000). Interface mutation. In *Mutation 2000 - A Symposium on Mutation Testing for the New Century*, pages 112–123, San José, California.

[20] Kov cs, G., Pap, Z., Viet, D. L., Wu-Hen-Chang, A., and Csopaki, G. (2003). Applying mutation analysis to sdl specifications. In Reed, R. and Reed, J., editors, *SDL 2003: System Design - 11th SDL Forum*, volume 2708 of *Lecture Notes on Computer Science*, pages 269–284, Stuttgart, Germany.

[21] Luo, G., Das, A., and Bochmann, G. (1991). Software test selection based on SDL specification with save. In *Proceedings of 5th SDL Forum*, pages 313–324, Glasgow. Elsevier.

[22] Maldonado, J. C., Delamaro, M. E., Fabbri, S. C. P. F., Sim o, A. S., Sugeta, T., Vincenzi, A. M. R., and Masiero, P. C. (2000). Proteum: A family of tools to support specification and program testing based on mutation. In *Mutation 2000 - A Symposium on Mutation Testing for the New Century*, pages 146–149, San José, California.

[23] Offutt, A. J., Lee, A., Rothermel, G., Untch, R. H., and Zapf, C. (1996). An experimental determination of sufficient mutant operators. *ACM Transactions on Software Engineering Methodology*, 5(2):99–118.

[24] Offutt, A. J. and Pan, J. (1997). Automatically detecting equivalent mutants and infeasible paths. *The Journal of Software Testing, Verification, and Reliability*, 7(3):165–192.

[25] Petrenko, A. and Bochmann, G. (1996). On fault coverage of tests for Finite State specifications. Technical report, Département d'Informatique et de Recherche Opérationnelle, Université de Montreal.

[26] Probert, R. L. and Guo, F. (1991). Mutation testing of protocols: Principles and preliminary experimental results. In *Proceedings of the IFIP TC6 Third International Workshop on Protocol Teste Systems*, pages 57–76, North-Holland.

[27] Simão, A. S. and Maldonado, J. C. (2000). Mutation based test sequence generation for Petri nets. In *Proceedings of III Workshop of Formal Methods*, pages 68–79, João Pessoa, PB.

[28] Simão, A. S., Maldonado, J. C., and Fabbri, S. C. P. F. (2000). Proteum-RS/PN: A tool to support edition, simulation and validation of Petri nets based on mutation testing. In *Proceedings of XIV Brazilian Symposium of Software Engineering*, pages 227–242, João Pessoa, PB, Brazil.

[29] Souza, S. R. S., Maldonado, J. C., Fabbri, S. C. P. F., and Lopes de Souza, W. (2000). Mutation testing applied to Estelle specifications. *Quality Software Journal*, 8(4):285–301. (Also published in the 33rd Hawaii Internacional Conference on System Sciences - 2000).

[30] Sugeta, T., Maldonado, J. C., Masiero, P. C., and Fabbri, S. C. P. F. (2001). Proteum-RS/ST – A Tool to Support Statecharts Validation Based on Mutation Testing. In *4th Workshop Iberoamericano de Engenharia de Requisitos e Ambientes de Software - IDEAS'2001*, pages 370–384, Santo Domingo, Costa Rica.

[31] Tanenbaum, A. S. (1996). *Computer Networks*. Prentice Hall, 3 edition.

[32] Ural, H., Saleh, K., and Williams, A. (2000). Test generation based on control and data dependencies within system specifications in SDL. *Computer Communications*, 23(7):609–627.

[33] Weyuker, E. J., Goradia, T., and Singh, A. (1994). Automatically generating test data from a boolean specification. *IEEE Transactions on Software Engineering*, 20(5):353–363.

[34] Wong, W. E., Maldonado, J. C., and Mathur, A. P. (1994). Mutation versus all-uses: An empirical evaluation of cost, strength and effectiveness. In *First IFIP/SQI International Conference on Software Quality and Productivity – Theory, Practice, Education and Training*, Hong Kong.

[35] Wong, W. E., Sugeta, T., Li, J. J., and Maldonado, J. C. (2003). Coverage testing software architectural design in SDL. *Computer Networks*, 42(3):359–374.

Execution of External Applications Using TTCN-3

Theofanis Vassiliou-Gioles[1], George Din[2], and Ina Schieferdecker[2]

[1]Testing Technologies IST GmbH,
Oranienburger Str. 65, D-10117 Berlin, Germany
vassiliou@testingtech.de
[2]Fraunhofer FOKUS, Kaiserin-Augusta-Allee 31,
D-10589 Berlin, Germany
{din,schieferdecker}@fokus.fraunhofer.de

Abstract. TTCN-3 allows an easy and efficient description of complex distributed test behaviour in terms of sequences, alternatives, loops and parallel stimuli and responses. The test system can use any number of test components to perform test procedures in parallel. Features which are not directly supported in TTCN-3 can be included by the use of external types, data and functions. However, the access to external test behaviour is rather limited as external functions are executed as plain functions only without being performed on test components. The combination of external functions and test components allows the extension of the communication between the TTCN-3 test system and the external behaviours towards complex send/receive patterns and supports the distribution of external behaviours on remote nodes. This paper discusses the concepts of external behaviours, proposes extensions to TTCN-3 to realise them and demonstrates its application by a concrete example.

1   Introduction

TTCN-3, the Testing and Test Control Notation, is the test specification and implementation language defined by the European Telecommunications Standards Institute (ETSI) for the precise definition of test procedures for black-box testing of distributed systems.

TTCN-3 allows an easy and efficient description of complex distributed test behaviour in terms of sequences, alternatives, loops and parallel stimuli and responses. The test system can use any number of test components to perform test procedures in parallel. One essential benefit of TTCN-3 is that it enables the specification of tests in a platform independent manner. TTCN-3 provides the concepts of test components, their creation, communication links between them and to the system under test (SUT), their execution and termination on an abstract level, yet together with TTCN-3 execution interfaces to provide the realisation of concrete executable tests on different target test platforms. Features and capabilities being beyond TTCN-3 can be integrated into TTCN-3 by the use of external types, data and functions.

TTCN-3 is currently been used in different domains, like in the telecommunications domain by network equipment vendors and carriers or in the service testing domain. Quite frequently it has been observed by these different user groups that the integration of external behaviour, i.e. non-TTCN-3 behaviour, is currently not foreseen

R. Groz and R.M. Hierons (Eds.): TestCom 2004, LNCS 2978, pp. 209–223, 2004.

within the language. As it will be shown in the following, the concept of external function lacks flexibility in order to integrate behaviour provided in different languages than TTCN-3 seamlessly. Although TTCN-3 offers strong concepts for black-box testing, management of test cases and verdicts, the inability to define the execution of arbitrary test scripts keeps potential users with an already existing stock of different test solutions from using TTCN-3. The possible translation of existing test scripts being defined for example in Perl, Python or Tcl is not feasible as there is no mapping available for every script language. Even if the mappings would have been available, the implementation of translators or migration tools would exceed current budgets allocated for testing. So, the overall goal was and is to provide a generic approach on how to integrate arbitrary scripts in a TTCN-3 execution environment.

Extending the TTCN-3 language with the capability of external behaviours requires extensions in the execution environments as well. Beside the language artefacts required for working with external behaviours, we present in this paper also a general strategy of how existing TTCN-3 tools can be extended to support this feature. Although handling external behaviours imposes some changes in the execution environment, our approach respects fully the specification of the TTCN-3 test system architecture defined in [1][2][3]. Having such a framework available, a broad range of new applications for TTCN-3 is opened. For example, TTCN-3 can be used more efficient as a test management language since e.g. existing scripts for traffic generation can be easily related to TTCN-3 test behaviours and controlled by TTCN-3.

At first, this paper motivates in Section 2 the need to extend TTCN-3 with the concepts of external component and external behaviour. Section 3 outlines implementations strategies based on the existing TTCN-3 execution interface specifications TRI and TCI. Section 4 presents a concrete example combining TTCN-3 efficiently with a test script written in the Perl programming language. Section 5 concludes the paper with a summary and an outlook on future work.

2   A Concept Framework for External TTCN-3 Behaviour

The TTCN-3 language defines several constructs for describing the functionality of a test system. The behaviour of the test system can be specified by using one of the following constructs: control, test case, function or external function.

The *control part*, as the name also suggests, is the part of the test system where the overall behaviour is controlled. From the control part, the test cases are executed and the final verdict can be collected. The control part is defined with the **control** construct.

```
control { ... }
```

A *test component* is the entity on which a test case or a function can be started. It may include in its type definition timers, variables, constants and ports, which can be accessed by any function or test case running on it. Test components are defined in TTCN-3 with the keyword **component**.

```
type component TestComponent {

    port PortType p;
    timer t1;

}
```

A *test case* is defined by the `testcase` keyword. It specifies the interaction with the SUT and/or the creation of test configurations using a number of parallel test components in addition to the main test component. It is able to instantiate types, to interact with the SUT by sending stimuli and receiving data, and to set verdicts. The communication with the SUT is realised via ports, which are defined by the test component on which it runs. In addition to the test component on which the test case runs, a system component can be specified which defines the interface to the SUT. If more than one test component is used by the test case, then the system component must be specified explicitly:

```
testcase T( ... ) runs on TestComponent system SystemComponent { ... }
```

A *function* defined by the keyword `function` is similar to a test case; it may deal with data, can access the variables, ports or timers of the test component on which it runs and may set verdicts. In the case where the function interacts with the SUT or with other test components, we call it a behaviour as compared to pure computational functions that do not interact with their environment. A behaviour differs from a test case by the fact that no system component is defined for it. A pure computational function has no runs on clause and no port parameters.

```
function F( ... ) runs on TestComponent { ... }
```

TTCN-3 has also the concept of *external functions*. An external function is introduced by `external function` keywords and defines the interface of a method whose implementation is outside the TTCN-3 test system. The glue between an external function and the TTCN-3 test system is realised in the platform adapter (PA) [3]. External functions can be called from control, test cases or functions. In contrast to a function, an external function does not run on a component and, because of that, cannot use ports to communicate with other test components.

```
external function F( ... );
```

For our purpose of using external behaviours flexibly, the language concepts seem not to be enough. Test cases or functions, the only behaviours which are allowed to run on components cannot be used to execute external behaviours.

As presented, the only way to define non-TTCN-3 code in TTCN-3 is the external function concept, but even this is limited to the signature (i.e. the interface) of the external function. TTCN-3 explicitly forbids the communication between external functions and test components. Indeed, an external function can be used to run scripts defined outside TTCN-3; however we consider this not to be enough. At least, the following features should be supported by an external behaviour:

- The possibility to set verdicts from an external behaviour.
- An external behaviour may produce TCI errors, which cause the termination of the test execution.
- External behaviours may be distributed and started over many test hosts.
- An external behaviour shall use ports to communicate with other test components.

An external function, as defined in TTCN-3, can help only for the first two requirements as the return value can be used to return some termination status of the external function or to encode different error codes. The last one, which is probably the most important one, is not supported in TTCN-3 and can also not be substituted by any other construct.

Consequently, we were motivated to introduce the concepts of external behaviour and external component. The principal architecture for a test system using TTCN-3 test components and external test components is depicted in Fig. 1.

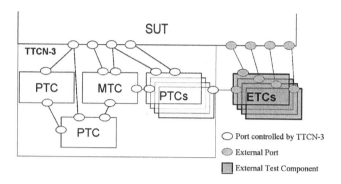

Fig. 1. Architecture for a test system using TTCN-3 test components (MTC – main test component and PTC – parallel test component) and external test components (ETC)

An external component is defined by using the keyword **external** with a component type definition:

```
type external component ExternalComponent {
    port PortType p;
}
```

An *external behaviour* is an external function which runs on a test component of type external:

```
external function F( ... ) runs on ExternalComponent;
```

An external function with a **runs on** clause is the construct for a behaviour defined in another language than TTCN-3, able to interact with the SUT by using specific operations and able to communicate with other TTCN-3 components by using TTCN-3 ports. An external behaviour is executed on an external test component having ports only since timers and variables are only meaningful within the TTCN-3 test system. External behaviours may not return values – neither via inout or out parameters nor via a function return. The only way to pass information between the TTCN-3 test system and the external behaviour is via the ports the external behaviour is running on[1]. External behaviours are started with a start operation called on an external component.

---

[1] Please note that also in TTCN-3 functions started on a test component cannot return values. Although the function might have defined a return type, a possible return is ignored when the function is being started on a test component.

The TTCN-3 language extension for external behaviour is defined below:

```
ExtBehaviourDef::= ExtKeyword FunctionKeyword FunctionIdentifier "("
[FunctionFormalParList] ")" RunsOnSpec ";"
```

We introduced in the TTCN-3 grammar the production of the non-terminal Ext-BehaviourDef. It is similar to ExtFunctionDef except that we introduced the RunsOnSpec, omitted the return ReturnType and allow only in parameters as parameters to the external behaviour function.

An external behaviour is considered to be running on an entity being outside the TTCN-3 test system having its own types and data. It uses technology specific possibilities to interact with the SUT and for the definition of its behaviour. An external behaviour may contain the notion of timers and local variables and may evaluate even verdicts. However, these concepts do not align with the concepts of timers, variables and verdicts as defined in TTCN-3 – they are specific to the external behaviour only. An external behaviour is considered a test component by itself which we want to integrate into a TTCN-3 test system. By combining them, we understand the possibility that a TTCN-3 test system may create and start external behaviours locally or remotely, may exchange data with it and by doing so may get its result. A TTCN-3 test system should not share the local variables or constants, timers or functions with the external behaviour. We refer to the external behaviour as an application (script or program) written independently of TTCN-3. Thus, for example, any Perl or Tcl script can be integrated with TTCN-3 and no further extension or adaptation for it is needed.

The following items characterise an external behaviour:

- It may be an application which may run independently of TTCN-3.
- Therefore, no access to TTCN-3 data, types, timers, functions should be possible.
- An external behaviour communicates with the TTCN-3 test system by using ports. This is the reason why an external behaviour is started on an external component whose ports are used for communication with the TTCN-3 test system.
- Within the external behaviour no direct reference/use of TTCN-3 ports is possible, but rather the communication between the TTCN-3 ports and external behaviour is realised via an adapter – the platform specific wrapper (PSW) - that relates the communication interfaces of the external behaviour to the TTCN-3 ports they are connected to.
- The wrapper handles the communications with the application; as defined, the external behaviour has no access to the internal TTCN-3 types and data. In order to be able to receive and send, data encoding and decoding of TTCN-3 values must be performed by the PSW.

Since an external behaviour is not allowed to access timers or variables, it cannot be executed on regular components. Thus, we define the concept of external component as a restricted TTCN-3 test component.

An *external component* is a TTCN-3 test component on which external behaviours run. An external component may contain only ports which may connect to other TTCN-3 ports, but no map operation is permitted. Communication of the external behaviour with the SUT is completely defined by the external behaviour. No timers, variables or constants are allowed. Below we present the TTCN-3 language extension for external component definition:

```
StructuredTypeDef::=
    RecordDef
    | UnionDef
    | SetDef
    | RecordOfDef
    | SetOfDef
    | EnumDef
    | PortDef
    | ComponentDef
    | ExtComponentDef
```

A `StructuredTypeDef` contains now also the non-terminal `ExtComponentDef`. It is similar to `ComponentDef` except that it is prefixed by the `ExtKeyword`.

```
ExtComponentDef::= ExtKeyword ComponentKeyword
ComponentTypeIdentifier BeginChar [ExtComponentDefList] EndChar
```

Instead of a `ComponentDefList`, the `ExtComponentDef` uses an `ExtComponentDefList` non-terminal.

```
ExtComponentDefList::= { ExtComponentElementDef [SemiColon] }
```

The `ExtComponentDefList` is defined through the `ExtComponentElementDef` non-terminal which contains only the `PortInstance` non-terminal.

```
ExtComponentElementDef::=
    PortInstance
```

From the TTCN-3 view, an external component is functionally a minimised component. Except the few constraints presented before, external components are compatible with normal test components: they run in the TTCN-3 Executable (TE), are handled by the TCI component handling (CH) and may connect via ports to other TTCN-3 test components.

3   Implementation Guidelines

This section explains how to realise technically the concepts presented previously. We experimented with our Java based implementation of the test system architecture as presented in ETSI standard [1] by extending it to support the execution of external behaviours. In the practical setup, we used the Perl language to describe external behaviours. Based on our experience, we present subsequently a general approach, of how to extend existing TTCN execution environments with external behaviours.

The main design requirement for our system was to follow strictly the TTCN-3 execution interfaces TRI [2] and TCI [3]. This way, our approach is general and reusable. A different implementation can follow the same patterns of implementation.

3.1   Test System Architecture

Firstly, we describe the implementation of the ETSI Test System Architecture and its related interfaces. The general structure of a distributed TTCN-3 test system is presented in Fig. 2. A TTCN-3 test system is build up of a set of interacting entities, which manage the test execution, interpretation or execution of TTCN-3 code, realise the communication with the SUT, implement external functions and handle timer operations.

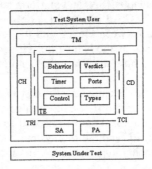

Fig. 2. General structure of a TTCN-3 test system as defined in TCI [3]. The test system contains the TTCN-3 executable (TE), which in turn communicates with the test management system (TM), the component handling (CH) and the coding/decoding (CD) via the TTCN-3 control interfaces. Communication with the SUT is performed using the TTCN-3 runtime interfaces (TRI), which define the interfaces between the TE and the system adapter (SA) and the platform adapter (PA).

The 6th part of the ETSI TTCN-3 standard [3] provides a standardised adaptation of a test system to a particular test platform by means of the management and handling of test components and encoding/decoding and defines the interaction between the three main entities: test management (TM), test component handling (CH) and coding/decoding (CD)[2]:

- *TTCN-3 executable (TE)* interprets or executes the compiled TTCN-3 code. This component manages different entities: control, behaviour, component, type, value and queue, entities which are the basic constructors for the executable code.
- *Component handling (CH)* handles the communication between components. The CH API contains operations to: create, start, stop test components, establish the connection between test components (map, connect), handle the communication operations (send, receive, call and reply) and manage the verdicts. The information about the created components and their physical locations is stored in a repository within the Execution Environment.
- *Test management (TM)* manages the test execution. It implements operations to execute tests, to provide and set module parameters and external-constants. The test logging is also realised by this component.

---

[2] We refer to the entity that provides encoding and coding functionality also as Codec.

- *Coding/decoding (CD)*: encodes and decodes types and values. TTCN-3 values are encoded into bitstrings before being sent to the SUT. Received data being also bitstrings are decoded back into the corresponding TTCN-3 values.

According to this architecture, a test can be distributed over many test hosts and different test behaviours can be executed in parallel and simultaneously. As it is conceived within the standard, on each host an instance of the test system is created. In detail, the TTCN-3 execution (TE) must be installed on each host with its own coding and decoding (CD), system adapter (SA) and platform adapter (PA).

The 5th part of the ETSI TTCN-3 standard [2] defines the TTCN-3 runtime interfaces for the communication between the TE and the test adapter (TA) and platform adapter (PA). This part defines methods how the TE sends data to the SUT and manipulates timers and methods how the SA and PA notify the TE about received test data and timeouts.

Our implementation of that architecture is represented in Fig. 3. A Java and CORBA-based platform is the platform used to implement the *execution environment* (EE). The EE contains the additional entities needed to manage the test system entities. The interaction between EE and the test system components is tool specific and depends on the underlying technology. For example in Java, it is very easy to implement the EE as a static class which can be accessed from everywhere. The TE is a standalone process, which instantiates components, timers, ports and behaviours. TE gets a reference to EE by which the CH, TM, SA and PA are accessible. The timers, ports and behaviours are also seen as parallel processes which are managed by the TE. Basically, the ports, timers and behaviours belong to a component, which is an object global to them and contains some global information such as identifier, local verdict, etc.

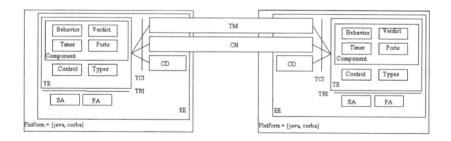

Fig. 3. Implementation view of a distributed TTCN-3 runtime environment. While the TTCN-3 execution environment is available on each test device (see [3]) only once, possibly distributed instances of the test management (TM) and the component handling (CH) entity exist.

In our implementation, the platform consists of the JVM (Java virtual machine) and the CORBA communication middleware included in Sun's Java 1.4 SDK. The EE running on that platform is the implementation of the test system entities. The CH, TM, CD, SA and PA are main entities providing the specified methods for communication, management, user interaction etc. They can be required by any built-in entity of EE; EE is seen as a global entity. TE instantiates and manages the ports, timers and behaviours which are implemented as Java threads; at creation each entity knows the TE so that it may use the other test system entities CH, TM etc.

As described in the general approach of the execution environment and as realised in the Java based implementation, behaviours are standalone processes running in parallel with other behaviours and/or entities. They may access ports or timers from the test component to which they belong.

An external behaviour is implemented by a different technology than the one used to implement the execution environment. However, the external component technology can be the same as the EE technology. Therefore, we use a *platform specific wrapper* (PSW) able to interconnect the external component in the TE with the external behaviour executing on the EB platform. An external component uses such a wrapper to communicate with the external behaviour but is also able to communicate with the other entities of the platform like a normal test component.

Fig. 4 shows an extension of the test system architecture where the external behaviours are deployed in a PSW (Platform Specific Wrapper).

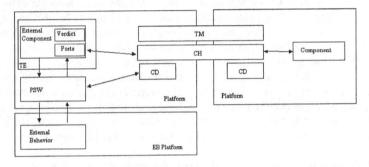

Fig. 4. Handling of external behaviours through PSW. An external behaviour runs on an external behaviour platform and interacts with the remaining test system via the PSW. The PSW is designed for a particular type of external behaviour platforms and not for a particular behaviour. It manages "incoming" CH communication and forwards the communication after translation into the external behaviour platform. Communication originating from the platform is mapped to the appropriate CH operations and thus forwarded into the TTCN-3 test system.

An external component maintains the characteristics of a normal test component (management of ports and verdicts) and uses additionally the PSW. Depending on the external behaviour technology, the wrapper is more or less difficult to realise. The problem is basically to find a mechanism to communicate between an application written in the EE technology (in our case the PSW) and an application written in the EB technology (in our case the external behaviour). The interaction may be either synchronous or asynchronous. Some possible strategies are:

- Create the external behaviour as a process and use for communication the input, output or error buffers.
- Use sockets to communicate via ports. In this case, one may have to define an own protocol to establish the communication.
- Use native communication interfaces. For example, Java has the JNI (Java Native Interface) to communicate with C applications.
- Use a communication middleware like CORBA.

The external component may support several types of external behaviours: Perl, Python, etc. Therefore, a wrapper for each type of behaviour is needed. A component decides which PSW to use depending on the type of behaviour that runs on it. Only one behaviour can run on the external component at once, thus, only one PSW is instantiated, namely the one associated to the type of the external behaviour.

3.2   Operations with External Components

An external component is very similar to normal components. It can be created, can have ports, may execute external behaviours and can be stopped. In order to adhere to the TTCN-3 standard, all these operations should be compatible with the TCI interface specifications.

To be aligned with the TCI standard, an external component should be managed by CH. While the external component has still access to the native TTCN-3 data type representation (via the TCI value interface) the communication with the external behaviour has to be performed using encoded data. The CH should be able to handle an external component in the same way as it handles a normal component. Almost all operations, the CH applies to normal components (creation, start of a behaviour etc), are also applicable to external components. An external behaviour can access the component on which it runs, via the PSW, and therefore can conceptually access the local verdict and ports as well. The ports of the external components are used to realise the communication between an external behaviour and other TTCN-3 test components. Since the data format in the external behaviours is different from the TTCN-3 data, a codec is needed. This is the reason to establish a link between the PSW and the CD.

Fig. 4 shows how the external components are managed by CH and how they can interact with other external components or normal components.

Almost all TCI CH operations can be re-used for the management of external components and for the execution of external behaviour purposes; they only require minimal extensions. Next, we describe some of the operations of CH and present how they are used to work with external components and behaviours. First, we consider the operations performed from a TE on another TE running an external component.

To create an external component, the TE uses the `tciCreateTestComponentReq` method of CH. The CH checks if the component is an external one; if this is the case, the external component and a platform specific wrapper are created. The PSW is associated to the external behaviour type. The created external component functionality is seen as a normal component, since it provides the same interface to CH, TM etc. In a similar way, `tciStopTestComponent` is used when an external behaviour is stopped.

The ports of the external components are accessed via PSW from the external behaviour. This enables the external behaviour to use the ports to connect the external component ports with other components ports. The connection of two ports is realised through the `tciConnectReq` method. Since the ports are TTCN-3 ports (the external components use normal TTCN-3 Ports), the `tciConnectReq` implementation does not require further extensions. The `tciDisconnectReq` method behaves equally when it is used to disconnect a port.

To send data to a port of an external component, the `tciSendConnected` method of CH is used. CH accesses the TE of the external component and asks the PSW to deliver the data to the external behaviour. The same strategy applies for the `tciCallConnected` method.

To start an external behaviour, TE uses the `tciStartTestComponentReq`. The `TriComponentId` is the identifier of the external behaviour. The external behaviour is identified by the `TciBehaviourId` argument of the `tciStartTest-ComponentReq` method and can be started by parameters specified in the `Tci-ParameterList`. Its implementation is complex, since it has to validate if the `TriComponentId` and the `TciBehaviourId` are external. If these values are not valid, error messages are returned. The external behaviours are started in the form of parallel processes and can be monitored or managed through PSW.

To check whether an external component is running, the `tciCreateTestComponentReq` is used. This method checks if the external process, used to start the external behaviour, is alive or not. The `tciTestComponentTerminatedReq` and `tciTestComponentDoneReq` work similarly.

Now we describe the operations an external behaviour can perform. To communicate with other test components, an external behaviour needs to access the ports of the external component where it runs. The external behaviour accesses the ports via PSW. Next, the PSW asks the external component to execute the requested operations which are: send, call etc. This is performed by using the CH methods: `tciSendConnectedReq`, `tciCallConnectedReq`.

The termination of the external behaviour is notified to the external component where it runs, which calls the `tciTestComponentTerminatedReq` method. This way, the verdict of the `ExternalBehaviour` is communicated to CH.

Some operations of TCI can not be called from the TE running external components since their corresponding operations are not possible:

- `tciCreateTestComponentReq`: an external behaviour cannot create other test components.
- `tciStartTestComponentReq`: an external behaviour cannot start behaviours on other test components.
- `tciExecuteTestCaseReq`: an external behaviour cannot start test cases.
- `tciMapReq`: the ports of an external component cannot be mapped to Test System Interface ports. The system component cannot be accessed by EB at all.
- `tciEncode`: there is no need that the EB uses the TCI codec as it uses a different type and value system.

3.3   Coupling with the SUT

External behaviours connect to the SUT by using proprietary technology specific mechanisms. An external behaviour should not be able to communicate to the SUT via the TTCN-3 TRI test adapter. The test adapter belongs to the TTCN-3 test system; it makes no sense that the external behaviours may access it. This is also underpinned by the fact that the external behaviours typically communicate already directly with the SUT which is simpler than going via TTCN-3. Basically, the EB does not/may not need a TRI adapter to communicate with the SUT. This is why we usually opt for using an external behaviour since it allows reusing existing assets for testing the SUT and often simplifies the communication with the SUT.

The stimulus and the received data are managed by the external behaviour itself. Beside the verdict (which can be returned to the test system as seen in previous chapter) other data can be transferred to the TTCN3 test system. The external behaviour runs on an external component whose ports can be accessed. If the external component has ports connected to other TTCN-3 test components, the external behaviour may use them to deliver data to the TTCN3 test system.

If transferring data from/to EB to/from the test system a codec is needed. This codec can be the default one provided by the platform specific wrapper or another one defined by the user.

4   An Example of Integrating Perl Scripts into a TTCN-3 Environment

In this section, we show how a possible application of the concepts introduced above might look like. For this, we are using a Perl script that performs an ftp-download as external test behaviour.

The following script defines a complete downloading procedure using Perl.

```
#!/usr/bin/perl -w
use Net::FTP;
my($ftp) ;
$ftp = Net::FTP->new("a.server.com");
die($ftp->message()) if( !($ftp->login("foo","bar")) );
die($ftp->message()) if( !($ftp->binary()) );
die($ftp->message()) if( !($ftp->get("AVeryBigFile.bin"")) );
exit(0);
```

As it can be seen, the test behaviour is defined in a very compact way using only built-in operations available in Perl. This is typically what in practice is being encountered, simple scripts developed for a particular purpose without being designed for a particular test framework. The presented script shows also some very common scripting techniques. On success the scripts is executed without any output and returns with an exit code of zero. In any other case, some diagnostic output is provided and the script returns with a non-zero exit code.

The following TTCN-3 extract shows type definitions for defining the necessary external test component and behaviour in order to handle the above introduced Perl script.

```
// type definitions
type port STDERR message { out charstring ; }
type port STDIN  message { in charstring ; }

type external component ScriptComponent {
    port STDERR stderr ;
}
```

```
type component MainTestComponent {
    port STDIN  fromScript ;
}

external function scriptStart(charstring scriptName)
    runs on ScriptComponent ;
```

Basically, the fragment defines the environment of the script as having a single port, in this case the stderr buffer. Thus, the external behaviour, i.e. the Perl script, can communicate with other test components, in this case the main test component (MTC) via this port. The MTC has only a single port, which receives data that has been provided by the external component via its stderr port.

For starting the script, the external behaviour scriptStart has been declared. scriptStart runs on the ScriptComponent. Therefore, its ports can be connected to MTC ports.

The following TTCN-3 fragment shows how a functional test case can be defined.

```
// test case definitions
modulepar { charstring SCRIPT_NAME := "download.pl" ; }

testcase functionalTest() runs on MainTestComponent {
    var ScriptComponent p := ScriptComponent.create ;
    connect(mtc:fromScript, p:stderr) ;
    p.start(scriptStart(SCRIPT_NAME));
    var charstring logMessage ;
    alt {
      [] p.done { stop }
      [] fromScript.receive -> value logMessage {
      log(logMessage) ;
      if (lengthof(logMessage) != 0) setverdict(fail);
      repeat ;
      }
    }
}
```

The functionalTest() test case running on the MainTestComponent creates a ScriptComponent component and connects MTC's fromScript port with the stderr port of the script component. The external behaviour is started by executing TTCN-3 start command on the external component. The actual Perl script is referenced by the module parameter SCRIPT_NAME. After starting the external behaviour, the MTC waits for the termination of the external test component. The test case verdict is being determined by the exit code of the Perl script. For this, the PSW exports the script's stderr buffer to the stderr port as defined in the external component definition.

The presented functional test case can now be easily extended to a load test for an ftp server. The following TTCN-3 fragment shows an example for replicating the same external behaviour on numerous external test components.

```
testcase loadTest(integer load) runs on MainTestComponent {
    var integer i := 0 ;
    var ScriptComponent p ;
    for(i := 0 ; i < load ; i := i + 1 ) {
        p := ScriptComponent.create ;
        connect(mtc:fromScript, p:stderr) ;
```

```
            p.start(scriptStart(SCRIPT_NAME));
        }
        var charstring logMessage ;
        alt {
          [] all component.done { }
          [] any port.receive -> value logMessage {
          log(logMessage) ;
          repeat ;
          }
        }
      }
```

This example shows how TTCN-3 can be used efficiently only for the instantiation of multiple scripts which are executed on many components. The code could also be written completely in Perl, but this would require the implementation of a distributed execution environment to be able to execute distributed test campaigns as described in [4]. For this, reusing existing TTCN-3 infrastructure for distributed test management can significantly reduce the complexity as the TTCN-3 execution environment hides the technical complexity.

```
control {
    if(execute(functionalTest(),2.0) == pass) {
        execute(loadTest(100), 10.0) ;
    }
}
```

This TTCN-3 code fragment displays further possibilities in order to reuse existing TTCN-3 infrastructure for the control of test campaigns.

5   Conclusions

This paper discussed the concepts of external behaviour and external component. External behaviours define non-TTCN-3 behaviours whose execution is controlled from TTCN-3. An external behaviour runs on an external component. Since the external component should not have access to timers or local variables, the concept of external component was introduced.

Extensions to existing TTCN-3 test system implementations to support external behaviours are possible along the standard TTCN-3 test system architecture. A common strategy of how to extend the actual TTCN-3 execution environments based on TCI was presented.

Our approach provides a generic adaptation method for running external behaviours. The adaptation is made in the TTCN-3 test system itself by means of technology-specific PSWs, which are reusable for any external behaviour provided in that technology.

Future work will demonstrate the applicability of our approach to cases where non-TTCN-3 applications different to Perl scripts will be included. A comparative study of the gain (in terms of development efforts and performance) in accessing external behaviours directly rather than to translate them into TTCN-3 will be done.

References

[1] ETSI ES 201 873 – 1, v2.2.1: "The Testing and Test Control Notation TTCN-3: Core Language ", Oct. 2002.

[2] ETSI ES 201 873-5 V1.1.1: "The Testing and Test Control Notation version 3; Part 5: TTCN-3 Runtime Interface (TRI)", February 2003.

[3] ETSI ES 201 873-6 V1.0.0: "The Testing and Test Control Notation version 3; Part 6: TTCN-3 Control Interfaces (TCI)", March 2003.

[4] I. Schieferdecker, T.Vassiliou-Gioles: Realizing distributed test systems with TCI, IFIP 15th International Conference on Testing of Communicating Systems (TestCom 2003), Sophia-Antipolis (France), May 2003.

[5] The Perl directory: Online documentation. available at http://www.perl.org/docs.html.

Author Index

Lecture Notes in Computer Science

For information about Vols. 1–2848

please contact your bookseller or Springer-Verlag